COMPOSING
AID

Activist Encounters in Folklore and Ethnomusicology

David A. McDonald, editor

COMPOSING AID

Music, Refugees, and Humanitarian Politics

OLIVER SHAO

INDIANA UNIVERSITY PRESS

This book is a publication of

Indiana University Press
Office of Scholarly Publishing
Herman B Wells Library 350
1320 East 10th Street
Bloomington, Indiana 47405 USA

https://iupress.org

Parts of chapters 1 and 6 were published as "'How Is That Going to Help Anyone?': A Critical Activist Ethnomusicology," by Oliver Y. Shao, in *Transforming Ethnomusicology: Methodologies, Institutional Structures, and Policies*, volume 1 (2021), edited by Beverley Diamond and Salwa El-Shawan Castelo-Branco, 87–100.

Manufactured in the United States of America

First Printing 2023

Cataloging is available from the Library of Congress.

ISBN 978-0-253-06764-7 (cloth)
ISBN 978-0-253-06765-4 (paperback)
ISBN 978-0-253-06766-1 (ebook)

CONTENTS

Acknowledgments   *vii*

List of Abbreviations   *xi*

Introduction   1

1. Belonging   20

After Relief

2. Pleasure   41

3. Labor   63

For Protection

4. Immobility   91

5. Security   115

6. Peace   141

Recomposing Aid   164

Bibliography   *175*

Index   *187*

ACKNOWLEDGMENTS

I extend my deepest gratitude to the individuals living and working in Kenya's Kakuma Refugee Camp who helped me with this project. While I cannot name you all for purposes of maintaining confidentiality, I am immensely grateful to each and every one of you for your kindness and generosity in allowing me to conduct this research project. I am humbled by your trust and willingness to share your stories and insights. I am also aware of the difficulties of accurately representing your personal experiences, so please forgive me if I have made any mistakes. I am forever indebted to you all for your support. Thank you.

I am thankful to various organizations in Kenya that made important contributions to this research and to my overall well-being. Thank you to the Ministry of Foreign Affairs, the Department of Refugee Affairs, and the UN Refugee Agency (UNHCR) for allowing me to conduct research in the Kakuma camp. Thank you to the staff at Burn for your hospitality in Nairobi while I waited for my research visa. Thank you to everyone at the Lutheran World Federation for providing space to carry out engaged research. Thank you to the Octopizzo Foundation and FilmAid International for helping me research the role of popular music in Kakuma. Thank you to the medical personnel at the Kakuma Mission Hospital, the International Rescue Committee, and IsraAid for performing my emergency appendectomy in Kakuma. Thank you to IsraAid for providing me with accommodations and social engagement. Thank you to all my former colleagues at the International Rescue Committee for your kindness, collegiality, and professional support.

I am deeply grateful for the support I have received from my colleagues, my students, and the administration at the School of the Art Institute of Chicago.

Thank you to president Elissa Tenny, provost Martin Berger, former dean of faculty Jefferson Pinder, current dean of faculty Camille Martin-Thomsen, former chair of faculty Beth Wright, and current chair of faculty Shaurya Kumar for providing me with the institutional support required to work on this project. Thank you to Christina Gómez, chair of the Liberal Arts Department, and Adam Mack, former chair, for your support and guidance. Thank you to Karen Morris, chair of the Institutional Review Board, and other IRB members involved in approving my research project. Thank you to professors Suma Ikeuchi, Kirin Wachter-Grene, Emily Hoyler, Zachary Tavlin, and Jennifer Lee for helping me draft the book proposal for this project. A special thank you to Suma for reading and commenting on a draft version of my introduction. Thank you to Patrick Lynn Rivers for sharing your insights and academic resources with me. Thank you to Kirin, Mika Tosca, and Sarah Zhou Rosengard for your professional and social support as early career scholars. Thank you to all of my colleagues in the Liberal Arts Department, and especially the music faculty for your inspiring work. And thank you to the students who provided feedback on various draft chapters during class discussions.

I received a great deal of support while working on this research project at Indiana University Bloomington. I offer my deepest gratitude to David McDonald, chair of my committee, for his unwavering support and critical engagement with my research. My other committee members—Daniel Reed, Ruth Stone, Jane Goodman, and Elizabeth Dunn—provided immensely constructive feedback during individual meetings and at my defense. I am especially thankful for my IU colleagues in the Department of Folklore and Ethnomusicology, the Department of Anthropology, and the African Studies program. Colleagues at Indiana University who helped shaped this research include Tania Bulakh, Sara Friedman, Maria Grosz-Ngaté, Clara Henderson, Michelle Moyd, Beatrice Okelo, Alwiya Omar, Fernando Orejuela, Doug Peach, Elena Popa, Georgina Ramsey, Deo Tungaraza, and Sue Tuohy. Collectively, these individuals helped me hone my thinking and advance this research project through institutional support and personal feedback.

I also received support for this project from individuals working in other academic institutions and on related projects. Thank you to the faculty, administration, and staff at Moi University, and especially Professor Mellitus Nyongesa Wanyama, for facilitating my research permits in Kenya. Thank you to Lieven Corthouts for sharing the insights you gained from working on your documentary film *The Invisible City: Kakuma*. Thank you to Angela Impey, Lucy Durán, Ilana Webster-Kogen, Rachel Harris, and Richard Williams at the School of Oriental and African Studies (SOAS); former SOAS faculty Elena

Fiddian-Qasmiyeh at the University College London; Steve Howard, Omar Hashi, and Bose Maposa at Ohio University; and Theo Randall at Indiana University South Bend. Thank you to Anne Rasmussen, Olivier Urbain, Elaine Chang Sandoval, Svanibor Pettan, Salwa El-Shawan Castelo-Branco, and Beverley Diamond for your academic support. Thank you to members of the African Music Section, the Applied Ethnomusicology Section, and the Crossroads Section for Difference and Representation organized by the Society for Ethnomusicology. Thank you to my cohort at SOAS, and in particular Kadambari Chauhan, Michele Banal, and John Crockett for our engaging conversations in classrooms and public houses in London. Thank you to Margaret Rowley, Esther Viola Kurtz, David Fossum, and Andrew Colwell for making conferences both stimulating and fun. Thank you also to Esther for your intellectual and emotional support during our reader/writer's retreat. Thank you to Indiana University Press and the blind reviewers, editors, and staff who provided me with invaluable feedback for improving the quality of this manuscript.

In terms of financial assistance, I acknowledge and thank the following institutions and programs: the Mellon Innovating International Research, Teaching, and Collaboration; IU's Office of Vice President of International Affairs; IU's College of Arts and Sciences; the United States Department of Education Foreign Language Area Studies; and the School of the Art Institute of Chicago.

Finally, I am deeply thankful to my family. To my grandparents, aunties, uncles, and parents, I am eternally grateful to you all for enduring the difficulties that came from being forcibly displaced from China and for providing me and our family with opportunities in Europe and North America. To my mother, Grace, I cannot express in words how much I am thankful to you for raising me. Your strength and resilience have motivated and inspired me throughout my life. To my father, I appreciate your early guidance and support. To my brother Jon and sister-in-law Nicole, both of you have provided me with an immense amount of help and encouragement. To my nieces Olivia, Soleil, and Diane, you have helped remind me of the meaningful things in life and the need to create a better world for the future generations that will inhabit it.

ABBREVIATIONS

AP	Administration Police
CPA	Comprehensive Peace Agreement
DJ	Disc jockey
DRA	Department of Refugee Affairs
DRC	Danish Refugee Council
EAC	East African Community
ECHO	European Commission Humanitarian Aid
ECS	Episcopal Church of the Sudan
EU	European Union
FAI	FilmAid International
FAO	Food and Agriculture Organization of the United Nations
GTZ	German Technical Cooperation
HIV/AIDS	Human immunodeficiency virus/acquired immunodeficiency syndrome
IDP	Internally displaced persons
IOM	International Organization for Migration
IRC	International Rescue Committee
IRR	International refugee regime
JRS	Jesuit Refugee Service
KSEDP	Kalobeyei Integrated Social and Economic Development Program
KYPA	Kakuma Youth Peace Ambassadors
Ksh	Kenyan shilling
KTN	Kenyan Television Network

LGBTQ	Lesbian, gay, bisexual, transgender, queer
LWF	Lutheran World Federation
MC	Master of ceremony
MP	Member of parliament
NCCK	National Council of Churches of Kenya
NGO	Nongovernmental organization
NRC	Norwegian Refugee Council
OAU	Organisation of African Unity
OCHA	United Nations Office for the Coordination of Humanitarian Affairs
OCPD	Officer in charge of the police department
OF	Octopizzo Foundation
OVC	Orphans and vulnerable children
PLWHA	People living with HIV and AIDS
PRS	Protracted refugee situation
PwD	Persons with disabilities
R&B	Rhythm and blues
RCK	Refugee Consortium of Kenya
SGBV	Sexual and gender-based violence
SPLM	Sudan People's Liberation Movement
STI	Sexually transmitted infection
TfD	Theater for development
UDG	United Drama Group
UN	United Nations
UNAIDS	Joint United Nations Programme on HIV/AIDS
UNFPA	United Nations Population Fund
UNHCR	United Nations High Commissioner for Refugees
UNICEF	United Nations Children's Fund
UNRWA	United Nations Relief and Works Agency
US	United States
USD	United States dollar
WBG	World Bank Group
WFP	World Food Program
WHO	World Health Organization
WRD	World Refugee Day
YC	Youth center
YEPD	Youth Education Programme Development
YIF	Youth Initiative Fund

COMPOSING
AID

INTRODUCTION

World Refugee Day, 2011

Music and dance transformed the Napata Fairground's bare dirt courtyard into a vibrant spectacle. It was June 18, 2011, and hundreds of visitors and residents had gathered at the Kakuma Refugee Camp in northwestern Kenya for the annual World Refugee Day (WRD) events. From morning to afternoon, performing groups put their artistry on display. Dinka and Nuer dance groups from South Sudan elicited loud applause with their powerful and elegant leaps. Audience members hollered when the Equatoria dance group rapidly stomped their feet on the ground, enveloping themselves in a massive dust cloud. The Somali Music Band grooved on electrified guitar and bass and a well-worn drum kit, fusing elements of Western rock with Somali folk music. Congolese lingala dancers elicited ululations when they provocatively shook their hips in time with the Youth Education Programme Development (YEPD) band's bright, percussive, up-tempo guitar riffs and syncopated beats. Oohs and ahhs were generated by the Burundian cultural troupe when their acrobats flipped and flew across the courtyard in sync with the pounding rhythms that resonated from the sun-stretched skins of large barrel drums. Smiles shone across the faces of government officials and aid workers who received fresh popcorn during an Ethiopian coffee ceremony replete with Eskista dancers rolling their shoulders and jilting their chests to the danceable rhythms of a recorded track. Audience members cheered when the Kenyan-Turkana choir powerfully sang out in unison and call and response over the clanging timbre of metal shakers, shifting their feet, shaking their hips, and bouncing their bodies in rhythm with each other. Impressed by these performances, a leading government official

1

enthusiastically remarked that even Kenya's capital, Nairobi, could not match the level of cultural diversity in Kakuma.[1]

Through their artistry, the performers created a celebratory mood, providing welcome relief for the aid workers and refugees charged with handling the difficulties of the camp's day-to-day operations. A slew of visitors—diplomats, donors, state officials, aid staff, celebrities, and journalists—flew in from Nairobi for this highly anticipated occasion. As the sun's hot rays blanketed the courtyard, most of the invited guests and agency staff took cover in plastic chairs arranged under the protective shade of makeshift awnings crafted from wooden poles and worn white tarpaulin sheets. Meanwhile, a host of refugees and local Kenyans crowded together in the open air toward the back and sides of the staged area. The Office of the United Nations High Commissioner for Refugees (UNHCR) in Kakuma holds a WRD event every year to raise awareness about refugee issues and secure funding for camp operations. And as with prior years, the 2011 event proved to be both entertaining and educational.

WRD has historically served as an annual occasion in the Kakuma camp for not only raising awareness about refugee issues but also acknowledging the efforts of the Kenyan state and the UNHCR. "Kenya is providing asylum in accordance to international standards," announced the district commissioner of Kakuma, speaking on behalf of the honorable minister of the Ministry of State for Immigration and Registration.[2] "We have done so much together," the head of the UNHCR-Kakuma suboffice proudly stated. "I arrived in the camp when security was bad, when refugees were not able to sleep in their homes in peace but now they can have serenity in their homes."[3] Positive sentiments toward the UNHCR were also conveyed in a praise song performed by a choir group from one of Kakuma's secondary schools, when they sang, "Thank you, thank you, and may God bless you, UNHCR and the other partners." The choice to sing a praise song in English and in unison was aimed at appealing to the ears and aesthetic tastes of the Euro-American agencies and donors in attendance. The song's lyrics, in conjunction with the event's spatial layout, were telling of who was being celebrated. The Lutheran World Federation (LWF) set up the covered seating area especially to give dignitaries a comfortable and direct view of the performances.

Not everyone, however, benignly accepted a celebratory view of the camp's administrative arms. Three young men with sunglasses and smeared white face paint stepped onto the stage area for the event's final performance. They were from a local youth group in the Kakuma camp organized by the LWF. It was their turn to educate, entertain, and showcase their culture. Two of the dancers wore trousers and oversized dress shirts stuffed with pillows to make themselves look fat. Moving to the up-tempo beats of an East African–style electronic dance track, the performers gyrated their hips and legs rapidly and rhythmically, kicking up dust and generating ululations and applause from the appreciative crowd. Amid the cheering and clapping, however, a few attendees questioned the performance's meaning. "Is this dance connected to their traditional culture?" asked one of the foreign visitors to her colleague. "I don't know," she responded. "Ummm, I think they are making fun of us," remarked one of the other attendees.[4]

On the day that Kakuma received the most visitors of the year, the youth group's performative piece sought to rupture the event's dominant messaging. The depiction of bloated aid officials in whiteface signified a common perception among many refugees I met, who believed and felt that they were being forced to belong in an unequal, racialized system—a system funded by American and European governments and organizations in which UNHCR and NGO staff disproportionately benefited from the business of regulating refugees. Crucially, the dance track's uplifting beats and melodies infused the performers' transgressive theatricality with just enough ambiguity to avoid condemnation from camp officials, while sending a not-so-subtle message about the socioeconomic and racial inequality of the camp system.

Some of the visitors departed Kakuma by plane later that afternoon. Others left in the day or two after. Actress and UNHCR goodwill ambassador Angelina Jolie, in the "Do 1 Thing" campaign video released in 2011, compassionately stated that "one child growing up in a camp is too many."[5] And yet despite this altruistic rhetoric, the WRD event's function as a fundraising activity for the Kakuma camp's continued operations contradicted the sentiment. Moreover, there was an unspoken expectation among attendees that the camp's refugee population would be present at public gatherings for World Refugee Day for many years to come.

The proceedings at the 2011 WRD event convey several challenges that have plagued the Kakuma camp's governing operations. Forced migrants in Kenya have been compelled to belong for years—some, even decades—in a camp system that has paradoxically both helped and harmed them (Verdirame and Harrell-Bond 2005). Originally established in 1992 as a temporary destination for forced migrants in East Africa, the Kakuma camp has since turned into a protracted site that is still in operation in 2022 despite numerous attempts to close it. Public speeches during the WRD event in 2011 highlighted Kenya's and the UNHCR's roles in upholding asylum and creating security for refugees. And yet these same institutions administered a site wherein refugees faced not only material inequality but also police brutality, demeaning headcounts, and infringements on labor and movement.

Within this difficult environment, I witnessed how its inhabitants used music, dance, and performance to negotiate and contest the camp system. Creative expression thus provides a unique lens through which to interrogate and rethink how refugee camps function. Indeed, the youth group's performative critique of the camp administration raises several probing questions: Why does a system that claims to offer protection and care for refugees suffer from such criticism? What roles do performing artists and their communities play in addressing state- and humanitarian-induced precarity and inequality? Why might listening to the worldviews and creative capacities of Kakuma's camp inhabitants help rethink and transform the debilitating aspects of long-term refugee camps and the existing migratory order?

Music, Refugees, and Humanitarian Politics

"We *even* have a music scholar here," chuckled a director from one of the Kakuma camp's leading aid agencies.[6] He made this remark about me during a welcome dinner held in the main NGO compound for the visiting directors who had recently arrived at the camp in August 2013.[7] The hint of laughter in his voice was indicative of his impression of music research as lacking a sense of seriousness in a refugee camp. In general, I have found that both camp officials and researchers consider music, and expressive culture more broadly, as ancillary to more pressing problems of security, healthcare, protection, and resettlement, to name a few. In a similar vein, Tania Kaiser suggests that while anthropologists have long found the study of "material and aesthetic worlds" socially significant, they have ignored these aspects of refugee camps, deeming them "too frivolous, or insufficiently solution-oriented in such contexts" (2006, 186).

Conversely, scholars who have examined the role of expressive culture in refugee camp settings have offered important insights on a range of pressing issues. These studies have shown how forced migrants establish senses of normalcy in the face of loss and trauma (Brower 2020); how they deal with the challenges of reconstituting social rituals in new territories (Kaiser 2008); and how they express, constitute, and negotiate sociopolitical identities within exilic contexts (McDonald 2013; Kaiser 2006; Diehl 2002; Reyes 1999; Malkki 1995a). Many of the ethnomusicological studies in particular offer rich accounts of the varied and dynamic aspects of music that address the politics of exile. Adelaida Reyes's (1999) study of refugee camps in the Philippines elucidates how and why members from various Vietnamese communities strategically constituted national identities through popular music styles as well as public and private performances. David McDonald's (2013) study of the poetics of protest songs in Palestinian refugee camps demonstrates myriad ways music reflected and shaped dynamic and multifaceted aspects of national identity. Keila Dhiel's (2002) study of music in Dharamsala, India, the home of Tibet's government-in-exile, unpacks how Tibetans grappled with issues of cultural change and ethnic purity within the context of political self-determination. These studies offer keen analyses of the complex relationship between music and national identity formation in various displacement contexts.

From a different perspective, this analytical orientation has resulted in less focus on the systematic forces involved in the global regulation and control of forced migrants. As a counterbalance to music studies focused primarily on national identity politics in exile, I offer in this book a critical account of music, dance, and performance in the lives of people who inhabit the margins of the nation-state system in one of the largest and oldest refugee camps in the world. Rather than conceiving of humanitarianism as an apolitical intervention, it is crucial to recognize that the institutional practice of assigning forced migrants to a demarcated territory is an intensely political process. In keeping with this view, I approach the study of sonic forms of expressive culture in the Kakuma Refugee Camp with critical attention to the politics of belonging. This perspective elucidates why the musical practices I observed were of paramount importance for structuring how camp inhabitants were expected to belong—and for constituting and voicing how they desired to belong—within a humanitarian-governed site of migratory control.

While many people picture refugee camps as temporary structures replete with tarpaulin tents and emergency facilities, their appearances and operations vary. The Buduburam Refugee Camp located on the outskirts of Accra, Ghana, for example, has come to resemble a city suburb, while the older areas of the Meheba refugee settlement in northwestern Zambia looks like a collection of villages (Bakewell 2014, 129). Kenya's refugee camps have taken on characteristics of medium-sized towns and rural farmlands. In a prototypical closed camp, the UNHCR and its contracted agencies administer food rations to migrants with restricted mobility. In agricultural settlements, the state allocates plots of land for subsistence cultivation. In Kenya, Kakuma and Dadaab operate as closed camps, while the recently built Kalobeyei functions as an agricultural settlement. And while these sites may look different and have different names, their locations within demarcated territories share the similar goal of separating and controlling migrants, a governmental practice that Oliver Bakewell terms "encampment": "A policy which requires refugees to live in a designated area set aside for the exclusive use of refugees, unless they have gained specific permission to live elsewhere. The host state is obliged to ensure that the human rights of refugees are upheld, including the rights to shelter, food, water, sanitation and healthcare, and education, but how these are delivered varies enormously" (2014, 129).

An unintended outcome of the establishment of encampments in the twentieth and twenty-first centuries is that many of these sites are still in operation, including Cooper's Camp in West Bengal, India (est. 1947); the Palestinian camps in the West Bank (est. late 1940s); the Mae La Camp in Thailand (est. 1984); and the Dadaab and Kakuma camps in Kenya (est. 1991 and 1992) (Finch 2015). These encampments are some of the oldest still in operation at the time of this writing. To reflect the increasing length of time that forced migrants have spent in these kinds of conditions, the UNHCR has coined the term "protracted refugee situation" (PRS). The UNHCR defines a PRS as "one in which 25,000 or more refugees from the same nationality have been in exile for at least five or more consecutive years in a given host country" (UNHCR 2021, 20). PRSs are far from an anomaly; the 2021 UNHCR *Global Trends* report indicates that 15.9 million out of 27.1 million total refugees are living in thirty-one host countries and fifty-one protracted situations.

As refugee camps have persisted and expanded, a new kind of government has emerged: a humanitarian government (Agier 2011; Fassin 2011 and 2007; Walters 2010). According to Didier Fassin, humanitarian government may be understood as "the administration of human collectivities in the name of a higher moral principle which sees the preservation of life and the alleviation of suffering as the highest value of action" (2007, 15). And yet Fassin argues that beyond the seemingly just aspects of this goal, humanitarianism poses a paradox whereby the "politics of compassion" is also a "politics of solidarity" and a "politics of inequality" (2011, 3). This paradox has given rise to situations in which beneficial outcomes of humanitarian interventions have emerged with, reproduced, and obscured institutionally constituted precarity and social control.

In one sense, the politics of compassion and solidarity undergirding camp operations help alleviate human suffering. Camps are places where the weary migrant can receive relief, where the persecuted can find refuge, and where the vulnerable can access social services. In the summer of 2011, for example, major news agencies circulated heartbreaking images and sound bites of social suffering in Somalia and eastern Kenya. Soon after, fourteen tons of food and supplies appeared in Kenya's Dadaab Refugee Complex, due in large part to the media's displays of emergency and a sense of moral responsibility to help people facing conflict and hunger. The UNHCR has also historically pressed signatory states to uphold non-refoulement, the right to not be forcibly returned to dangerous situations in the country from which one has fled. These facets of the refugee camp are indicative of humanitarianism's supportive features. On closer inspection, however, there is more to the story than care and concern.

Refugee camps have also produced discriminatory, undignified, and precarious conditions. Policymakers have used camps to restrict forced migrants' capacity to move freely and access formal labor markets (Agier 2011; Verdirame and Harrell-Bond 2005). Locating camps in impoverished areas has fostered conflict over scarce resources (Aukot 2003). UN agencies have demeaned refugees through headcounts and degraded food rations (Besteman 2016; Harrell-Bond 1986). Donors and NGOs have administered an aid system that is often erratic and unpredictable. During my research in the Kakuma camp in 2015, for example, I witnessed multiple occasions when the World Food Program (WFP) slashed food rations in half and gave refugees only twenty-four hours' notice!

And yet it is necessary to consider that the refugee camp is more than just a site of hardship. In Kenya, the Kakuma and Dadaab camps have become places for the formation of new identities (Agier 2002; Grabska 2014) and new kinds of urbanism (Jansen 2018; Rawlence 2016; Agier 2002; Montclos and Kagwanja 2000). Camp residents have graduated from schools, built businesses, and raised families. They have forged complex social networks linked to other parts of Kenya, Africa, and Western resettlement countries (Jansen 2018, 197; Horst 2006). Far from being passive subjects of humanitarian rule, refugees in Kenya and elsewhere have coped with, resisted, and shaped the regulation of camps (Brankamp 2021; Jansen 2018; Jaji 2012; Ramadan 2012; Horst 2006).

Recognizing refugees' ability to use the camp system to suit their needs is crucially important; however, doing so should neither downplay the challenging conditions in camps nor obfuscate their overarching purpose as a spatializing technology of control (Agier 2011; Jaji 2012; Ramadan 2012; Hyndman 2000; Malkki 1995b). Gerawork Teferra, a scholar of development economics and a long-term resident of the Kakuma camp, has noted that the camp's "urbanlike" qualities "should not disguise the precarity of camp life, nor the consequences of instability borne by refugees struggling to live there in increasingly permanent fashion" (2022, 164). In his study, Teferra (2022) argues that many refugees face a life of "pseudopermanence" constituted by short-term administrative plans, an unstable leadership system, substandard educational and healthcare services, temporary housing structures, discriminatory business and labor policies, and unrealistic hopes for resettlement. Controlling Kenya's camp inhabitants has also consisted of militarized forms of policing through checkpoints, permission letters, and physical abuse (Brankamp 2019). These findings point to humanitarian encampment's capacity to simultaneously protect human life and engender a "slow" and "liberal" form of violence (Brankamp 2021, 107–108).

It is with these ideas in mind that I approach the study of music, dance, and performance in the United Nations–administered Kakuma Refugee Camp. Specifically, I infuse this research with critical scholarship on humanitarian-enabled migratory control while recognizing camp inhabitants' creative capacities to alter, oppose, and negotiate the encampment system. In doing so, I add to the nascent scholarship on music, migration, and border regimes (Western 2020; Impey 2018; Chávez 2017; Kun 2000; Rasmussen 2019 et al.; Bohlman 2011) and to the growing body of work on music, charity, and humanitarianism (Ndaliko and Anderson 2020; Ndaliko 2016; Dave 2015; Helbig et al. 2008; Impey 2002). Humanitarian arts initiatives in Africa have tended to emphasize issues of "utility and urgency" instead of considering how "aesthetics of intervention" may support the intervener's goals, marginalize local views, and exacerbate uneven power dynamics (Ndaliko and Anderson 2020, 2). In the realm of music and human rights initiatives, it has become commonplace for institutions to hold erroneous assumptions that music is a universal expression for creating positive change while ignoring music's actual effect on people's lives (Dave 2015, 1–2). Cognizant of the limitations and dangers of these dominant views and approaches, ethnomusicologists have offered a range of corrective methods, including supporting a more constrained perspective on music's beneficial impacts (Dave 2015); placing heightened emphasis on scrutinizing the politics of production and the wider socioeconomic and political impacts of arts interventions (Helbig et al. 2008; Ndaliko 2016; Dave 2015); and advancing participatory modes of research attuned to local viewpoints and wider power imbalances (Ndaliko 2016; Impey 2002). Building off these approaches, I endeavor to move beyond an analysis of the intended, immediate utility of music and arts initiatives in the Kakuma camp and toward a more critical and collaborative methodology that addresses the politics of music production and the social and material realities of people actively negotiating humanitarian social control.

Interweaving approaches from ethnomusicology, folklore, anthropology, political science, sociology, sound studies, and performance studies, I apply aesthetic and social analysis to the "humanitarian border," a specific form of border making constituted through humanitarian government (Walters 2011). This approach elucidates how the Global North has externalized its borders in the Global South by funding music and arts projects in refugee camps. It examines the ways forced migrants have used music, dance, and performance to negotiate and challenge the disciplinary schemes of humanitarianized forms of security. It homes in on how and why musical practices have reproduced, resisted, and resignified the affective forces of humanitarian governmentality. An ethnomusicology of migration focused on the borders and biopolitics of humanitarianism provides a rich understanding of the cultural lives of people labeled as "refugees" and "asylum seekers" while engaging with the uneven systemic forces involved in the transnational regulation and control of cross-border movements.[8]

Although scholars have long critiqued the visual representation of the refugee figure in films, news media, and charity marketing campaigns (Bleiker et al. 2013; Wright 2002; Malkki 1996), it is crucial to consider that migration and borders are also sonic phenomena. More than just a different way to represent forced migration, "sonic perspectives," writes musicologist Tom Western, allow "for an unsettling of storytelling, where the messiness of life across borders overtakes reductive tropes of refugeeness; and circulation, encounter, and friction are placed front and center in the mix" (Western 2020, 296). Focusing on sound can thus offer insightful ways for understanding the complex and multifaceted experiential realities of people living in long-term refugee camps. With an "ethnographic ear" (Erlmann 2004), one can hear how songs and dances provide forced migrants with important ways of thinking, communicating, and feeling in places rife with precarity and inequality.

A critical ethnomusicology of migration centered on interrogating the unequal workings of humanitarianism allows for studies of places like refugee camps that have historically been conducted by disciplines such as political science, geography, economics, and international relations. This approach aims to collapse what Achille Mbembe refers to as a false dichotomy between the "cultural symbolic" and the "economic material" (2001, 4). In this regard, I consider some of the following questions: Why did hip hop musicians who performed in an NGO social campaign publicly reject brand-new mobile phones in a site with scarce resources? Why has no significant nighttime music scene been established in an urbanized place that has existed for almost three decades? Why did a camp run by Christian organizations forbid refugees from engaging in traditional forms of Christian worship during the Christmas to New Year's holiday period? How has the proliferation of peace songs reproduced institutional forms of violence? Answering these questions requires bridging ethnographically grounded social and aesthetic analysis with a political-economy approach that interrogates the inequality of the camp system. It requires elucidating what is often obscured by the "feel-good factor of art" and scrutinizing the politics of production behind NGO-organized music projects (Ndaliko 2016,

151). Ethnomusicological approaches privilege listening to and understanding individual lived experiences and the meanings, identities, and emotions made manifest in musical practice. By reframing the dominant ways forced migrants are heard and, thus, treated, it is my hope that this book may prove useful for those opposing the debilitating aspects of humanitarian encampment and those working toward the creation of more just approaches.

Follow the Music, Follow the Campaign

During my research visit to the Kakuma camp from July to August 2013, the main Somali market in Kakuma One was often a hive of activity. Passersby and customers walked across the bumpy dirt roads lined with storefronts selling household wares, foodstuffs, and garments. Multicolored fabrics suspended below the ceilings of clothing shops painted the monochromatic tin sheet walls and rooftops. Webs of black electrical wire strewn atop high wooden poles carried juice for the rumbling generators that powered light bulbs, TVs, and refrigerators in the local shops. Each evening, Cabdi stood by his samosa stand and Fatuma by her bread cart. It was Ramadan, and they, like the surrounding cafés, restaurants, and food vendors, prepped for customers coming after sundown. During this period, I regularly ate dinner in the market's cafés and restaurants. One evening, my presence by the food stalls and mobile-phone shops attracted a chattering crowd of approximately fifteen young and middle-aged Somali men. I was a strange and curious sight because of my East Asian features, prompting many questions about my role in the camp.

"Do you work for the UNHCR or one of the NGOs?" asked one of the
    young men.
"No, no, no," I responded. "I do research."
"Really? About what?"
"About music and dance."
"How is that going to help anyone?" he replied with a slight chuckle.
"He is a collector," mumbled another man.
"What did he say?" I asked.
"He said that you are a collector."
"Oh no, I don't just collect information about music and dance. I do re-
    search to understand how the conditions of the camp restrict the music
    and dance practices of refugees."
"Ahhh, I see. OK, yes, you are a researcher, but even so, how is researching
    our problems going to help us?"[9]

After I explained that my reasons for coming to the Kakuma camp involved more than just collecting data about music and dance, the group appeared to take my work more seriously. Yet they were still unsatisfied with my approach. They were skeptical about the benefits of another foreigner documenting their plight. Some scholars may suggest that the act of writing critically about the oppression of marginalized groups is a sufficient means of giving back to communities in need. Critical scholarship can indeed generate significant social benefits across time and space, and scholarly knowledge has the potential to transform how we think about and act toward a specific issue. My conversation with the Somali men reported above, however, indicates that researchers writing about the suffering of others may not serve as an adequate form of reciprocity for those living in difficult conditions. As Frantz Fanon has powerfully suggested, "What matters is not to know the world but to change it" (2008 [1952], 17). With these issues in mind, I trace the circumstances that brought about my shift toward a politically engaged ethnomusicological approach.

In 2011, I worked for six months as an intern for the International Rescue Committee (IRC), the largest health provider in the Kakuma camp. As part of my role, I assisted in developing programs for mobilizing music and dance to transform health-related behaviors of refugees. I documented and analyzed how different theater for development (TfD) groups employed culturally specific forms of drama, music, and dance as a means of sensitizing camp residents to issues concerning malaria, nutrition, reproductive health, and sexually transmitted infections (STIs). I was tasked with translating qualitative and quantitative data from my research findings into grant proposals and final reports to build on the existing arts-based component of the IRC's health programs. I found that music, dance, and drama most effectively addressed health issues when tailored to audiences' lived realities and cultural nuances, a finding in line with those of other ethnomusicologists doing similar studies (see Barz and Cohen 2011; Van Buren 2010; Barz 2006).

Strongly committed to applied research, I contemplated continuing to support edutainment activities with subsequent research projects. Yet as I spent more time learning about the logics, practices, and deleterious effects of the international humanitarian/refugee industry and the Kenyan state's refugee policies, it became clear that I had to do more than merely apply my research findings to camp programming initiatives. Drawing on the work of feminist and critical race scholars, I reflected on my own position and involvement within interlocking systems of oppression and inequality based on race, citizenship, nationality, gender, and class (Madison 2011; Collins 1998). In doing so, I began to realize that I was part of a humanitarian-constituted social hierarchy in which NGO workers presented themselves as custodians of proper behavior and refugees as incomplete beings requiring reform. I believed my involvement in these programs might reinforce uneven relations of power in ways that justified the unequal treatment of certain people over others.

After much reflection, the approach that I have found the least exploitative and the most productive has involved combining ethnographic critique with activist engagement. Anthropologist Charles Hale has argued that while the cultural critic's goals are aimed at the academy, the activist researcher has "dual loyalties—to academia and to a political struggle" (2006, 100). Hale calls for a merging of cultural critique and activist research to negotiate these twin demands. Some critics have claimed that activist research is biased and, thus, less valid than scientific approaches that strive to be objective (Oring 2004). In contrast, proponents of activist research have argued that it is more rigorous and generative of richer analysis both theoretically and methodologically because of the difficulties that come with striving to solve wide-scale social problems (Greenwood 2008; Lipsitz 2008; Hale 2006). Activist scholars have also critiqued some types of applied work, not on intellectual grounds but on the capacity of these projects to bring about meaningful social transformation (Lipsitz 2008, 95). A critical activist approach, on the other hand, works toward addressing immediate needs and advancing social transformation, providing greater potential to generate both theoretical innovation and alternative solutions. Building off these ideas as well as my experiences in Kakuma, I have sought to conduct a critical activist ethnomusicology—a mode of participatory research focused on sonic cultural practices, conducted through a critical engagement with asymmetrical power dynamics, and designed and activated to pursue social justice.

During each of my three visits to the Kakuma Refugee Camp between 2011 and 2015, I lived in a small cement-block room in the NGO compound run by the Lutheran World Federation. My residence there was crucial to understanding the dynamics of humanitarian government and establishing close links with aid agencies. I spoke with managers and support staff from the LWF, FilmAid International (FAI), the National Council of Churches of Kenya (NCCK), the Octopizzo Foundation (OF), the IRC, the Jesuit Refugee Service (JRS), IsraAid, the Refugee Consortium of Kenya (RCK), the Department of Refugee Affairs (DRA), and the UNHCR. During the latter half of my third visit, I moved to the camp area in April 2015 after members of El-Shabaab threatened to bomb the UN and NGO compounds. As a safety measure, the UN security team allowed me to live in my teacher Alier's South Sudanese Dinka neighborhood in Kakuma One. The block where I resided was one of the earliest parts of the camp settled by refugees. And while the block's inhabitants have changed over time, living in a long-standing, Dinka-populated area enabled me to hear stories and narratives spanning Kakuma's history from its inception to its current operation. My time with this community helped me better understand both the normalcy and hardships of living in a long-term encampment and was integral (though never fully successful) to reducing the physical and social barriers created by my status as a US citizen and my association with the UNHCR and its contracted agencies. Throughout my stay, I walked back and forth between the Dinka compound and the NGO compound, creating some confusion among refugees and aid workers as to where my allegiances fell.

On my second visit to Kakuma, from July to August 2013, and my third, from October 2014 to August 2015, I acted as an ethnomusicologist with no formal attachment to an aid agency. In this role, I sought to conduct a different type of research, still focused on the arts but with greater attention toward examining how refugees deploy cultural resources within the context of encampment. I was interested in better understanding how music, dance, and ritual operate as forms of aid (broadly construed), an endeavor I thought would offer a nice counterpoint to the oft-repeated narratives of refugees as helpless victims requiring external assistance. A central part of my methodology has thus focused on understanding Kakuma's diverse musical worlds. Many of my techniques could arguably be classified as conventional ethnomusicological research methods. During my third visit, I established a research routine. In the early mornings, I would attend Dinka language and culture lessons with my teacher Alier Manyang Jok. He was instrumental in helping me translate song lyrics and understand Dinka music and dance in their cultural contexts. Studying and performing Dinka songs and dances allowed me to better understand the performative processes, meanings, and nuances of these activities during public events. When I was learning songs with Alier, he would often call in friends and elders, both men and women, to provide further insight into their meaning. This process of learning a foreign music as a musician, what Mantle Hood (1960, 55) termed a "bi-musicality" approach, proved invaluable for understanding the creative processes of song composition and reception. In the afternoons and evenings, I would frequent market areas and meet with hip hop artists, ox song singers, community leaders, and NGO workers. I would also use this time to conduct formal and informal discussions, attend public festivals, and observe workshops on popular music production.

In addition to researching music, carrying out the demands of everyday life was critically important for partially experiencing how it felt to inhabit a refugee camp. The chronic diarrhea, the bouts of malaria, the cold bucket baths,

the sweat from daily temperatures in the high nineties, the blasts of sand on my
face from windstorms, the trash-filled puddles of water against my legs when
walking on flooded roads, the guilt of paying for injera dishes in the Ethiopian
and Somali markets while my Dinka friends and neighbors mostly ate food
rations, and the thirst I felt when the water taps broke down all contributed to
an embodied knowledge (Holmes 2013). "Embodied experience," anthropologist Seth Holmes suggests, "offers thickness and vividness to the ethnographic
description of everyday life, including such critical realities as social suffering,
inequality and hierarchy, and local and global solidarity" (2013, 57). Indeed, my
body and mind were inseparable from my understanding of life in the Kakuma
camp. Though I only experienced a fraction of the precarious conditions camp
residents faced and continue to face, my attempts to better understand these debilitating conditions motivated me to make my research relevant for addressing
immediate concerns and for exposing larger systems of inequality extending
across and beyond the Kakuma camp's physical territory.

It was during my third visit that I decided to work in solidarity with performing artists and community leaders to address their grievances with the
encampment system. Through research, I became keenly aware of several administrative procedures that impinged on the daily lives of camp residents, providing the impetus for an activist engagement. Despite the UNHCR's hiring of
Kenyan police to provide security in the camp, some police officers generated
insecurity for refugees. They did so by beating and detaining young people
who violated evening curfews and charging organizers illegal fees for social
activities conducted at night. The heads of the police administration also halted
Dinka Christian activities and weekly dance practices, claiming they caused
violence and insecurity. Furthermore, the UNHCR and its contracted agencies
failed to provide fair financial compensation to performing artists involved in
their social campaigns. The UNHCR also drastically reduced resettlement
quotas for citizens from South Sudan. As a result, select leaders asked if I could
assist in redressing these issues, so I designed my research process to fit the
needs of the respective campaigns. It is important to note that the resettlement campaign involved neither studying nor advocating for music and dance;
however, my support for greater resettlement numbers aligned with my politics
and fostered greater trust and respect among my South Sudanese colleagues
and friends. Overall, this problem solving–based approach to research required
working in collaboration with members from local communities, the UNHCR,
the LWF, the AP, and the DRA.

"Follow the music" is an age-old adage for conducting ethnomusicological
research. Musical events, ethnomusicologist Ruth Stone argues, are important

social contexts for observing and understanding the ways participants communicate and make meaning through music (2010 [1982], 1–7). I, like many ethnomusicologists, inquired about and sought out performances, social rituals, and recording sessions in the Kakuma camp. I attended a wide array of musical events, from hip hop shows and multicultural performances to Dinka weekly dances and Christian ceremonial processions that my interlocutors called marches. My attendance at these events helped me hear, feel, see, and understand the significance of music-making and its wider social meaning for performers, audiences, and their communities. Had I not been present at the Christian marches, for example, I would potentially have been less inclined to advocate in solidarity with church pastors to reverse the police's ban on this communal activity.

And yet I found that the requirements of the different social campaigns I joined largely drove my research agenda. Prior to my arrival, I had no intention of studying police bans on Christian activities and Dinka traditional dances or, for that matter, the labor rights of hip hop artists, the consequences of police brutality, or the process of resettlement. An ethics of responsibility oriented toward addressing injustice and supporting the interests of my interlocutors required me not only to attend musical performances and interview musicians but also to visit police stations, government offices, and UN compounds. I participated in strategic planning meetings with Christian pastors, hip hop musicians, and Dinka youth leaders. This approach differed from research projects aimed at testing a specific social theory about a musical sound or collecting information about a musical tradition receiving scant attention in academia. Music was undoubtedly an important part of my research, but of utmost concern was the necessity to follow the campaign. In some ways, this "follow the campaign" approach contributed to a thinning out of the types of "thick description" (Geertz 1973, 6–10) commonly associated with "the anthropology of music" (Merriam 1964). Contrastingly, I believe my commitment to rectifying social injustice makes the stories and experiences of my research participants more audible and legible compared to the work of a researcher whose objectives fail to question the practicality of encampment.

"Write this down," said Thon Mariar, a prominent leader, activist, journalist, and educator living in Kakuma One. "The refugee camp is like a garden."[10] We were seated across from each other under an awning of trees behind the cement-block youth center in the Hong Kong market. He made this statement during our discussion about police officers halting the Dinka weekly dances to extract bribes from youth leaders keen on holding these communal activities. He explained that the concept of the garden elucidates the exploitative process of refugees existing as "crops" for corrupt administrators to cultivate wealth. Long after our meeting ended, Thon's understanding of the Kakuma camp as a garden has continued to reverberate in my head. His critical concept vividly articulates other refugees' complaints about the ways aid workers and academic researchers alike have built their careers after temporarily working in the camp. Many refugees, meanwhile, have had to endure numerous years living within a precarious and unequal encampment system. Thon's concept of the garden thus serves as a critical assessment of the unequal relations of power constituting a UNHCR-governed space. It has also helped remind me of my own ethical responsibility to take continuing action with what I have learned from the Kakuma camp's social actors.

On *Composing Aid*

This book's title, *Composing Aid*, conveys several important aspects of this research project. First, aid in the Kakuma camp has generally consisted of more than just the external delivery of food, shelter, healthcare, and other services. Camp inhabitants also helped themselves and others through creative means. This book documents both the compositional processes involved in making music and dance and the role of these expressive practices in creating meaningful, enjoyable, and dignified lives. Second, this study has genealogical ties to Barbara Harrell-Bond's (1986) book *Imposing Aid*, a pioneering publication in forced migration studies critical of the aid system's impact on refugees in East Africa. *Composing Aid* builds on Harrell-Bond's critical assessment of humanitarianism by adding an ethnographically grounded analysis of expressive culture. In the chapters that follow, I document how and why music, dance, and performance functioned as potent social forces through which to reproduce, refigure, and contest humanitarian rule. Third, while I have attempted to portray the ideas and experiences of my interlocutors as accurately as possible, I recognize that I have made compositional choices on how to represent their stories and the aid system as a whole. The phrase *composing aid* thus highlights my active role in shaping this ethnographic account of music and encampment in Kenya. And finally, conceiving of the aid system and the wider refugee regime as a socially constructed and dynamic process is crucial for recognizing that it is not a static system but rather one that can be transformed into something better.

With these ideas in mind, it is important to mention some of my compositional approaches. For purposes of confidentiality, I have changed the names of everyone described in this book except for public officials and select popular musicians who have made their refugee status and music known in public media. All of the conversations and quotes are based on recordings from structured interviews, handwritten notes of actual events, and secondary sources. Most importantly, I learned that many refugees were skilled in documenting and depicting their own experiences through mediums including audiovisual recordings and written prose. Recognition of the capacity of Kakuma's inhabitants to tell their own stories led me to deploy a variety of data collection techniques. Throughout this book, I have included the voices and views of the Kakuma camp's inhabitants as expressed in their music as well as in *Kanere*, an online newspaper established and run by refugees living in the Kakuma camp. Chapter 2 includes findings from an essay writing contest I organized wherein I requested that Kakuma's inhabitants submit critical commentary about how camp operations affected music, dance, and rituals. I have also drawn from data sources that emerged from the various social campaigns in which I participated. Chapter 3 incorporates findings from an informative video about the cost of musical labor in Kakuma's camp economy that I made in collaboration with filmmaker John Baraka and musicians King Moses and E-Squad. Chapter 4 includes narratives drawn from letters Dinka youth leaders sent to the Kakuma camp's governing authorities during their campaign to overturn the police's ban on weekly dances. And chapter 5 includes the responses of select Dinka Christian leaders seeking to reverse the police's halting of marching activities and midnight mass services. Collectively, these data sources elucidate the desires and worldviews of the musicians, dancers, and community leaders I met in the Kakuma camp as well as their perspicacious insights on the inequalities of encampment.

Another important compositional issue concerns the kinds of voices and experiences present and absent in this study. English-speaking young men from the Democratic Republic of the Congo and South Sudan are the most represented demographics in this book. There are several reasons why this is the case. A major reason is that all the music- and dance-oriented social campaigns I joined were led by individuals from these backgrounds. My commitment to only conducting research that had an immediate impact for individuals and groups desiring research assistance thus resulted in less focus on the music of other social groups in the Kakuma camp. Additionally, my subject position as an unmarried foreign man gendered my research focus. In the Dinka neighborhood where I resided, it was considered taboo for unmarried men to socialize in women's spaces. For this reason, I exclusively ate with and conversed with other young, unmarried men. My gendered subjectivity and habitation of mostly male spaces contributed to a greater inclusion of male voices and experiences in this book. And while I studied and conversed in Dinka, Somali, and Swahili language on a daily basis, I was not proficient enough in these languages to have complex conversations with native speakers. This limited my involvement with elders, many of whom were not fluent in English. Each of these interconnected factors has resulted in me representing only a partial view of the complex and diverse sociocultural lives of Kakuma's inhabitants.

The musicians, dancers, community leaders, and individuals I met in the Kakuma camp—my teachers and consultants, my caregivers and friends—are those whose experiences and views I have attempted to accurately represent in this book. I do not aim to "give voice to the marginalized" through this work, a phrase that I have long found paternalistic and misleading. I often witnessed Kakuma's inhabitants fighting for and achieving recognition of their rights and related practices. They held planning meetings, wrote letters to the UNHCR and DRA, and lobbied campaigns in front of governing officials. By acting and writing in solidarity with them rather than on behalf of them, I seek to be just one of many individuals involved in redressing the ill effects of encampment. I witnessed members of Afrostars Entertainment, the Dinka weekly dances, and the Episcopal Church of Sudan challenge uneven power structures and stereotypical perceptions of what it means to be a refugee. Their friends and families as well as their colleagues and communities have long known what they offer to the world. This book aims to build on this recognition by mobilizing research about their lifeways and pursuits of dignity, well-being, and social justice. With these ideas in mind, I invite individuals and institutions to read and critique the stories and analyses in this book and to reflect on their choices in responding to the problematic effects of humanitarian encampment.

Notes

1. Throughout this book, I use the term Kakuma to refer to the place where *both* the Kakuma camp and Kakuma town are located.

2. Kanere, "World Refugee Day 2011," *Kakuma News Reflector*, August 21, 2011, https://kanere.org/world-refugee-day-2011/.

3. Kanere, "World Refugee Day 2011."

4. Author's personal observation, June 18, 2011, Kakuma Refugee Camp, Kenya.

5. Angelina Jolie, "Do 1 Thing: Angelina Jolie." *The UNHCR, the UN Refugee Agency*, November 10, 2011, video, 0:36, https://www.youtube.com/watch?v=VUz5HOOfLzw.

6. Author's personal observation, August 4, 2013, Kakuma Refugee Camp, Kenya.

7. The main NGO compound was referred to as the "LWF compound" because it was administered by the LWF.

8. Roger Zetter (1991 and 2007) uses the concept of "labelling" to elucidate the bureaucratic processes involved in the social construction of the refugee subject.

9. This dialogue is a summary of my conversation with a group of young Somali men in the Somali market area of Kakuma One on July 16, 2013.

10. Thon Mariar, personal communication, March 2014, Kakuma Refugee Camp, Kenya.

1

∿

BELONGING

"I Belong to Hip Hop Music"

Musafiri Balabala's fans anointed him with the nickname King Moses because of how impressed they were with his rap skills. As a teenager, he often competed in and won music competitions that the Lutheran World Federation (LWF) and FilmAid International (FAI) held during school break periods. By his early twenties, he had established himself as one of the most well-known and accomplished rappers in the Kakuma Refugee Camp. His songs "Mkali" and "Maesabu Yasiku" ignited audiences to cheer, dance, and rap along at his shows in LWF youth centers and local *hoteli* in the market areas. His role in the musical collective Afrostars Entertainment compelled other young rappers to follow his lead. Due to his status and influence, managers from the UNHCR, FAI, and the Octopizzo Foundation regularly asked King Moses not only to participate in their projects but also to help organize other rappers and singers.

I first met King Moses in 2014 as part of my research on hip hop and humanitarian politics in the Kakuma camp. He had been living in the camp since 2011, having arrived from conflict areas in the eastern region of the Democratic Republic of the Congo. Over the course of my research, he graciously invited me into his musical world. I went to his live shows. I attended meetings organized by Afrostars Entertainment. And I frequently conversed with him about his artistry and experiences living in a UNHCR camp. Since my last departure from Kakuma in 2015, we have kept in contact via WhatsApp messenger. The COVID-19 pandemic put a halt to my original plan to revisit Kenya in 2020 and 2021 for follow-up research. Nevertheless, King Moses and I were still able to converse over the phone.

During one of our conversations in June 2021, I asked him where he felt he belonged in the world.[1] He responded by saying he felt "countryless." He explained how ongoing war in Congo made it impossible to go back. He said that if he were to be provided citizenship in Kenya, he would appreciate it because of his affinity for Kenyans, especially the ones he knew in Nairobi. However, obtaining Kenyan citizenship was not likely. I then asked him, if he did not feel a sense of belonging to a country, whether he felt any kind of belonging to a hip hop community.

KM: "Yes! Exactly! Yes!" he exclaimed.

OS: "Can you explain?"

KM: "Yeah. First of all, I am a lyricist. And . . . ah . . . hip hop culture is rhyming, it rhymes. I can rhyme. I can make sense. I can talk to my community, and they can understand what I am saying. I can be a teacher. 'Cuz a rapper is a teacher, and my words work to correct people who are wrong and people who are right. I am the mirror of my society. So, I belong to hip hop music. Because I provide what they want to be provided."

OS: "What is it that they want to be provided?"

KM: "The thing that they want to hear from a hip hop artist is what I am giving them—if it's the street word I give them, if it's hustling, if it's love, if it's sadness, if it's whatever advice, I do them. That's what they want . . . they want from an artist. You can give them love. You can give them street life. You can give them sadness. You can make them cry. You can make them love to make love. You can make them . . . to remember the street."

For King Moses, hip hop culture provides a meaningful way to constitute a sense of belonging within a nation-state system that fails to do so. His roles as a lyricist and artist empowers him and allows him to occupy a position of social strength in a place and political environment where he has often felt excluded. His social role as a rapper enables him to make sense of the world for both himself and his audiences. Crucially, the social and sensorial aspects of musically constituted belonging are significant not only for King Moses but also for many of the individuals I met in northwestern Kenya facing the difficulties of forced migration and the refugee regime.

Sonic Politics of Belonging

Belonging is a central concern in situations of displacement. Debates often revolve around when and how forced migrants can return to their national homelands. For many individuals and institutions, this objective is a top priority. And yet while this goal has its benefits, it can also have harmful effects. The belief that a person's rightful place of belonging is the country from which they fled has contributed to establishing an exclusionary border regime. Contrary to popular perception, states and international agencies have constructed refugee camps not merely for altruistic purposes but also for controlling unwanted migrants, a process anthropologist Michel Agier (2011, 4) refers to as "managing the undesirables." As refugee camps persist far past their intended lifespan, it is necessary to better understand (1) how people are made to belong in these sites; (2) what kinds of belonging camp inhabitants create and desire; and (3) how and why different forms of belonging reproduce and contest structural inequality. One insightful way to unpack these issues is by focusing on a type of expression that constitutes a kaleidoscopic range of belonging—music.

In the face of rupture, music can serve as a powerful means through which to constitute multiple types of belonging. Forced migration often entails fleeing one's home with few personal possessions. Music can help in such situations because it can be transported and circulated through the body and technology, then recalled and recontextualized in new locales. Listening to and performing music can evoke feelings and memories that forge old and new senses of belonging to people and places located near and far. The affective capacities of music can have a "presencing" effect, reintegrating individuals with embodied and situated pasts (Impey 2018, 26). The ideational qualities of music can constitute "ideologies of belonging" in the face of social marginalization (Webster-Kogen 2018, 12). Individuals dealing with similar ordeals can use music to gather in shared spaces, reflect on shared histories, and feel shared experiences. The repetition of rhythmic grooves and familiar sounds can put people in "social synchrony" with each other (Turino 2008, 44). Over time, regular engagement in musical activities can establish meaningful attachments not only to social groups but also to the places where they are performed (Feld 1996). Ultimately, the capacity of music to foster social membership is vital for individuals separated from family and friends, communities and countries.

This capacity to create belonging is also what makes music highly political. During my research in the Kakuma camp, I observed how music fostered participation in diverse social worlds, ranging from popular music scenes and religious congregations to ethnic communities. The subjectivities forged from these social worlds, however, became enmeshed with institutional forces designed to assign and control where forced migrants belonged within the nation-state system. To better understand these processes, migration scholar Nira Yuval-Davis's (2011) ideas on the "politics of belonging" are particularly apt for elucidating the intersection between music, power, and subjectivity in a long-term refugee camp. According to Yuval-Davis, the politics of belonging consist of "specific political projects aimed at constructing belonging to particular collectivity/ies which are themselves being constructed in these projects in very specific ways and in very specific boundaries" (2011, 10). More than a uni-directional flow of power, this process comprises subjection to and resistance by political agents (2011, 20). Through this framework, refugee camps may be understood as subject-making political projects within a wider political project of migratory control, as well as sites of contestation. With these ideas in mind, I approach the study of music, dance, and performance in the Kakuma camp through the sonic politics of belonging—complex social processes of belonging through which enactments of music and sound uphold, negotiate, refigure, and contest the political project of humanitarian encampment.

Processes of inclusion and exclusion were main facets of the sonic politics of belonging in the Kakuma camp. Not all forms of musicking were valued and treated the same.[2] Certain musical practices were considered pleasing to the ear, while others were perceived as noise. More than just personal tastes, valu-ations of music-making and musical aesthetics were interwoven with norms of belonging within the space of encampment. Music deemed pleasing to camp officials benefited from financial, administrative, and public support, while mu-sic considered unwanted noise was censored and delegitimized. The symbolic power of seemingly benign forms of music was involved in regulating social behavior. The recurrent use of certain narratives and musical aesthetics and practices worked at subtle and subconscious levels, normalizing hegemonic systems. The regular display of ethnonational dances during UNHCR events, for example, reproduced political boundaries that legitimized the refugee camp's existence. UNHCR/NGO-funded songs depicting forced migrants as subjects requiring humanitarian support reproduced dominant ideas on what constituted a real and ideal refugee.

The valuation and treatment of music in the Kakuma camp were manifes-tations of what performance studies scholar Leonardo Cardoso refers to as "sound-politics"—"sounds as objects that are susceptible to state interven-tion through specific regulatory, disciplinary, and punishment mechanisms" (2019, 1). Part of understanding how sound-politics operated in the camp re-quires recognizing that sound and listening are culturally positioned within wider power dynamics (Martin 2021; Cardoso 2019; Chávez 2017; Ochoa-Gautier 2015). As Alex Chávez states in his work on music and migration at the US-Mexico border, "sound is heard through culturally and historically situ-ated forms of listening, that is, through aural modes of attention that circulate within social fields of meaning and experience contoured by power, politics, and economy" (2017, 7).

Drawing on these ideas, I approach the sonic politics of belonging through an intersectional approach that considers an individual's mutually constitutive social locations—race, class, gender, sexuality, age, ability, religion, nation, and other facets of identity (see Martin 2021; Yuval-Davis 2011; Crenshaw 1990). "Intersectional listening," writes Alison Martin, "enables us to interrogate music, sound, and noise, as well as what lies in between these distinctions in their relation to broad understandings of space and place" (2021, 108). For example, I found that several of the Kakuma camp's high-ranking security officials deemed Dinka weekly dances as a dangerous cultural practice that should be halted. Their decision was shaped, in part, by a belief that these dances consisted of overly aggressive young Dinka men from pastoralist areas of war-torn South Sudan. In other words, intersecting identifications of age, ethnicity, gender, class, livelihood, and nationality influenced how these security officials heard, understood, and treated the Dinka dances. An intersectional framework thus provides critical insights on how and why valuations of musically mediated social belonging in the Kakuma camp were subjective and contingent on intersecting social locations and the hierarchy of humanitarian government.

Crucially, attunement to the sonic politics of belonging makes audible instructive moments of dissonance and dissent. "Sound and listening," Brandon LaBelle argues, "are situated as the basis for capacities by which to nurture an insurrectionary sensibility—a potential found in the quiver of the eardrum, the strains of the voice, the vibrations and echoes that spirit new formations of social solidarity" (2018, 5). Indeed, critical awareness of discord associated with music-making in Kakuma elucidates how certain subjectivities challenged and refigured normative ideas of belonging within the territory of encampment. Dissonance and dissent were not just disruptive occurrences that needed to be managed and silenced. Rather, attuning one's ear to noise and the oppositional forces of music manifested within the margins of the nation-state system illuminates the kinds of disqualified knowledges and utopian ideas necessary for redressing the detrimental effects of using the long-term refugee camp to sort, monitor, and control forced migrants.

The Protraction of Encampment in Kenya

The Kakuma Refugee Camp lies seven hundred kilometers northwest of Kenya's capital, Nairobi. It is situated between the political borders of South Sudan, Uganda, and Ethiopia in the semiarid desert region of Turkana County.

During the twentieth century, the area shifted from serving as a seasonal grazing area for seminomadic Turkana pastoralists to a British colonial outpost and finally a small town located next to a sprawling encampment administered by the UNHCR. Originally established in 1992 to provide relief and refuge for migrants fleeing southern Sudan, Kakuma's camp area has since turned into a catchall site for managing forced migration in the region.[3] Individuals who arrived in the early nineties would have mostly heard Swahili, English, and Turkana, the dominant languages of the aid agencies and local Kenyan population. They would have also heard Arabic, Dinka, and Nuer, the languages of the first refugees from southern Sudan. Even more languages from across the region entered Kakuma's soundscape during the 1990s and 2010s. During my research between 2013 and 2015, Somali, Amharic, Oromo, Acholi, Kirundi, and Congolese Swahili were among the languages I heard on a daily basis. Tens of thousands of Kenyan citizens also settled the town of Kakuma, largely to take advantage of the financial inflows accompanying a UNHCR-governed space.

As Kakuma's camp area diversified and expanded into one of the largest refugee camps on the globe, the UNHCR created increasingly planned out and bureaucratic systems of social control. Officials designated the camp's main sections Kakuma One, Two, Three, and Four, which they further divided into zones and blocks (formerly known as groups). The different layouts of each main section are indicative of the UNHCR's institutional shift toward greater levels of planning and oversight. The narrow, crooked, and jig-sawed pathways in Kakuma One resulted from spontaneous settlement of the camp's oldest parts. The paths and roads designating blocks and zones for Kakuma Two and Three became more rectangular and squared. The camp area doubled in size after an alleged political coup in South Sudan set off another civil war in 2014, bringing the camp's total population to approximately 175,000 people. The UNHCR catered to this newer group by constructing Kakuma Four, which has the largest and most ordered layout in terms of roads, housing plots, and service facilities.

Many people think of refugee camps as temporary sites for migrants fleeing persecution and conflict. They typically imagine that these places provide short-term care and relief and that once the emergency period ends, the camps will close, and the refugees will return to their countries of origin. In reality, many forced migrants have lived in these sites for years and some for decades. What factors have led to the existence of the long-term refugee camp? Has forced migration always been a facet of humanity? And if so, why is the refugee camp a relatively recent invention? More specifically, why have UNHCR camps that were originally designed for temporary relief in Kenya existed for three decades?

Part of understanding why the refugee camp emerged in Kenya in the late twentieth century requires examining the effects of European colonialism. The current perception of cross-border migration in Kenya can be traced back to 1895, when British imperialists set up the East African Protectorate. It was during this period that the present-day borders of East Africa emerged. Conflict and displacement occurred during the colonial and postindependence periods due to the ill-conceived borders drawn by European colonialists more interested in resource extraction than cultural sensitivity. From the 1920s to 1950s, hundreds of thousands of Rwandans and Burundians fled state-imposed forced labor and physical abuse for refuge in Uganda and, in lesser numbers, Kenya. Conflict and war between the Sudanese government and the southern Sudanese compelled refugees to seek safety in Uganda and Kenya in the 1950s and for many years onward. By the 1960s, a majority of African countries had achieved independence from European control—Somalia and the Democratic Republic of the Congo (1960), Tanzania (1961), Uganda (1962), and Kenya (1963). The 1960–1967 civil wars in Congo and Mobutu's repressive regime forced tens of thousands of refugees to migrate, mostly into Uganda but also to Burundi, Tanzania, Sudan, and Kenya. Colonialism thus produced two main conditions enabling the establishment of refugee camps: national borders and violent conflict.

For the refugee camp to materialize, however, these two factors required another component—a shift in attitude toward migrants. In the aftermath of Kenya's independence, the government enacted a laissez-faire approach to forced migration (Verdirame and Harrell-Bond 2005, 31). State officials allowed refugees to settle rather freely in towns and cities and to earn livelihoods as best they could with little infringement; the Kenyan government took few actions to restrict basic rights to movement, work, and education, enabling refugees to start businesses and find jobs in universities and the health sector; and while xenophobic attitudes toward refugees did exist, public sentiment was largely supportive of refugees (2005, 32). By the late 1980s, however, the government became increasingly more distrustful of ethnic Somalis in Kenya, resulting in the forced deportation of approximately three thousand Somalis to Somalia (Hyndman 2000, 49–50). Kenyan officials' persistent refusal to encamp forced migrants would also not last. After armed factions toppled the Somali government of Siad Barre, Somalis began to arrive in larger numbers into Kenya and later Uganda. In the early 1990s, the need to accommodate four hundred thousand refugees from Somalia, along with approximately seven thousand refugees from Sudan, prompted the Kenyan government to appeal for assistance from the UNHCR. With formal approval from Kenyan officials, the UNHCR set up camps around Mombasa for Somalis before moving them to Dadaab, a camp in Mandera for Ethiopians, and another in Kakuma for minors fleeing war in Sudan. Between 1995 and 1997, tension between Kenyan and Somali traders led to the closure of the Mombasa camps, and until recent years most refugees have resided in either Kakuma or Dadaab. In 2018, the Kalobeyei camp settlement was officially launched to cater to the increasing number of refugees arriving from South Sudan and to decongest the Kakuma camp. In recent years, the UNHCR has expanded its urban refugee program in Kenya's cities, though the vast number of officially registered refugees still reside in encampments. State officials in Kenya have operated these camps through what some scholars term a "containment" approach (Verdirame and Harrell-Bond 2005, 31; Hyndman 2000, 23–24). Refugee policies have mandated that most forced migrants reside in camps, where they are required to wait until they can either return to their so-called countries of origin or obtain official residency in Kenya or another country.

More than just a national project, the establishment of Kenya's encampments stems from a far-reaching international system. The legal category of "refugee" is a relatively recent state invention. The aftermath of war in Europe in the mid-twentieth century resulted in the creation of a new juridico-political subject codified into international law. The UN 1951 Convention considers a refugee to be a person who "as a result of events occurring before 1 January 1951 and owing to well-founded fear of being persecuted for reasons of race, religion, nationality, membership of a particular social group or political opinion, is outside the country of his nationality and is unable or, owing to such fear, is unwilling to avail himself of the protection of that country; or who, not having a nationality and being outside the country of his former habitual residence as a result of such events, is unable or, owing to such fear, is unwilling to return to it" (Article 1).

The "events" in Article 1 specifically pertain to Europe's postwar period in the mid-twentieth century. The 1967 Protocol removed the temporal and geographic restrictions of the 1951 Convention, providing the legal basis for more expansive institutional reach and influence. The legibility of the refugee as a distinct political subject has become reaffirmed and reproduced through what scholars have termed the "international refugee regime" (IRR)—a system of institutions, legal instruments, and norms administered through the UNHCR and deployed to regulate the movement of forced migration across international borders (Besteman 2016, 58; Scalettaris 2007). This regime dictates the terms through which people categorized as refugees face differentiated treatment within the nation-state order. Its blueprint for regulating migrants consists of what the IRR has dubbed "durable solutions"—"repatriation (return to the country of origin) local integration (permanent residency or naturalization in the first country of asylum) and resettlement (ordered migration to a third country)" (Long 2014, 476). These solutions are grounded in the idea that refugees are incomplete and out of place. They are based on a logic and understanding of the nation-state as the only viable form of belonging. Such ideas are rooted in what Liisa Malkki (1995b, 509) calls a "sedentarist bias," a predisposition that links people and belonging to state territories and overlooks the regularity of forced migration.

Numerous political factors over the last several decades have affected the IRR's capacity to execute its durable solutions. Some scholars have argued that northern states have historically used the refugee regime for their own political objectives (Besteman 2016; Chimni 1999). From 1945 to 1980, the United States resettled two million refugees, 90 percent of whom came from Communist countries (Besteman 2016, 212). The US and its European allies shifted toward repatriation as their preferred solution during the post–Cold War era because it was no longer politically advantageous to accept refugees from Communist adversaries. The Bush administration enacted even tighter procedures for resettlement after the 9/11 attacks, moving toward a security model wherein refugees are regarded with deep mistrust. Obama's administration strove to resettle more refugees to the United States, especially during the final years of his second term: the official quota in 2017 reached 110,000. In a sharp reversal of this mandate, the Trump administration's resettlement quota of 30,000 in fiscal year 2019 and 18,000 in fiscal year 2020 (which started October 1, 2019) is indicative of many Americans' continued xenophobia toward refugees. Moreover, northern states have used political and economic influence to externalize their borders by funding UNHCR-administered encampments across the Global South. The preference of many states for repatriation over resettlement and local integration has resulted in turning the relief camp from a temporary structure to a more permanent fixture across the contemporary political landscape (Besteman 2016; Long 2014). And despite the fact that on average, no more than 1 percent of refugees are resettled each year, many refugees in Kenya have come to view this process as a viable means for migrating to Western countries during a period when other legal entryways have become limited (Jansen 2008 and 2018). This belief has altered the intended purpose of resettlement and contributed to extended stays in Kenya's refugee camps. Besteman has argued that, far from being an altruistic system, the "[IRR] is setup to maintain inequality, disempower refugees, and protect the borders of the global north, in addition to providing care for displaced people while global powers determine where they will be allowed to go" (2016, 64).

In another caveat to this issue, refugee camps have persisted because of their political functions. For example, closing the Palestinian camps operated through the United Nations Relief and Works Agency (UNRWA) would diminish claims for establishing a Palestinian state in the face of Israeli occupation. This same issue has applied to the city-like camps for Tibetans in Dharamsala, India, and for Sahrawis in western Sahara, for example. And while the Kenyan state and the UNHCR have operated the Kakuma camp as an apolitical catchall site for housing forced migrants from across the region, in practice, the camp has played a potent political role for refugees seeking national self-determination. For many South Sudanese refugees, for example, the camp functioned as both an important symbol of political struggle against North Sudanese oppression and a crucial socioeconomic resource for establishing a sovereign South Sudan in 2011. Similarly, Oromo nationalists seeking to separate from the Ethiopian state have used the Kakuma camp to bring greater international attention to their political struggle.

Since its inception, the Kakuma camp has contracted and expanded, but it has never closed, despite multiple attempts. A significant portion of its population migrated to South Sudan in the late 2000s after the 2005 Comprehensive Peace Agreement (CPA) between the Sudan People's Liberation Movement (SPLM) and the government of Sudan. In the following years, increasing outflows of migration created speculation that the camp would shut down. The pending closure created anxiety among aid workers fearful of losing their jobs, among the remaining refugees fearful of where they would be relocated, and among Kenyan business owners fearful of how they would earn an income if donor money stopped. The Kenyan government eventually decided not to close the camp. It instead bused in tens of thousands of Somalis from Dadaab, in the eastern part of the country, which at the time was the site of the most highly populated refugee complex on the globe. Increasing numbers of forced migrants also arrived from conflict areas in the eastern region of the Democratic Republic of the Congo. Over the last several years, conflict and instability in South Sudan has caused greater numbers of South Sudanese to arrive. In July 2022, the Kakuma camp's total population was 188,000, with just over 50 percent hailing from South Sudan. In recent years, Kenyan state officials have threatened to shut down all refugee camps on the grounds that they pose a security risk. Such threats prompted calls by the UNHCR and partner agencies for the Kenyan state to rethink its demands on the grounds that camp closures would create a humanitarian crisis. Undeterred, the Kenyan government announced in March 2021 that it would close both the Dadaab and Kakuma camps by June 30, 2022. This deadline has since passed and both camps, as of February 2022, are still in operation.

The Diversity of Sonic Belonging

With its long-term function as a catchall site for regulating forced migrants from eastern and central Africa, the Kakuma camp turned into a sprawling area with a sonically diverse population spanning different countries and cultures, regions and religions, ecologies and economies. Every year, ethnonational cultural groups—Burundian drummers, Congolese lingala musicians, Somali dhaanto dancers, Oromo coffee ceremony actors, and Acholi, Nuer, Dinka, Nubian, and Equatoria singers and dancers—performed at events for UN-recognized international days at the Napata Fairgrounds and the International Organization for Migration (IOM) Peace Centre. Every weekend, the collective singing of Christian choirs and congregations from a range of denominations filled local courtyards. Every day, the sacred sounds of the Islamic call to prayer emanated from speakers perched atop the corrugated iron roofs of the numerous mosques strewn throughout the camp. The sounds of secular music, most notably hip hop, R&B, and reggae styles from East Africa, Nigeria, and North America, emanated from audio technologies. Bongo flava music from Tanzania blasted from speaker systems in bars and restaurants. Video shops screened the latest music videos from MTV Africa. Rap music blared from portable radios affixed to motorcycle taxis and from the mobile phones of teenagers and twenty-somethings on their way home from school. Amid this urban soundscape, Kakuma's long history as a grazing area for cattle herders was also audible. The long legs of camels trotted across the sandy passageways located along the sundrenched banks of the Tarach River Basin. Turkana pastoralists dressed in cloth tunics and short-sleeved shirts shouted directional commands to their herds of bleating goats, bellowing cows, and grunting camels. Senses of belonging to rural lifeways resonated in the dancing fields of Dinka, Nuer, Nubian, and Equatoria communities keen on carrying out their cultural traditions.

In an area officially owned by the Kenyan state and governed by the UNHCR, sonic and musical practices transformed the unfamiliar territories of Turkana County and the standardized packages of relief aid into socially active and culturally meaningful places of belonging. During the early morning hours, the swishing sounds of brooms clearing away the previous night's debris emanated from blocks and zones, while the shuffling feet and chattering sounds of children and market workers filled the dirt roadways. By afternoon, the sizzle of potatoes and goat meat in skillets and pots of hot oil at Ethiopian and Somali restaurants mixed with the whirring of electric razors hooked up to car batteries at neighboring barbershops. The loud rumbling of dried maize pulverized in electric grinders competed with lively conversations and daily Al Jazeera telecasts beamed in through satellite dishes in homes, cafés, and restaurants. The Kakuma camp was a place where Ethiopian *hoteli* were turned into Somali wedding halls; where courtyards became sacred sites of Christian, Islamic, Jewish, and African indigenous religious worship; and where riverbeds were football pitches one day and Dinka and Nuer dancing fields the next.

Crucially, the capacity of music and dance to circulate across temporal and spatial boundaries enabled Kakuma's camp inhabitants to forge connections with people, places, and ideas beyond the camp's physical location. Dinka choir members from the Episcopal church, for example, learned new hymnal songs by sharing cassettes, compact discs, and MP3s with newly arrived migrants from South Sudan. The transmission of songs during weekly choir practices and church services enabled members of the congregation to forge ties to their local communities and to a wider transnational Christianity. And while social membership forged through singing and dancing was often organized along South Sudanese Dinka affiliations, I found that many worshippers held universalistic views of faith that extended beyond national and ethnic boundaries. In a similar fashion, many young people felt senses of belonging to capitalistic lifestyles exemplified in commercial music styles circulated between and across Africa, the Caribbean, and North America. Smart Djaba and King Moses, leaders of the musical collective Afrostars Entertainment, organized and performed live hip hop and R&B shows in local venues—Francos, the Green *hoteli*, and the Nile *hoteli*. They used these venues to forge communal ties with like-minded performers and audiences. Through these social spaces, they could not only imagine but also enact their participation in the wider East African commercial music scene. These findings align with Arjun Appadurai's (1996, 33) writings on identity formation in the late twentieth century, and in particular the effects of a diverse array of -*scapes* constituted through the global movement of humans, media, technology, financial capital, and ideology. "These cultural flows," he argues, "are the building blocks to imagined worlds—multiple worlds that are constituted by the historically situated imaginations of persons and groups spread across the globe" (1996, 33). And while music's mobile capacities enabled diverse soundscapes to circulate across and beyond the Kakuma camp's physical locale, it is crucial to recognize that in a place characterized by extreme social control, sonic frictions were also a part of everyday life.

Sounds of Segregated Care

Over time, a particular kind of sonic environment manifested in Kakuma— one born out of the seemingly contradictory practices of humanitarian care and regulated mobility. On the one hand, the Kakuma camp was a place where refugees could obtain support from the aid system. On the other hand, it was a place designed to separate, sort, and control forced migrants. Over the course of my research, it became clear to me that acts of care were not contradictory to—but rather, complimentary of—a segregating mandate.

The camp's humanitarian soundscape was unlike anything I had ever heard. Social messages—concerning domestic violence, sexual exploitation, early marriage, substance abuse, HIV and AIDS, disability, nutrition, and sanitation—echoed through speaker systems fitted to the backs of roaming white Land Cruisers and Land Rovers. Aid workers and refugees regularly gave speeches about these issues during school functions and public events for World Refugee Day, World AIDS Day, World Water Day, World Earth Day, World Toilet Day, Day of the African Child, International Women's Day, and 16 Days of Activism. Songs, dances, poems, and dramas became mediums through which to circulate social messages because of their perceived capacities to entertain, educate, and empower refugees.

In one sense, the widespread audibility of these messages points to a system of care and concern for the well-being of vulnerable peoples. A critical understanding of arts-based humanitarianism, however, offers a very different perspective. In Ndaliko's study of NGO art projects in the Democratic Republic of the Congo, she observes that the "feel-good factor of art and culture" coupled with the rhetoric of "global interconnection" overshadowed the details of artists' material realities (2016, 188). In the Kakuma camp, a similar phenomenon occurred whereby the feel-good factor of artistic displays of singing and dancing during UNHCR events obfuscated the structural inequalities constituting encampment. The rhetoric of global interconnectedness masked the actual disparity between the relatively unencumbered mobility of humanitarian aid and the heavily constrained mobility of refugees (see Hyndman 2000, 60). Furthermore, the seemingly positive idea that edutainment projects help refugees had the effect of normalizing their status as subjects requiring rehabilitation, simultaneously positioning UN officials and aid workers as the people in power with the skills, knowledge, and technologies necessary to offer them a productive and healthy life. The rhetoric, aesthetics, and affective dimensions of the discourse of care thus contributed to the function of the Kakuma camp as a spatializing technology of management and social control (Jaji 2012; Hyndman 2000).

Within this space, the discourse of care materialized into a peculiar socioeconomic environment. On the one hand, the sounds of material well-being emanated throughout the bustling market areas. Speeches at public UN events often announced the success of new social programs and income generating projects. Overall, financial inflows created through the aid system provided a level of material wealth that exceeded the wider region of Turkana County. And yet a closer listening elucidates the precarity of camp life. The intermittent roars and rumbles of gas-powered generators strewn throughout the camp area and agency compounds permeated the air on a daily basis in a place without public utilities. Commotion was a common occurrence among frustrated patrons vying for positions at overcrowded food ration centers and water taps. Feedback squeals and distortion emanated from the speakers of low quality portable public address systems used during UNHCR/NGO events.

At first listen, one might think the reverberation of precarity in the Kakuma camp was simply due to the operational challenges of underfunded charities. Attention to the political-economy of humanitarian aesthetics, however, provides a more critical perspective. As the protraction of large-scale refugee situations persisted, the UNHCR initiated steps in the 1990s to incorporate a development agenda into its operations (Gabiam 2016, 45). Elements of this agenda materialized in the Kakuma camp as evidenced by the creation of robust market areas and NGO-sponsored business and education programs. And yet Kenya's refugee camps have been constituted through a widespread belief among members of the Kenyan government, UN, and refugee population that camps are meant for temporary habitation despite their more permanent operations, a paradox that has contributed to instability in the lives of refugees (Teferra 2022; Rawlence 2016). State officials, for example, ordered an NGO to demolish newly built houses for refugees in the Dadaab complex on the grounds that they looked too nice and would promote long-term settlement as well as generate animosity among the more economically disadvantaged host community. One could argue that the government was attempting to generate socioeconomic equality between refugees and Kenyans; however, this line of thinking does not hold up if one recognizes that the government placed no regulatory limits on local Kenyans' material well-being. The only paved road in Kakuma, for example, ran through the less populated town area. The socioeconomic threshold placed on Kenya's refugee camps meant that even if the UNHCR/NGOs had been provided with the best specialists, the best technology, the best operational plans, and unlimited capital, they would not have been able to deploy them to their fullest degree. At another level, the Kakuma camp's location in one of the poorest regions in Kenya allowed camp administrators to say something to the effect of "Do you see how well we treat the refugees? They are much better off than the Kenyan-Turkana." While this claim elucidates the difficult problems Kenyan-Turkana faced in this region, this type of reasoning pits the economically disadvantaged against each other, providing comfort to the more affluent. The sonic precarity that proliferated throughout the camp area was thus neither an error nor a capacity issue. Rather, it was the intended and planned result of a humanitarianized space governed through logics of liminal care.

Given the Kakuma camp's wider function as a site for segregating and sorting migrants within a borderland area, it is perhaps unsurprising that the camp area itself was segregated. Over the years, acts of gross sexual misconduct have become a troubling pattern of behavior among aid workers and UN peacekeepers working in crisis and humanitarian situations. From conflict areas in the Balkans in the 1990s to refugee camps in West Africa in the early 2000s to Ebola-affected towns in the Democratic Republic of the Congo in 2018 and 2020, such abuses have manifested from power imbalances between aid workers/UN peacekeepers and the populations they are charged with assisting. In a global effort to address this problem, the UNHCR has established operational procedures designed to protect refugees from the violence of sexual misconduct (IASC 2002). In the Kakuma context, camp policy dictated that refugees and nonrefugees be kept separate from each other during evening and nighttime hours to prevent UNHCR/NGO workers from sexually exploiting and abusing refugees. The sonic manifestation of social segregation in Kakuma could be heard each evening when UNHCR and NGO vehicles rumbled and rolled through the camp area on their way back to the compound or the town of Kakuma and when the squeaking gates of the NGO compound opened and closed for the refugee incentive workers to leave before sundown. Even with this policy and practice in place, acts of sexual misconduct still occurred. What materialized, then, was a system that operationalized the discourse of care in ways that naturalized social segregation due in part to the fundamental power imbalances of humanitarian work.

Social divisions were also shaped by a widespread belief that refugees posed a danger to the safety and security of Kakuma's entire population. Evening curfews mandated that all refugees be in their compounds shortly after sundown for their own safety and for the overall stability of the camp and the surrounding areas. This policy muted the sounds of sociality emanating from roadways and most of the bars and restaurants in the camp area. Curfew restrictions did not apply to Kakuma's town area; however, only nonrefugees were allowed in town at night. The police often restricted refugees from engaging in nighttime music and dance activities on the grounds that such activities caused conflict and insecurity. Refugees who violated curfews and cultural restrictions were subject to police roundups and financial exploitation at the hands of corrupt police officers. Meanwhile, aid officials regularly held all-night dance parties replete with booming music behind the securitized walls of the UNHCR and NGO compounds. The sonic revelry emanating from town and UNHCR and NGO compounds contrasted sharply with the quietude of the camp area.

Various interlocking forms of care thus had the effect of normalizing the segregating effects of encampment. The proliferation of music and arts programs designed to rehabilitate and educate refugees obfuscated and legitimized the refugee regime's control over camp inhabitants. The enforced separation of refugees and aid workers was necessary to ensure the well-being of a camp population subject to the dangers of a humanitarian system plagued with sexual exploitation and abuse. An ideology of liminal care manifested in the sounds of precarious infrastructures that signified and reproduced the dividing lines between refugees and citizens. Meanwhile, police officials could easily legitimize curfews and cultural restrictions by claiming protection trumped the need for social activities in a place of planned precarity, a place intentionally operated to deter long-term settlement by fostering discontent.

Dissonance and Dissent

In August 2015, the first ever Youth Congress was held in the Kakuma camp. The UNHCR and LWF organized this event in the Catholic-run Don Bosco compound, one of the few organizations whose offices and accommodations were located in the camp's interior. The purpose of the Youth Congress was to provide a platform for young people to voice their concerns in front of the camp's main governing agencies. The UNHCR was there. The Kenyan police administration was there. The officials in charge of water, the Norwegian Refugee Council (NRC); housing, the National Council of Churches of Kenya (NCCK); food, the World Food Program (WFP); and education, the Lutheran World Federation (LWF), were also there. By early morning, over fifty refugees in their teens and twenties had trickled into the large timber and cinder block building. They sat in plastic chairs arranged in a circle near the large open windows in the center of the crowded hall. For one of the first sessions, the master of ceremony (MC) invited a top police official to dialogue with the attendees. The officer entered the circle, introduced himself, and welcomed any questions. The upbeat tone in his voice, however, suggested that he did not expect what was about to occur.

At first, the invitees were reluctant to voice their complaints. The MC recognized their apprehension, so he pulled out slips of paper from a brown envelope containing anonymous comments the attendees had submitted beforehand. One by one, he read aloud damning accounts of exploitation and abuse. Soon after, rapper and youth leader King Moses stood up. With passion and poise, he conveyed the ways police officials extorted money from performing artists. He explained how the police charged him and his fellow musicians cash payments for what were supposed to be free performance permits. He also used the moment to decry the aid agencies for their unwillingness to provide fair financial compensation to working musicians. Buoyed by King Moses's bravery to publicly confront a high-ranking police officer, other young women and men stood up. With anger and resentment in their voices, they recounted the ways police officers addressed curfew violations and fights at football games. They told the stunned crowd of aid workers how police officers beat their friends and family members, detained them in jail cells, and charged fees for their release. The UNHCR's protection officer held an emergency meeting later that night. She returned the next day and announced that the UNHCR was implementing a formal process whereby refugees could submit complaints about the police directly to the UNHCR's Protection Office.

This brief account demonstrates that Kakuma's camp inhabitants, far from being passive subjects, were vocal critics of how they were treated and mistreated. In his ethnographic study of humanitarian governance in Kakuma, Hanno Brankamp argues that militarized policing has transformed the refugee camp into an "occupied enclave" wherein the Kenyan police enforce a "humanitarian violence" on refugees living in a place of precarity and limited movement (2019, 71). Rather than accept these difficult conditions, refugees fought against their subjection to this unjust system (see Brankamp 2021). Dissonance in Kakuma's soundscape often occurred when they felt their rights and related practices were impinged on by both the heavy-handed tactics of militarized policing and the subordinating effects of aid delivery. Turning an ear toward dissonance, and in particular to the ways refugees dissented against the camp system, elucidates how they constituted and fought for desired ways of belonging.

Musical dissent manifested in the Kakuma camp in different ways. A main form of opposition entailed vocalizing claims to practice marginalized music activities. King Moses's critique of the ways police officers extorted money from performing artists offers just one example of the ways refugees made claims to camp officials. Another form of dissent manifested through performative protests. The youth group's transgressive piece described at the outset of this book highlights how select artists creatively voiced grievances with the inequities of the camp system through theatrical aesthetics. A less obvious though no less impactful form of dissent involved the very act of making music. In particular, forging spaces of pleasure through music was a political act in a place where refugees were expected to suffer in order to access social and material aid.

It is important to note that dissent was not merely a binary process pitting refugees against camp administrators. Power struggles were diffuse and context specific. The very reason Kenyan managers at the LWF organized the Youth Congress in the first place was to provide refugees with a platform to voice concerns over not only the police but also the new biometric food distribution system, the healthcare system, the school system, and the protection program. After learning of the extreme acts of police brutality that plagued the camp's youth population, members of the UNHCR Protection Office acted quickly to help ameliorate the situation. Examining acts of musical dissent thus requires attending to how allies from across the refugee, UNHCR/NGO worker, and Kenyan populations worked in tandem to advance social justice.

With these ideas in mind, it is crucial to consider that acts of dissent are relationally constituted within wider fields of power. Camp residents who campaigned for rights and related practices often did so by negotiating the institutional structures of humanitarian government. When the attendees at the Youth Congress announced their grievances toward the police's heavy-handed tactics, they did so at a UNHCR- and LWF-organized event. They consented to go through the bureaucratic process of having their claims heard at an official gathering. In this sense, their public complaints reaffirmed the governing authority's schemes of protection, surveillance, discipline, and control. An understanding of the sonic politics of belonging as a process of subjectification is thus crucial for elucidating and interrogating the ways acts of musical dissent intersect with the wider disciplinary forces of humanitarian rule.

Finally, listening to dissonance and dissent raises another vital issue—the possibility for social and political change. When musicians at the Youth Congress voiced dissatisfaction with not receiving fair financial compensation for their musical labor, they were enacting possibilities for reconfiguring the economic paradigm governing forced migration in Kenya. Although some might argue these actions stemmed solely from subjection to state, humanitarian, and capitalistic forces, I would reply that these musicians also challenged the status quo of humanitarian encampment. This issue is vitally important because if scholars only elucidate the subjectification of hegemonic forces, they may fail to recognize the emergence of new politics of possibilities for addressing forced migration.

When it comes to understanding the efficacy of music and dance in refugee camp settings, too much emphasis has been placed on their utility for rehabilitating the refugee subject, and too little attention has been placed on their roles in relation to the wider political project of encampment. Attuning to the sonic politics of belonging in the Kakuma camp offers a unique perspective for addressing the latter. Why did camp officials and refugees believe that certain kinds of musicking belonged in the Kakuma camp while others did not? What can listening to moments of silence and noise reveal about disqualified ways of belonging? How did camp inhabitants express how they desired to belong through songs, music videos, and dances? The stories and ideas in the subsequent chapters in this book are grounded in the fundamental idea that the task of making sense of the political project of encampment requires listening to and learning from the teachings of musicians and dancers, individuals often responsible for publicly and creatively expressing ideas and behaviors that resonate with their communities. "I can make sense," said King Moses when explaining why he felt a sense of belonging to hip hop culture. "I can talk to my community, and they can understand what I am saying. I can be a teacher."[4]

Notes

1. King Moses, phone interview with author, June 15, 2021.

2. The term "musicking" conveys the idea that music is not an object but an activity. Examples of musicking include performing, listening, rehearsing, composing, providing materials for performance, and dancing (Small 1998).

3. The UNHCR initially set up an emergency camp in the border town of Lokichoggio. A few months later, the camp was moved to Kakuma for security reasons (Grabksa 2014, 40).

4. King Moses, phone interview with author, June 15, 2021.

AFTER RELIEF

2

PLEASURE

On Music, Pleasure, and Refugees

I first met rapper and R&B singer Smart Djaba in July 2013 in the tree-canopied courtyard of the Turkana cafeteria, a communal space the Lutheran World Federation (LWF) operated in Kakuma One. We agreed to meet so that I could learn more about his musical life. He began our conversation by describing the circumstances that had brought him to Kenya. While he spoke, his torso shifted downward as he cast his eyes toward the dirt ground. With a somber tone in his voice, he conveyed the tragic way his family members had been attacked by local militias in the eastern region of the Democratic Republic of the Congo. The air felt heavy. After a brief pause, I suggested we shift our conversation to his music. Within seconds, a smile broke across Smart's face. His chest lifted. His voice became more animated and self-assured as he described his musical accomplishments. The mere act of remembering and recounting his music transformed his emotional state from one of grief to gratification.

This chapter provides an ethnographic account of the multifaceted ways commercial popular musicians experienced pleasure within the Kakuma camp, a site where suffering was a fundamental facet of humanitarian operations. Focusing on the experiences of these musicians is instructive for this discussion because the music industry has historically valued what the aid/refugee industry has delegitimized: wealth, style, and fun. And yet despite this difference, aid agencies in the Kakuma camp widely supported popular music initiatives. Why were hip hop projects so pervasive in a refugee camp setting? What role did popular music's pleasurable elements play in meeting the needs of the camp's young people *and* its authorities? What were the limits and consequences of making music for pleasure in a site where suffering was highly valued?

"Pleasure" is not typically the first word that comes to mind when thinking about refugees. Neither are words with similar connotations, such as "entertainment" and "joy." "Trauma," "loss," and "suffering"—these are terms more often used for articulating the experiences of forced migrants. In the *Oxford Handbook of Refugee and Forced Migration Studies*, the word "suffering" appears in twenty-one out of fifty-two chapters (Fiddian-Qasimiyeh et al., 2014). The word "pleasure" appears once. Anthropological studies on forced migration include evocative documentation of everyday hardships, fieldwork methods attentive to knowledge gained from embodied pain, and critical theories that expose the uneven political-economy of suffering in humanitarian discourse and practice (see Dunn 2017; Holmes 2013; Fassin 2011; Malkki 1996). Each of these approaches provides critical, meaningful, and insightful analyses for approaching the complexities of suffering in the lives of forced migrants.

And yet it is important to consider that while anthropologists have long studied the complex and diverse dimensions of human emotions (see Lutz and White 1986), ethnographic accounts of forced migration have disproportionately focused on suffering. Why? Perhaps studies on suffering are considered serious work, which in turn makes studies on happiness and pleasure seem frivolous. Perhaps the documentation of suffering is rooted in an activist and moral imperative aimed at mobilizing solidarity with forced migrants. Perhaps the focus on suffering is part of a disciplinary shift in anthropology aimed at redressing a fraught history of cultural Othering.[1] Or it could plainly be that suffering *is* a prominent empirical reality faced by forced migrants, a population subjected to the violence of war and persecution. In a similar vein but from a more critical angle, it could be that suffering undergirds the fundamental makeup of the wider refugee regime and, as such, requires heightened scrutiny.

In keeping with this latter view, it is crucial to consider the consequences of such a widespread discourse of suffering. Rather than bridging cultural divides, representations of suffering can result in voyeuristic accounts that reproduce the migrant Other. Additionally, if scholars accept the idea that humanitarianism and the wider refugee regime expect forced migrants to conform to a life of suffering, then academic discourses of suffering may inadvertently reinforce the very system scholars seek to critique. An analytical focus on suffering can lock scholars into the same inquiries of the humanitarian enterprise—the effects of which can result in defining displaced people in relation to an aid process wherein it is the "job" of beneficiaries to suffer (Dunn 2017, 15). Similar to how the label of "refugee" may reduce the complexity of what it means to be human to a monolithic legal category, an amplified discourse of refugees as suffering subjects can obscure other meaningful emotions and identifications.[2]

With these perspectives in mind, I situate the lives of popular musicians living in the Kakuma camp within what feminist and postcolonial scholar Sara Ahmed (2014 [2004]) has termed the "cultural politics of emotion." Her approach focuses on the ways emotions and politics shape subjectivities. According to Ahmed (2014 [2004], 8, 11–15), emotions work through "affective economies" consisting of signs that, when circulated over time, increase in "affective value." This process, in turn, creates social and material effects in people's lives. Through this framework, I approach pleasure not merely as a depoliticized sense of joy or satisfaction, but rather as an affective force interwoven with a humanitarian political-economy wherein suffering is highly valued. Instead of adhering to a dichotomous worldview that sees refugees as either suffering or enjoying themselves, I analyze the multifaceted, relational, context-specific, entangled ways suffering and pleasure intersect with popular music and politics within the interconnected realms of musical events, institutional practices, and everyday life.

Pleasure from music can be deeply political. More than an individual feeling, musical pleasure can work at collective and public levels in ways that are both inclusive and exclusive. The pleasure that audiences and performers feel through music performances can be a "productive force" that fosters distinct skills, knowledges, values, and social formations (Guilbault 2010, 17, 31). Sharing experiences and ideas of pleasure can affect the ways people understand and engage with social life and, in particular, how they form alliances and forge collective memories and goals (Dave 2019, 2). Performances can engender "feelings and emotive responses" that can alter "habits and potentially produce social or political redress" (Perman 2010, 446). Conversely, it is important to temper romanticized ideas about music's oppositional qualities by recognizing that pleasure through music can reaffirm and reproduce repressive politics (Dave 2019).

In a camp system undergirded by principles of relief and deterrence, musicians like Smart Djaba and members of his musical collective, Afrostars Entertainment, drew on their senses of belonging to local and transnational music scenes to satisfy their needs and desires. The pleasure they generated through music reproduced, resignified, and challenged an encampment system wherein suffering held great currency. Examining the times aid officials celebrated and suppressed moments of musical pleasure elucidates the norms of belonging and the unequal power relations at play in upholding a site of migratory control. Moreover, attuning to the experiences and insights of popular musicians in the Kakuma camp can help to reimagine stereotypical ideas of refugees as *only* suffering subjects, provoking new ways for thinking about pleasure and for approaching the debilitating aspects of the refugee regime.

Suffering Conflict and Encampment

Smart Djaba's arrival to Kakuma was a result of ongoing conflict and political instability in the eastern region of the Democratic Republic of the Congo. Conflicts in the North and South Kivu Provinces have stemmed from competition over land and economic resources with competing groups jockeying for political power and influence through the lucrative mineral trade. Many of these conflict minerals have gone toward the production of mobile phones, cars, airplanes, and jewelry, linking local conflicts in Congo to consumerism in the Global North and global capitalism more broadly. These contemporary conflicts have historically manifested from a range of factors including economic exploitation, political disputes, Western intervention, and long periods of conflict (see Turner 2007; Ndaliko 2016). From the mid-1990s to the early 2000s, the Democratic Republic of the Congo was embroiled in two wars—the First Congo War (1996–1997) and the Second Congo War (1998–2003), also known as Africa's Great War due to the involvement of nine African nations, most notably Rwanda, Zimbabwe, Namibia, and Angola. Though the Second Congo War ended in 2003, instability has persisted. Whereas the Democratic Republic of the Congo used to be a country that attracted numerous African migrants, the Migration Policy Institute has determined that since the 1980s, emigration has outpaced migratory inflows (Flahaux, and Schoumaker 2016). By 2015, main sites of relocation included Uganda, Rwanda, Burundi, South Sudan, Tanzania, and Kenya.

Located in Turkana County, far from Kenya's major metropolitan cities, lay a sprawling urbanized site surrounded by a semiarid desert landscape, pocketed with shrubs and crisscrossed by rocky hills. The living conditions I witnessed in the Kakuma camp were striking. Each day, pedestrians, drivers, and bicyclists traveled over dilapidated dirt roads. They passed mud-brick housing compounds with perimeter walls made from thorn-covered branches erected to stem off criminal activity. During the rare times when it rained, camp inhabitants walked through knee-high polluted puddles on their routes to home, school, and work. Windswept grains of sand blasted people's faces amid daily temperatures that hovered in the high nineties. In general, camp inhabitants faced limited public services—overcrowded schools, overflowing pit latrines, and congested water taps.

This lived reality was neither a mistake nor an accident. Feelings of hardship were the planned outcome of humanitarian government. If made too comfortable, refugees might never leave. If made too lucrative, economic migrants would arrive in large numbers. In fact, the latter outcome would call into question the very logic and purpose of the entire refugee regime. The idea that refugees should feel a certain level of discomfort was also tied to the issue of security. "We try not to make it too comfortable for refugees," said a UNHCR official in response to a Kenya Television Network (KTN) reporter's comment about international aid in Kakuma.[3] With this response, the UNHCR official sought to placate the reporter's critique regarding the UN's disproportionate amount of aid for refugees and simultaneous neglect of the more impoverished Turkana "host community" (see also Aukot 2003). Throughout Kakuma's history, aid-induced inequality has stoked conflict between refugees and surrounding residents. Cognizant of this dynamic, camp officials believed that limiting refugees' material wealth was essential for reducing envy and conflict. This practice elucidates how bureaucratic limits on pleasure were justified through a discourse of security that pitted disadvantaged groups against each other.

The more I learned about camp operations, the more it became clear that suffering had significant affective value. All new arrivals, with the exception of South Sudanese and Somali refugees granted prima facie status, had to convince UNHCR officials that they required protection from harm during the process of refugee status determination. The more clearly an applicant seeking resettlement could demonstrate and prove their suffering to forces beyond their control, the greater their chances for relocation. In terms of programming, the aid agencies made it a point to identify and offer services for persons they referred to as "vulnerable populations"—persons with disabilities (PwD), people living with HIV and AIDS (PLWHA), people subjected to sexual and gender-based violence (SGBV), and orphans and vulnerable children (OVC). In one sense, the widespread use of acronyms to designate these groups signified sentiments of care for oft-marginalized social groups. In another sense, they signified the humanitarian system's preoccupation with identifying categories of suffering subjects in order to legitimize itself. Suffering also served important political agendas. Nell Gabiam uses the term "the politics of suffering" to describe how suffering became a means through which Palestinian refugees in Syria attained political legitimacy and rights (2016, 9). A similar politics of suffering manifested in the Kakuma camp, most notably among South Sudanese and Oromo nationalists seeking to establish independent states. In another caveat to this discussion, aid officials labeled the Kakuma camp a "hardship post," a designation aid workers used to justify taking vacation time every six to eight weeks and receiving extra pay on top of their regular salaries.

Forced migrants in Kenya thus had to endure multiple hardships. Individuals fleeing the crippling effects of conflict and persecution had to endure a humanitarianized system wherein they were compelled to both experience and display suffering and discontent. It was within this context that commercial popular music emerged as a meaningful expression.

The Politics of Entertainment

Beyond the exit roads leading away from the UN and NGO compounds, other lifestyles resonated with young people living in the Kakuma camp. Smart Djaba and his friend and music partner King Moses, for example, knew that the places where their musical icons lived—Nairobi, Kinshasa, Dar el Salaam, Toronto, and New York City—made up a different world from the debilitating conditions of segregated care. In the mid-2010s, many young people had access to Safaricom and Airtel's internet services via their phones and to a lesser extent their laptops and tablets. With this technology, they would download popular tracks—such as "Number One" by Diamond Platnumz and "Started from the Bottom" by Drake—onto their phones and MP3 players. They would play these commercial hits while walking to food distribution centers or resting at home in their designated blocks and zones. On a regular basis, Smart Djaba and King Moses would gather at their friend's mud-brick house in Kakuma One to sit and watch music video recordings of R&B, rap, dancehall, bongo flava, genge, and boomba on a dust-covered TV set hooked up to a gas-powered generator. They would frequent the video-screening shops in the market areas to watch MTV Africa. Through TV and social media, they learned about the latest musical styles and fashion trends emerging from East Africa, Nigeria, North America, and the Caribbean. The world they saw, a world consisting of diamond-encrusted gold jewelry, flashy sports cars, and beautiful people, exuded style, glamour, and wealth.

On the surface, it would appear that there is nothing uniquely remarkable about young people's consumption of commercial popular music in a refugee camp setting. Critics might even suggest that the hypermasculine and ostentatious imagery of entertainment-oriented pop music is misogynistic and classist, at its worst reinforcing inequalities and at its best doing little more than providing refugees with a fantasy-driven distraction from real life. And while there is some validity to these claims, it is important to recognize that there is more to consider when it comes to the effects of commodified

entertainment—"experience that can be sold to and enjoyed by large and heterogeneous groups of people" (Barnouw and Kirkland 1992, 50). Folklorists
Erik Barnouw and Catherine Kirkland suggest that, rather than functioning
as either a "pleasant diversion" or an "escape from reality," "entertainment is
attentive to the norms, myths, and fears of its audiences but also serves to shape
and reshape them; it reflects social trends but also nudges them into being and
reinforces and furthers them. It provides a social repertoire of characters, relationships and outcomes that is used in the ongoing attempt to make sense of the
world" (1992, 52). This framework elucidates commercial entertainment's role
in helping audiences shape, navigate, and grapple with the world around them.

Consider the case of kwaito music in South Africa. A host of critics have
dismissed kwaito on the grounds that it ignores the dismal social and political
realities of the postapartheid period. Contrastingly, Gavin Steingo has argued
that when kwaito musicians and listeners ignore their actual social conditions,
they do so intentionally, to "forge another body and another way of hearing"
(2016, 6). This perspective shifts the perception of kwaito as an illusion that
hides reality toward an illusion that generates a "new sensory reality" (2016, 6).
In this regard, it is precisely kwaito's disconnection from political messages and
reflections of societal structures and conflicts that makes it political (2016, 7).
As Achille Mbembe (2005, 72) has argued, the measure of the "aesthetic sig-
nification" of a musical work does not simply lie with its ability or inability to
elucidate social alienation. Rather, its revelatory qualities lie with how the work
connects to a "world of sensations."

Moreover, it is crucial to consider how commercialized forms of entertainment are relationally constituted within wider political contexts. The norms,
myths, and fears of audiences and producers may be both antithetical to and
supportive of established political orders. How fans and musicians make sense
of the world through commodified entertainment may reproduce, contradict,
or oppose the worldviews of governing authorities. New sensory realities forged
through commercial music are recognizably meaningful and distinct in relation to existing political realities. Such perspectives suggest that although
commercial music entertainment in the Kakuma camp may seem superficial
and devoid of political content, in reality, its consumption, production, and
circulation were highly political.

Refashioning the "Refugee" Label

"Afrostars is a group of young artists living in Kakuma Refugee Camp trying
to help themselves, to promote themselves."[4] This was the mantra Smart used

to convey the purpose of his musical collective, Afrostars Entertainment. He, along with King Moses, Chris Black, and other popular musicians from the Great Lakes region, formed this collective to advance their musical aspirations, sell their music, and enhance their visibility among their fans and the aid agencies. Growing up in a refugee camp, a place where inhabitants are often expected to conform to stereotypical aspects of the refugee figure, Afrostars' members drew on the stylized and pleasurable aspects of popular music to express more complex emotions and identities.

Bureaucratic discourse obscured the complexities of Kakuma's camp inhabitants through a process of refugee labeling (Zetter 2007 and 1991). Terms such as "refugee" and "asylum seeker" made bodies legible for aid delivery and state monitoring while masking more intricate, personal "co-existing and contrasting identities" (Zetter 1991, 60). Musical self-styling, on the other hand, offered performing artists empowering and enjoyable ways to express aspects of their personhood often muted within humanitarian discourse. As hip hop scholar Tricia Rose has argued, "taking on new names and identities offers 'prestige from below' in the face of limited access to legitimate forms of status attainment" (1994, 36).

In 2013, I met with Smart Djaba in his neighborhood in Kakuma One for one of our first conversations about his role as a hip hop and R&B musician. When we discussed the issue of addressing dominant stereotypes associated with refugees, he said, "I have to be well dressed, you know. Even though I am a refugee, but it doesn't mean that a refugee must be dirty—you know, bad clothes. I'm an artist, of course. I have to be Smart, like my name, you know."[5] Smart was well aware of the stereotypical images of disheveled refugees displayed in media coverage and NGO marketing campaigns. Indeed, his stage name was in direct response to these reductive depictions. While his parents in the Democratic Republic of the Congo gave him the name Salumu Djabir, his friends in the camp nicknamed him Smart because of his fashionable attire. He could be seen wearing black thick-rimmed vanity glasses, baseball caps, long zippered shirts, and skinny jeans on stage and in his daily life. His fashion consciousness shaped not only his friends' impressions of him but also his public persona as an artist.

Similarly, other popular musicians fashioned personalized stage names that signified empowerment over victimhood. Musicians King Moses and Queen Lisa and the breakdancing crew King of the Dance evoked tropes of royalty with their musical personas as a way of signifying high levels of musicianship and fame. As another founding member of Afrostars, King Moses was a leader among young, up-and-coming artists in the camp. He was considered one of

Kakuma's best rappers among his fans and musical peers. Queen Lisa gained recognition among her peers and the aid agencies for her singing skills during her teenage years. She made it a point in her twenties to draw on her popularity and leadership skills to help empower and mentor young girls. Consider also singer and rapper Chris Black and the hip hop dancing group Black Snake Swagger and their use of stage names to express racial pride. Chris was another leading figure in Afrostars and the commercial music scene more broadly. As such, he was often called on by both local entertainment producers and NGO managers to lend his voice to their projects. Through stage names, performing artists exuded pride and pleasure from self-fashioning chosen musical identities. At each NGO and private event I saw these artists perform, they exhibited confidence, joy, and "swagga" on their faces and in their bodily comportment whenever their stage names emanated from the loudspeakers.

Through their music-making, Afrostars' members had a wider goal of unifying musicians from across the African continent. The satisfaction they gained from making music for entertainment advanced a Pan-Africanist ideology that brought together individuals from the Democratic Republic of the Congo, Burundi, Uganda, Sudan, and South Sudan during live performances. This phenomenon supports Guilbault's idea that the pleasure derived from music can be generative of "public intimacies" that bring together individuals from disparate ethnicities and nationalities (2010, 17). In this sense, commercial popular music, and hip hop in particular, was a potent force in challenging a refugee regime dominated by a nation-state order. Moreover, the group's emphasis on entertainment was a collective aspiration that provided an important counterpoint to dominant perceptions of refugees as a primarily vulnerable population.

Musical self-labeling offered a meaningful and pleasurable alternative to dominant forms of bureaucratic identification. Whereas the administration's assignment of ID and ration card numbers aimed to reduce the cultural specificity of refugees, hip hop monikers were based on personal preferences. Whereas labels such as "refugee," "beneficiary," and "aid recipient" connoted marginality and dependency, stage names evoked senses of empowerment and self-worth. Crucially, the pleasure that Afrostars' members felt from their senses of belonging to the aesthetic values and norms of the East African music industry was often in contradistinction to those of humanitarian programming.

"We Can't Always Sing about Peace"

The popularity of hip hop youth culture was not lost on the Kakuma camp's aid organizations. Many young artists gained their first taste of recognition during youth talent competitions the LWF and FAI organized during school breaks. These contests were extremely popular, attracting hundreds of young people who would crowd the doorways and aisles of packed seating areas in the camp's youth centers. The LWF typically organized these events around thematic social concerns such as peace and conflict, drug and alcohol abuse, HIV and AIDS, and early marriage. Successful artists often moved to the next level of performing in UNHCR-sponsored public festivals where they could showcase their musicianship in front of peers as well as diplomats, donors, and celebrities. FilmAid International also created opportunities for artists to record their music. Activist and rapper Emmanuel Jal, for example, worked with FAI and local musicians to produce a peace song entitled "Kakuma Rocks." For another project, FAI recruited several of Kakuma's rap and R&B singers to record a song about malaria for circulation on the local IOM radio station.

Each of the above projects demonstrates the ways aid organizations sought to do more than offer handouts. They positioned artists as agents actively ameliorating their communities' social problems. We may think of these music projects as contributing to the sonic signs that made up the Kakuma camp's affective economy of pleasure. Entertaining songs aimed at addressing health concerns and mitigating conflict had the potential to advance the twin effects of fostering lively social environments and reducing social suffering. And yet despite the promise of these projects, they never fully satisfied the musical desires of some artists.

In April 2015, I met with Smart Djaba to discuss his musical career and life ambitions. We began our conversation on the Tarach Riverbank in Kakuma town. Halfway into our talk, it started raining, so we walked to the courtyard located just outside the UNHCR compound. We found cover under an iron sheet awning amid individuals waiting to have their cases heard by UNHCR officials. As raindrops pattered against the corrugated iron sheeting above us, Smart and I continued our conversation about the meaning behind his musical repertoire.

"For whom is this song?" I asked in reference to "Nimedata," a song Smart composed about finding love in a music club.
"This is just for moving. You know, moving people, making them moving. We can't always sing about peace. *Nini nini*, people need some time to forget, to destress themselves."[6]

Smart's explanation of the social value of "Nimedata" articulates an important facet of music that addresses humanitarian concerns. In his mind, the aid agencies' need for refugees to repeatedly sing and listen to songs about peace imposed a sense of stress on refugees. These types of songs reminded forced migrants about the suffering they endured instead of expressing what they could gain from life's pleasurable experiences, such as finding love. From this perspective, educational songs that leveraged the pleasurable elements of entertainment still contributed to an affective economy of suffering. These songs normalized the perception of refugees as incomplete beings requiring rehabilitation and impinged on their psychological well-being.

It is crucial to recognize that songs aimed at addressing refugees' social problems reproduced social stratification. To put this into perspective, consider that the UNHCR/NGOs never once commissioned refugee performing artists to compose songs and dramas aimed at altering the instances of alcohol and drug abuse, sexual predation, and corruption in their own ranks. Doing so would have destabilized social hierarchies between aid workers and refugees, blurring social divisions that normalized their separation as two distinct social groups requiring differential treatment.

On the whole, Smart was not opposed to making music to address humanitarian concerns, but he desired more than to make music that reinforced the identity of a refugee as someone who suffers. He wanted to be recognized for his skills as a hip hop and R&B artist in the commercial music industry. For Smart, popular music offered a way out of the Kakuma camp's precarious conditions. Popular music provided a sense of hope and possibility for a future beyond debilitating conditions of unemployment and subpar social services. Inspired by the songs and images of his musical icons and buoyed by the praise he received from aid workers, musical peers, and audiences, Smart found a resource in music that helped him negotiate the difficulties of encampment.

Live from the Green *Hoteli*

It was early in the evening when I flagged down a motorcycle along the main road of Kakuma One just outside the food distribution center. I was headed to a hip hop show at the Green *hoteli* in the Ethiopian market. As it turned out, so was the motorcyclist. I hopped on the back of his bike and we plodded along the puddle-filled, dilapidated dirt roads that led to the show. Smart Djaba invited me to watch him and other artists from Afrostars Entertainment perform. When I approached the iron sheet entrance, I greeted the doorman and paid the 350 KSH ($3.50) VIP price. Most others paid 150 KSH ($1.50), while the artists' friends entered for free.

On entry, it quickly became clear that this event provided performers and patrons with a break from the monotonous rhythms of humanitarian programming. Instead of UNHCR officials and NGO workers, Smart and his older sister were the lead organizers for this show. Instead of banners with social messages, decorative red fabric hung on the back walls, and white party streamers were strung across the courtyard trees. In place of the World Food Program's (WFP) food rations, the audience gathered around plastic tables covered with bowls of popcorn and bottles of soda, beer, vodka, and whiskey. In place of songs about nutrition and peace, a DJ sat behind a laptop playing popular hip hop, R&B, and dancehall tracks, filling the air with bouncing beats and lyrical messages about money and fame, dating and partying. This was an event where young patrons could see and be seen. Young women put style on display in tight, form-fitting jeans and tank tops, heeled shoes, and flawless makeup. Young gents fashioned themselves with tilted baseball caps, slim-fit and slouching jeans, and chain necklaces, a collection of gear made to bolster their belonging to hip hop and youth culture more broadly. More than nonessential or unreasonable items, material goods were displayed and consumed in a pleasurable manner, giving credence to the idea that "luxuries and comforts" provided refugees in the Kakuma camp with important coping benefits through which to feel senses of normalcy and dignity (Oka 2014, 249, 253).

After a host of singers, rappers, and break-dancers performed throughout the event, Smart Djaba and King Moses served as the event's final acts. They knew that if they played to their audience's desire for fun and entertainment, they would generate joy and satisfaction through their music. Under the multicolored spotlights of a swirling disco ball strung in the courtyard's tree branches, King Moses broke into his song "Mkali" ("the baddest"; sharp, fierce, blazing). Several fans in the audience immediately applauded on hearing one of his signature songs. They jumped out of their chairs, moving and grooving their bodies to a pulsating hip hop track composed of a short and repetitive minor key melody line accented on the offbeat with a staccato percussive sound punctuating the downbeat. During the song's main chorus line, King Moses's most ardent fans swayed their hands in the air and energetically rapped along with him.

Original Version	Translated Version[7]
Hi sio bifu, ni league yamistari	This is not beef, it's a league of lines
League ya freestyle, siwaokopi ata kwa shari	On the freestyle league, I am not afraid of them whatsoever
Ivi amuja kubali, kwamba mimi ni mkali?	So you haven't accepted that I am the baddest?
Jeeh kwamba mimi ni mkali	Yeah that I am the baddest

Smart and King Moses then traded tracks, sharing the spotlight. Toward the end of their set, Smart launched into his upbeat song "Piga Photo," a song inspired by The Kansoul's "Dabotab," a recent hit in Kenya. "Piga Photo" encourages people to remember the special moments in life by taking photos with their phones. As Smart Djaba and King Moses worked the crowd by motivating them to follow the song's message, young men and women popped out of their seats and started snapping photos of themselves and the performers while dancing. Songs like "Piga Photo" have neither "heal the world" messages nor the melancholic, slow melodies that often accompany news media about refugees. Within these spaces, the sensuous melodies and syncopated rhythms of hip hop entertainment took over. Through their music, Smart Djaba and King Moses generated a sense of normalcy and joy among themselves and their fans.

Musically induced affective pleasure not only signified the audience's satisfaction with a particular performance but also served as a productive and collective force. Smart Djaba and King Moses used hip hop and R&B to bring people together in shared spaces of sociality wherein they could enjoy the entertainment factor of a live performance. Through their lyrics, musical sounds, and gestures, they put themselves at the center of attention for enhancing pleasure in their communities. The visible satisfaction these artists generated encouraged them to record more songs, arrange more shows, and even refrain from participating in NGO-organized music shows unless they received suitable compensation. In a site where refugees were often viewed as disempowered victims, engagement in hip hop cultural practices provided a medium through which to improve emotional states, raise social status, and contribute to a public sociality forged through communal entertainment. Moreover, the pleasure they and their audiences gained from popular music supports Lara Allen's assertion that "enjoyment can constitute a radical assault against destructive forces. To achieve joy and pleasure in a context in which one's humanity seems not to be recognized is fundamentally to contest the situation" (2004, 6).

Satisfying Musical Desires

A recurring pattern of sound was heard and felt at every popular music show I attended in the Kakuma camp. Whether at festivals commemorating a UN international day at the Napata Fairgrounds or smaller shows at the LWF youth centers, it became apparent that the sound quality during these performances was low. Feedback squealed from the speaker systems. Vocal lines came out distorted when sung at higher pitches. And singers' social messages competed with the rumblings of gas-powered generators. The recurring subpar sound quality of these events signified and reproduced precarity. When I asked aid workers why they did not invest in equipment for making higher quality music, they often told me that they were not in the business of producing professional musicians. Their mandates were to address refugees' pressing social problems, and making high-grade commercial music was not part of their mission.

Contrastingly, many of the popular musicians I knew decried the poor sound quality as insufficient for their musical needs and aspirations. Members of Afrostars Entertainment would often tell me that musicians in the camp needed access to better musical equipment: microphones, public address systems, and recording technologies. These artists heard and felt the deficiency in the songs they performed at the Napata Fairgrounds and other public spaces. They disliked the music that distorted from the dusty public address systems used at each event. They felt frustrated when their vocal lines competed with feedback squeals and noisy generators. In the same way that bland food rations and overcrowded schools were functional though far from satisfying, low-quality musical sounds and equipment reflected and reinforced a poor quality of life. Feedback, distortion, breakdowns, and rumblings were inextricably linked to affective norms that constituted the Kakuma camp as a site of displeasure and discomfort.

With the understanding that refugees were often critics of their own condition, I sought a formal means of gathering knowledge and insights in a manner that destabilized hierarchical relationships involved in the research process. In 2015, I held an essay-writing competition that requested refugees submit essays totaling 750–1,000 words critically addressing the marginalization of music and dance practices in the Kakuma camp. Aron, a refugee from the Democratic Republic of the Congo, submitted one of the more thoughtful essays elucidating the struggles that popular musicians faced in the camp. He was friends with several artists and had an intimate knowledge of their lives and musical desires. The thrust of his argument focused on what the UNHCR and the aid agencies needed to do to better support performing artists. The following quote from his essay pinpoints some of his interlocutors' concrete desires: "Just like the extensive investments made on other departments such as human rights, media by FilmAid and sports, the same capital investment should be done on dance and music in the camp. Dance and music demands a lot of capital ranging from recordings, video and clips, shooting, organizing shows, and very many other expenses and all this needs money including posting a video shoot on YouTube. Therefore, dance and music in the camp need capital investment since I can't believe neither an independent music artist nor a dance group can manage the cost."[8]

Aron's essay on popular musicians' desires is telling on several accounts when it comes to the realities of life in the Kakuma camp. Performing artists felt a sense of entitlement to programs that did more than just provide relief. They required capital investments in resources and programs that would enable musicians to make professional grade music. Aron's findings elucidate the manner in which the camp area shifted over time from a temporary site of emergency relief into a more permanent place where residents required fulfillment of higher-level needs—a place where ideologies and practices of development became part of the UNHCR's programming efforts.

Two aid agencies in particular, FAI and the Octopizzo Foundation, heard and recognized the repeated desires of Kakuma's aspiring professional musicians to make music for the entertainment industry. In 2013, Kenyan rapper Octopizzo began supporting projects that emphasized the commercial aspects of rap and popular music more broadly. He grew up in Kibera, an economically challenging area of Nairobi. As such, he recognized the ways charities too often focus on the social problems of disenfranchised populations. As a professional musician, he was also acutely aware of the benefits of music for music's sake. Through his leadership, he sought to offer what so many of Kakuma's performing artists living in both the town and camp area wanted—a chance to develop their musicianship as well as opportunities for career-minded musicians to gain greater entry into the East African music industry.

The pleasure that Kakuma's performing artists felt from these NGO music projects is exemplified in a two-day recording session that FAI and Octopizzo organized in 2015. One of Octopizzo's music producers based in Nairobi came to the Kakuma camp to conduct the recordings. One by one, young artists, both men and women, entered a cramped, makeshift studio located in Youth Center Two. After the artists laid down their personal tracks, the producer critiqued each musician like he would any other client. If they were off pitch, off rhythm, or lacking in confidence in their delivery, he told them to "do it again."[9] As word got around of a professional music producer's presence, hordes of young musicians crowded the backroom area hoping to get their chance. The demand for professional recording services was so great that several musicians who had waited eight hours on the first day to no avail returned the next day just as eager to record their songs.

After years of requests that the NGOs provide greater opportunities for artists to enhance their musical skill sets, increase their exposure in the commercial music industry, and move beyond making music for NGO social campaigns, FAI and the OF obliged. Soon after wrapping up the music production workshops in the Kakuma camp, the UNHCR flew eight musicians from Kakuma to Nairobi to perform live at Octopizzo's album release party. Octopizzo subsequently arranged for several of the more skilled artists to record audio tracks, film music videos, and conduct nationally aired TV and radio interviews. His organization then helped the artists produce a compilation album called *Refugeenius*. This project enabled performing artists from different regions and countries to engage in musical "collabos" with each other in an effort to generate social cohesion through the joys of music-making. Most of the songs on *Refugeenius* evoke feelings of fun, fantasy, and romance in their lyrics and upbeat backing tracks, musical aesthetics of sonic pleasure that resonate more with the entertainment industry than the aid industry. Songs such as "Ma Champagne" by King Moses and Queen Lisa, "Mapenzi Gani" by Queen Lisa and A Solution, and "Let's Party" by Street Boyz provide important counternarratives to the dominant discourse of social suffering and vulnerability often associated with the refugee figure.

In composing these songs, however, these musicians largely ignored the Kakuma camp's socioeconomic and political realities. In "Mapenzi Gani," for example, scenes of a rooftop swimming pool overlooking Nairobi's cityscape, a bathtub filled with rose petals, and a gravel-covered office parking lot surrounded by lush green trees provides the backdrop for Queen Lisa and A Solution's lyrical exchange about tensions involving infidelity in a romantic relationship.[10] In "Let's Party," the Street Boyz rappers strut and stroll through a market area in the Kakuma camp dressed in crisp white streetwear rapping about clubbing and partying through the night.[11] Critics might contend that these videos are forms of mere escapism from the difficult material and political realities of encampment. After all, none of the content in "Mapenzi Gani," visual or lyrical, expresses what it is like to live in a refugee camp. Meanwhile, the video for the "Street Boyz" provides a false impression that the Kakuma camp was a place where young people could party all night. And yet, similar to Steingo's (2016) argument about kwaito music in South Africa, the illusions expressed in these songs and videos may be understood as producing new sensory realities. More than just creating forms of escapism, these artists used music and visual art to generate desired ways of living—lifestyles in contradistinction to normative ideas about how refugees are expected to belong within the space of humanitarian encampment.

The making of entertainment-oriented commercial music was no small feat in a place where aid officials and visiting musicians historically expected refugees to produce humanitarian songs on topics such as peace and health, songs that normalized stereotypical ideas of refugees as suffering subjects. Joy and satisfaction came from making entertaining music—the kind of music that reminded Kakuma's camp inhabitants that their lives and aspirations consisted of more than what their refugee status often compelled them to convey. And yet despite this new direction in music programming, these kinds of arts interventions still had their limitations. To better understand why requires returning to the Afrostars show at the Green *hoteli*.

Limits of Music for Entertainment

As the sun's light dimmed to darkness, the staged event turned into a full-fledged dance party. The audience's movements were catalyzed by Smart Djaba and King Moses's closing performance and fueled by the DJ's digital playlist. The youthful crowd grooved to the rhythms and melodies of hip hop and R&B artists such as P-Square and Rihanna. Smiling faces, bouncing bodies, and intermittent hollers filled the dirt-covered courtyard under the spotted lights of the swirling disco ball. Just as the party began to build in emotional intensity, however, the bar's owner shut down the show. It was curfew time, and Smart's permit only lasted until 7:00 p.m.

The existence of multilevel clubs, open-air balcony bars, and late-night food stalls is just one of the reasons why Nairobi has become renowned for its nightlife. An entertaining night out might include gathering at a friend's flat before boarding a taxi or minibus (*matatu*) to a popular nightclub—K1 KlubHouse, iClub, Black Diamond. Even the town of Kakuma had several bars and restaurants that catered to local residents who wanted to drink, dance, and converse late into the night, such as White House. From Eldoret to Mombasa and Nairobi to Kakuma, nocturnal entertainment has long been crucial for city residents' social pleasure.

And yet the Kakuma camp, which several scholars have characterized as an urban or city-like space, lacked such areas for sustained nighttime entertainment (see Jansen 2018; Agier 2002; Montclos and Kagwanja 2000). Prohibition had long served as a governing instrument for regulating nocturnal activities. By sundown, taxi drivers had to cease working, and most refugees had to stay in their housing compounds. The police allowed refugees to conduct nighttime ceremonies for weddings and funerals as long as they obtained a permit. Yet when it came to holding events for the express purposes of entertainment, the police often restricted the right to evening hours while extracting illegal fees of 1000–1500 KSH ($10–15) from organizers. If shows went past the allotted curfew, the organizers and the *hoteli* owner were subject to arrest, detention, and fines. In the words of an NGO worker I knew, "the police have made a business out of the permit and curfew system."[12]

High-ranking administrators typically rationalized this situation through interlocking and obfuscating logics and discourses of security and deservingness. Liisa Malkki (1996, 384) has argued that a "performative dimension" to what constitutes a "real" refugee in the social imagination of most administrators is often generated through visual depictions of wounds and human tragedy. The musical signs that constitute hip hop entertainment—fashionable dress, lively dance beats, and lyrical expressions of wealth and play—are in contradiction to what Malkki has termed the "signs of social refugeeness" (1996, 385). On this topic, several administrators told me that refugees came for protection from harm, not for fun and play. They perceived refugees as excessively prone to violence as well as undeserving of the pleasurable excesses of entertainment.

The police's prohibition and exploitation of nighttime music scenes elucidates the limits of NGO music projects aimed at advancing the musical desires of performing artists. FAI and the OF could organize trainings, recording sessions, and live shows in the Kakuma camp and even in Nairobi, but at the end of the day, these projects failed to radically alter the workings of segregated care. Part of understanding these projects' shortcomings requires interrogating how significations of musical pleasure privilege certain forms of knowledge over others. Music videos and songs that signify partying and play create the impression that the Kakuma camp was a cool place for young people to live. And yet absent from these performative frames are critically conscious images and lyrics exposing the difficulties refugees faced from the policies and practices that naturalized the camp as a site of precarity and social control. The hip hop genre has become synonymous with providing artists a platform for delivering biting social criticism of inequality and oppression. Surely at least one rap song sponsored by the UNHCR/NGOs should have openly critiqued the socioeconomic injustices that plague encampment. And yet as far as I know, none did.

Part of understanding why this is the case requires delving into the politics of UNHCR/NGO music production in the Kakuma camp. During the OF/FAI music marketing workshops, a common narrative among trainers and trainees was that politically conscious music does not do well in terms of sales in the East African music industry. If the aspiring professional musicians in Kakuma wanted to garner attention from mainstream media and audiences, they would need to focus their energies and artistic capacities on making music that was cool, fun, and entertaining. In the same vein but from a different angle, there was a lack of demand among the UNHCR/NGOs for music that openly critiqued the camp system. In my conversations with refugees and aid workers, I found that it was okay and even expected for refugees to voice criticisms about the camp in front of UNHCR officials and aid workers.

Doing so enabled camp officials to resolve, or at least attempt to resolve, complaints. However, it was largely frowned on for refugees to publicly critique the UNHCR/NGOs. I asked a rapper who held a keen understanding of how the business of the refugee camp subjugated and exploited its inhabitants why he did not record and circulate a music track about his ideas.[13] He responded by explaining that the UNHCR and NGOs would never let him do that and that there would be consequences if he did. If one of the main strategies for negotiating the camp system was to leverage positive relationships with aid workers and UNHCR officials, then angering them by criticizing their work would be counterproductive.

What artists faced, then, was a situation in which their musical skills and desires frequently became co-opted by the Kakuma camp's governing officials. I often witnessed the UNHCR and NGOs parade performing artists in front of donors and diplomats. Such events highlighted the good work these institutions were doing to create healthy and happy refugees by providing projects for advancing refugees' artistic skills and talents and alleviating the stress and trauma of forced migration. However, these same events also ignored and masked the structural inequality of encampment. These findings are indicative of the ways musical signs of the affective economy of pleasure became instrumentalized to obfuscate and reinforce oppression and suffering through symbolic violence, a type of violence enacted through hegemonic discourses that reproduce discrimination and inequality (see Fast and Pegley 2012).

In Audre Lorde's essay "Uses of the Erotic: The Erotic as Power" (2007 [1984]), she foregrounds joy as a powerful means through which to nurture connection in the face of oppression. She understands the erotic as "an assertion of the lifeforce of women; of that creative energy empowered" (89). For Lorde, the power of the erotic becomes actualized through sharing deeply and opening oneself up to the capacity for joy. "The sharing of joy," Lorde writes, "whether physical, emotional, psychic, or intellectual, forms a bridge between the sharers which can be the basis for understanding much of what is not shared between them, and lessens the threat of their difference" (89). Lorde explains that when we neglect and misuse the power of the erotic, "we use each other as objects of satisfaction rather than share our joy in the satisfying, rather than make connection with our similarities and our differences" (91).

Lorde's ideas about the power of joy are instructive for unpacking the promises and limits of musically constituted social pleasure in the Kakuma camp. In one sense, NGO music projects created conditions for joy in the recording studio and on the performance stage. They enabled musicians from different ethno-national backgrounds, including ones with nonrefugee status, to share in the joy of collaborative music-making. NGO-supported music workshops strengthened the musicianship skills of artists like Smart Djaba and King Moses in ways that better equipped them to generate pleasure and joy during live sets in the camp's youth centers and local bars and restaurants. In another sense, however, a radical kind of shared joy cannot be fully actualized within a system of segregated care. The common NGO practice of parading happy refugee-musicians on stage during donor visits is indicative of how the power of the erotic can be used to turn refugees into objects of satisfaction. UNHCR-funded music projects positioned NGOs as providers and refugees as beneficiaries in ways that solidified the boundaries of encampment. This arrangement meant that joy manifested from music-making was not shared between different social groups in a manner that wholly removed the idea of the refugee as a threat of difference.

Making Pleasure Political

Within a humanitarian-governed system where suffering was highly valued, select popular musicians in the Kakuma camp generated moments of joy and pleasure with their artistry. Through their senses of belonging to local and transnational music scenes, members of Afrostars Entertainment stylized their hip hop personas in ways that redefined dominant perceptions of refugees as suffering subjects. These artists were proud of their roles as social critics and entertainers. The pleasure they derived from producing and performing popular music helped to advance their social status and create joyous spaces of public sociality in a site where refugees were expected to live in precarity.

While sustained discomfort is a main facet of places designed for temporary habitation, it would be a mistake to reduce the Kakuma camp to a draconian apparatus that restricted all forms of pleasure. In practice, aid agencies such as FAI and the OF supported various pleasure-making activities. Successful edutainment projects raised the confidence and self-satisfaction of select artists who felt empowered when they performed songs intended to ameliorate social problems in their communities. Initiatives like the *Refugeenius* project provided musicians with an artistic medium through which to generate new sensory realities consisting of stylized expressions of pleasure and play. Music workshops and recording sessions developed participants' musicianship and marketing skills, which in turn helped them generate joy and pleasure in the lives of their fans and audiences.

More than just acts of altruism, these kinds of pleasure-making projects received fervent support from Kakuma's camp administrators, and it is crucial to understand why. Like other aid services, these projects functioned in ways that positioned the UNHCR and its contracted agencies as the primary sponsors and caregivers of the suffering and vulnerable refugee. In this sense, pleasure was entangled with an affective economy of suffering that structured an unequal hierarchy between refugees and camp officials. Music projects were distinct from other forms of aid precisely because of the ways they wielded pleasure. Musical signs of joy, fun, and fantasy had the obfuscating effects of promoting pleasure in the lives of refugees without radically altering the larger goal of the Kakuma camp as a site of migratory control.

Some might contend that making refugee camps like Kakuma pleasurable places to live would encourage forced migrants to stay in Kenya, negating the very purpose of the temporary relief camp. In reality, long-term settlement has already happened, as many camp inhabitants hail from conflict areas that make it nearly impossible for them to return. Many of the teenagers and twenty-somethings I met were either born or raised in the camp, with little to no experiences living in their countries of origin. On average, only 1 percent of Kakuma's camp population has historically been resettled each year. And according to statistics from UNHCR's *Global Trends* report in 2016, repatriation figures have steadily declined since the early 1990s. What has resulted in Kenya and other parts of the globe is a refugee regime that has institutionalized the habitation of long-term sites of precarity and uncertainty—a humanitarian system that requires refugees to both experience and exhibit suffering and discontent in order to become audible and legible to the officials charged with regulating forced migration.

Reflecting on this issue reminds me of my initial conversation with Smart Djaba and the way his mood and emotions shifted when he began talking about his musical career. For him, popular music was a productive force for pleasure that had real tangible effects. Attuning to pleasure begs the following questions. What if, instead of suffering, pleasure became the primary modus operandi of the refugee regime? How would this affective shift alter the workings of humanitarianism and transform the way we engage with international migration? Perhaps instead of spending billions of dollars on making people feel discontented for decades with little end in sight, finances could be redirected toward creating pleasurable spaces and experiences in coordination with forced migrants and local residents. Perhaps instead of basing resettlement cases on the deservingness of who suffers more, state officials from wealthy countries could open their borders to forced migrants on the grounds of generating a life of pleasure, joy, and human flourishing. While I know that there are additional social, economic, and political concerns involved with making these kinds of changes, it is clear that transforming the debilitating aspects of the refugee regime will require more concerted efforts toward making pleasure political.

Notes

1. Joel Robbins (2013) has argued that in the early 1990s, anthropologists shifted their attention from studying societies radically different from their own to focusing on studies of trauma and suffering as a means of redressing anthropology's problematic history with cultural Othering. "Because of its universalistic quality," Robbins writes, "the suffering subject appeared to anthropologists not just as a something new to study, but as a solution to a problem that had in the 1980s appeared ready to condemn their discipline to irrelevance" (2013, 454).

2. My use of the term "suffering subject" has the same meaning as Joel Robbins's definition: "the subject living in pain, in poverty, or under conditions of violence or oppression" (2013, 448).

3. This quote by a leading UNHCR official in Kenya is from a news segment on KTN News Kenya aired in 2015.

4. Smart Djaba, interview with the author, April 2, 2015, Kakuma Refugee Camp, Kenya.

5. Smart Djaba, interview with the author, July 15, 2013, Kakuma Refugee Camp, Kenya.

6. Smart Djaba, interview with the author, April 2, 2015, Kakuma Refugee Camp, Kenya.

7. King Moses's friend Stephanie Abitho revised my initial translation of this song to more accurately reflect King Moses's intended meanings and phrasings of his lyrics.

8. Aron, essay sent to author, June 3, 2015, Kakuma Refugee Camp, Kenya.

9. Personal observation, May 25, 2015, Kakuma Refugee Camp, Kenya.

10. "Queen Lissa—Mapenzi Gani ft. Solution [ItsNambaNaneTV]," OCTOPIZZO, February 8, 2017, music video, 3:56, https://www.youtube.com/watch?v=CB4Kz2eLBBw.

11. "Street Boyz—Lets Party [ItsNambaNaneTV]," OCTOPIZZO, December 20, 2016, music video, 3:42, https://www.youtube.com/watch?v=ADveyY_udzo.

12. Anonymous, personal communication, November 20, 2014, Kakuma Refugee Camp, Kenya.

13. Anonymous, interview with author, June 15, 2015, Kakuma Refugee Camp, Kenya.

3

LABOR

"We Need More Than Appreciations"

An audience of children and young adults surrounded the hardtop basketball court located just outside the iron-sheet gates of the Ethiopian market in Kakuma One. Some came from the nearby Nuer and Congolese neighborhoods. Others came across the dried-out riverbed that separated the camp area from the town of Kakuma. Still others came through the Lutheran World Federation (LWF) compound's metal gates, with its white vehicles, public address systems, and banners emblazoned with messages about the problem of sexual and gender-based violence, a term widely circulated in the Kakuma camp used to discuss incidences and experiences of domestic abuse and sexual assault. The audience was there to watch a collection of hip hop, R&B, and dancehall performers address this pressing issue through music. The invited musicians, dressed in fashionable tops and jewelry, came to the stage area and performed their signature songs. With attitude, style, and confidence, they bobbed and paced around the hardtop court, rapping and singing to a crowd of young people who loudly cheered and applauded each performance. When the musicians' sets had all ended, the MC asked them to return to the stage. The aid agency's project managers wanted to publicly thank them for contributing their talents to the social campaign. The MC praised the musicians for their efforts and offered each a brand-new Nokia phone as a token of the agency's appreciation. Unexpectedly, all the musicians declined the phones, causing a minor public embarrassment for the sponsoring agency.

Why did musicians performing for a pressing social project publicly reject brand new mobile phones in a refugee camp, a site with scarce material resources? What did these musicians hope to make audible through their public dissent? One of the main organizers of the protest told me that he and his fellow musicians had received similar phones in the past, and they did not want more of the same. "We need more than appreciations," he explained. What they wanted was cash, a desire they repeatedly communicated to the organizing agency. They wanted financial recognition of their musical profession, not symbolic gestures of appreciation that did little to ameliorate their disadvantaged economic positions. Were these musicians right to turn down phones, or were their claims unwarranted? Were they immoral because they sought monetary compensation for their participation in support of a good cause? Were they selfish because they refused a luxury item in an already cash-strapped aid economy? Did they not understand that refugee camps are made for relief, not for developing music careers?

During my three visits to the Kakuma camp between 2011 and 2015, I often heard aid officials call for the upholding of a slew of rights: refugee rights, women's rights, LGBTQ rights, children's rights, the right to clean water, and the right to education. Slogans championing these rights were printed on billboards, posters, and T-shirts. They echoed from speakers during public speeches at school functions and UNHCR events. And yet often absent from this messaging was a commonly endorsed right, a right written into the UN Universal Declaration of Human Rights and the 1951 Convention, a right that most aid workers and UN officials probably believed in—labor rights.[1] A common rationale given to justify the UNHCR and its contracted agencies' silence on labor rights was that speaking up for refugees' right to employment would jeopardize the UNHCR's mandate to protect forced migrants. Many of the aid workers I knew reasoned that advocating for the labor rights of refugees would anger Kenyan officials and citizens to the point where the state would deport and turn away all refugees. From this perspective, the relative silence on labor rights stemmed from a humanitarian mandate to uphold other refugee rights, especially the right to non-refoulement. Attuning to the perspectives and experiences of some of Kakuma's commercially minded popular musicians, however, reveals that there was more to this story than sacrificing one right for another.

In East Africa, hip hop culture has served as a potent social force for many young people living in urban areas (Kidula 2012; Eisenberg 2012; Perullo 2011; Ntarangwi 2009). In his transregional study of hip hop and globalization, Mwenda Ntarangwi (2009) examines issues of power and identity, documenting the realities and philosophies of hip hop artists living in an array of cities—Dar es Salaam, Arusha, Nairobi, Mombasa, Kampala, Jinja, Moshi, and Kisumu, among others. In doing so, he argues that young people in urban centers have drawn on hip hop "as a means of retaining autonomy and the ability to act on their own behalf while influencing other people in political discourse and even economic activity in spite of the global forces of inequality and exploitation that they face" (2009, 3). Relatedly, Jean Kidula has discussed the unique communicative capacity of rap music for young people in Kenya, noting that its accessibility has made it the most viable way for them to express themselves musically in a range of urban spaces from schools and churches to dance halls and bars (2012, 172, 177).

The Kakuma Refugee Camp has become another urban center in East Africa where hip hop and related musical styles play communicative and agentive roles in the lives of young people facing global forces of inequality and exploitation. Urban music genres such as hip hop, R&B, and dancehall were precisely the kinds of music required for sustaining and surviving in the camp system. Listening to these musical styles on mobile phones, radios, and televisions—and performing them in bars, restaurants, youth centers, and schools—constituted subjectivities that aligned with the Kakuma camp's urbanized operation. At the same time, social imaginaries of fame and fortune stemming from the seductive influences of commercial media resulted in agonistic musicians resentful of a discriminatory system that forbade refugees from receiving money for labor. Rather than accept these conditions, select musicians voiced their concerns. Their sense of belonging to transnational music markets catalyzed a critical consciousness that manifested in concerted actions toward redressing an unequal humanitarian labor economy. Moreover, their stories and experiences elucidate the cohesion and disjuncture that occur when forces from the aid/refugee industry and the music industry collide and intertwine.

"From Refugee to Superstar"

With an air of both swagger and hesitation, Smart Djaba strode to the front of the crowd. Dressed impeccably in a fitted black dress shirt, silvery gray vest, and dark slacks, he surveyed the audience of UNHCR officials and agency staff, seated in a circular arrangement. As the soft piano lines of his signature song wafted through the speaker system, his nerves calmed and his confidence grew. With mic in hand, he crooned the song's introductory line, "I was born to shine," and when the beat dropped, he sang out:

Original Version	Translated Version[2]
Mimi nita wika	Me I will blow
Beat ita pigika	The beat will be played
Kila dakika	Every minute
Kwenye ma woofer na speaker	On the woofers and speakers
Mimi mtoto wa Afrika	Me the African child
Nita sikika	I will be listened to
Paka Amerika	in America
I was born to shine	I was born to shine

Feeling the groove of the hip hop beat and the increasing intensity of the clinking sounds of the melodic piano line, the audience roared with applause when Smart belted out the song's chorus.

I was born to shine
'Cuz I got a talent
I got a beautiful gift
It's my beautiful voice

On that warm July night in 2013, Smart was on privileged ground. The barbed wire–protected UNHCR compound, stationed with guards from the British multinational security company G4S, was typically off-limits to refugees after 5:00 p.m. Yet on that night, FilmAid (FAI) had organized a screening of film entries directed by refugees for its upcoming film festival. Managers asked Smart to perform because of his musical skills and involvement in FAI filmmaking programs. The UNHCR typically restricted refugees from entering the UNHCR and NGO compound areas past curfew hours unless an agency organized an event that enabled refugees to attend. Interestingly, most of these nighttime events involved musical performances—that is, music was often the medium for traversing the physical and social divisions that structured relations between refugees and aid workers. Smart was in good spirits that night. After his performance, I congratulated him, as did many other people in attendance. Shortly thereafter, he was transported back to the camp area. Meanwhile, the UNHCR and agency staff stayed for the party portion of the event, drinking bottles of Tusker and Whitecap beer and dancing late into the night to the grooves of popular bongo flava, hip hop, dancehall, and R&B songs pumped through the public address systems set up in the compound's outdoor bar area.

When I first met Smart Djaba, he had just started making hip hop and R&B music with the support of FAI and the LWF. Buoyed by the praise he received for his track "Born to Shine," he continued pursuing his passion and honing his craft by recording tracks, making videos, and performing shows. Recognizing his musical prowess, the aid agencies regularly asked to use his music in social campaigns to address issues such as HIV and AIDS, domestic abuse, sexual violence, and social conflict. In turn, I found that Smart was proud of his musical accomplishments and grateful to the agencies for supporting his artistry. FAI's projects empowered Smart, providing him with a platform through which to express himself and his ideas. In one of his early compositions with FAI, he expresses the power of filmmaking through his song "I Am the Director."

> No matter who you are
> No matter the story's yours.
> No matter you get money
> The film is mine because I am the director
> It's my vision. It's my conception. It's my vision.
> I'm the director ah

A notable message of this song is that monetary gains are secondary to filmmaking gains. Telling one's story, one's vision, is what matters most. The idea of intangible benefits from involvement in arts-based projects was a fundamental principle of the aid agencies operating in the Kakuma camp. For artistically inclined refugees like Smart Djaba, opportunities to make music and films were crucial for well-being and self-worth.

Smart Djaba's popularity as a musician in Kakuma grew quickly. The staff at FAI viewed him as one of the most talented and skilled performing artists in the camp. Crowds of young people loudly cheered for his performances during UNHCR events. They paid money to see him perform at the shows he and his friends organized in the market areas and LWF youth centers. Smart's confidence in his musical abilities grew as praise was heaped on him by fans and agency staff. He began to dream of transforming his life as a refugee through music, a desire openly stated in his song "From Refugee to Superstar."

> I gotta make it. That's all I need in my life.
> I know I gotta make it. From zero to hero, yeah
> I gotta make it. That's all I need in my life.
> From refugee to superstar
> I gotta make it

Smart's goal of shifting his subjectivity from refugee to superstar reflected and affected how he understood his position within the aid agencies' music and arts projects. In October 2014, I returned to the Kakuma camp and once again connected with Smart. We met in the neem tree–shaded courtyard of the Green *hoteli* in the Ethiopian market in Kakuma One. Over bottles of warm soda, he recounted his involvement with UNHCR/NGO music projects from a wholly different perspective compared to when we first met. He was no longer interested in making music for the UNHCR or the agencies. Though he admitted to benefiting from these projects, he felt he had reached a point in his career where he should receive payment for his labor. For Smart, there was an expectation that musicians should and need to be paid for their work.

To better understand why Smart felt this way, it is crucial to recognize the subject-making effects of hip hop and popular music in Kakuma and the wider East African region. A central facet of becoming a modern subject, for many of Kakuma's rappers and R&B singers, was the accrual of wealth, a common ideal and trope enacted in the songs and music videos they consumed on a daily basis. Such desires and behaviors resonated with the kinds of capitalistic subjectivities constituted within the popular music industry in East Africa. "Central to the commodification of music," notes Alex Perullo in his study of popular music and Tanzania's music economy, "is that it creates desires to pursue careers associated with the increasing financial value of songs. As local and international artists present images of wealth and prestige, people imagine a musical career as an opportunity to attain these social statuses. Even the notion of fame, relatively absent in the past, is now a sought-after ambition" (2011, 24). Perullo's (2011) study examines the multifaceted ways that participation in Tanzania's neoliberal economy is more than just a form of empowerment and has involved both economic advancement and economic subjugation.

A similar situation arose with humanitarian music projects in the Kakuma camp. Music empowered Smart. With every new track, performance, competition prize, and praise from NGO managers and fans, his confidence grew—as did his recognition of the value he provided to the aid agencies. NGO projects thus both supported Smart's ambitions and induced agonistic views toward the sponsoring agencies.

Reevaluating Musical Aid

I worked with some of the Kakuma camp's theater for development (TfD) groups in 2011 when I first began studying the role of musical aid. Through my research, I learned that some performers were better at addressing social concerns than others. Some groups spent more time than others tailoring messages to their communities. I knew this because I observed groups' shows, spoke with their members, and interacted with their crowds. I witnessed groups dressed in costumes with choreographed dance routines and topical songs whose main worries were to solve local health concerns through artistic means. Contrastingly, I knew other groups with less dedication to social causes whose main concerns were pocketing the 350 KSH ($3.50) stipend for lunch. Over time, I came to feel admiration for the former's dedication and frustration with the latter's apathy. Then, things changed. Through reflection and research, I came to better understand the discriminatory experiences of these performing artists. Reaching this perspective required rethinking what constitutes a successful musical aid project.

Artistic approaches to aid delivery circulated widely throughout the Kakuma camp's social environment. TfD groups spread messages about peace and public health by performing songs, dramas, and poems in local communities. Celebrity musicians taught rap skills to aspiring musicians during workshops held at LWF youth centers. Rappers composed songs about malaria for distribution on IOM's radio system. As the camp shifted from providing short-term emergency relief to existing as a more permanent site, its administrators understood the need to provide refugees, especially young people, with services extending beyond basic food rations, healthcare, and housing. The UNHCR, LWF, FAI, Octopizzo Foundation (OF), International Rescue Committee (IRC), National Council of Churches of Kenya (NCCK), Danish Refugee Council (DRC), Waldorf, and Kakuma Sound were all organizations that supported programs designed to use the arts—music, dance, poetry, crafts, fashion, drama, and filmmaking—in some manner to fulfill refugees' creative needs and ameliorate pressing social concerns.

To meet these goals, aid agencies operating in the Kakuma camp often supported arts-based projects that blended entertainment and didactic components. Known as edutainment activities in aid circles, these projects leveraged the fun and pleasurable aspects of the arts to shape a desired attitude and behavior toward a specific social problem. In contrast to top-down forms of aid delivery that risk fostering paternalism and irrelevancy, edutainment projects are designed to use bottom-up, participatory approaches that position and empower the artist-refugee as an expert and active agent charged with solving problems in their own community. In many ways, performing artists in the camp *were* uniquely suited for this task. They encountered similar problems as their peers. They shared similar needs, desires, and goals. They spoke the same languages and employed the same slang. They consumed the same media, wore similar clothes, and participated in shared activities. Furthermore, local artists had many of the skills aid workers lacked—language, social knowledge, and relatability—which they embodied and enacted through artistic expression. In other words, young artists were relatable to their peers and knowledgeable of local needs and worldly perspectives, a position folklorist Diane Goldstein has called "the voices and knowledge of vernacular culture" (Goldstein 2015, 126).

The kinds of bottom-up edutainment activities that NGO workers in the Kakuma camp often valued are exemplified in the projects that came out of the 2015 UNHCR Youth Initiative Fund. The UNHCR's *2015 Global Appeal Update* discusses the benefits, aims, and procedures of this initiative:

> Getting protection programming right for forcibly displaced youth can pay dividends not only for them, but also their families and communities. Such are the objectives of UNHCR's Youth Initiative Fund, launched in 2013. It asks displaced communities to design and lead projects to address protection challenges they have identified within their own communities (UNHCR 2015).
>
> The initiative takes a community-based approach to selecting and training coaches, and cultivating leadership among participating youth and adolescents, by enabling them to take on increased roles and responsibilities. It places the unique needs of youth and their communities at the centre of its design (UNHCR 2015).

For this initiative, UNHCR-Geneva invited applicants from various displacement situations across the globe to submit project proposals. In 2015, a TfD from the Kakuma camp called United Drama Group (UDG) was one of eight winners the UNHCR selected from a large pool of applications. Buoyed by this success, UNHCR-Kakuma decided to support the project ideas of other competing groups. One of these projects was a series of refugee-organized events aimed at using popular music to promote peace in the camp. Around that time, several conflicts had occurred between members of the Great Lakes and South Sudanese populations. UNHCR officials believed that a camp-wide music for peace project designed and led by refugees would create greater social harmony and stability.

The music for peace project was a main topic of concern at subsequent Afrostars Entertainment meetings. I had been attending these meetings at the behest of the group's leaders to learn more about the goals and challenges that came with making popular music in a refugee camp. Aftrostars Entertainment typically held its gatherings at LWF's YC2 in Kakuma Two, a common meeting place for youth groups in the area. Topics of discussion usually centered on planning and promotional ideas for upcoming shows. Yet discussions would at times turn to debate about whether or not to continue performing in NGO music projects. Such conversations arose whenever an aid agency asked the group to perform in a social campaign. The issue of participating in the new UNHCR music for peace project set off a heated debate during a meeting in 2015. Seated in plastic chairs and on the thick lower branches of the tree located near the gated entrance to YC2, musicians with competing claims and agendas held a tense conversation.

M1: "Why are you so upset?" one of the more established musicians asked, looking in the direction of a musician who had recently joined Afrostars.

M2: "Last week, we all agreed that we would stop performing for the NGOs unless we were paid. Didn't we?" a new Afrostars member replied.

M3: "Yes, we did. So what happened?" chimed in another musician.

M2: "Yesterday, I was at the show at Youth Center Two, and I saw her performing on stage," said the new Afrostars member. "Did they pay you?"

M4: "Don't point your finger at me!" responded the rapper who performed at the youth center.

M5: "This is not right!" yelled out another musician.

M1: "Listen!" yelled the established musician. "We have to be united. We have to stop fighting. We cannot keep performing for nothing."

M6: "I think we should perform," said another of the younger, less established musicians in the Kakuma camp. "You all have benefited from performing for the agencies. And we think by telling us to stop, you are preventing us from getting the same fame."

M1: "Trust me," the established musician replied, "you perform, but you get nothing—just broken biscuits and juice."

M6: "Well, we think it is OK to perform because we are still underground artists and need the same fame you have," answered the younger musician.

M1: "You are right—I have benefited. I cannot say that I have not. But imagine if we were all able to perform, and we also got money for our music. The only way to do that is if we are united!"[3]

This contentious conversation is similar to debates disgruntled factory workers have about striking for higher wages. Those in support of boycotting the agencies believed the UNHCR and aid agencies disrespected their talents, skills, and craft by not offering fair financial compensation. These musicians required more than "broken biscuits and juice," a phrase several musicians I knew often used to evoke the paltry appreciations refugees received for their musical labor. Others refused to quit working with the agencies, seeking the same fame as the more established artists. As a result, the large pool of underground (up-and-coming) musicians hungry for fame created barriers for forging a unified opposition. Tensions and infighting over even the most modest sums of money were a fact of life in a site with limited resources, especially among young people raised on the promises and imaginaries of humanitarian aid and capitalistic music.

The debate at the Afrostars meeting is instructive because it unsettles dominant assumptions about what constitutes a successful arts-based aid project. The aid agencies and their donors often evaluated edutainment projects by assessing the accuracy and persuasiveness of the musical message and identifying and analyzing audience size, demographics, and reactions. Such metrics are indicative of the tendency of international NGOs to focus on meeting a singular, specified project goal. In her study of music and aid in the Democratic Republic of the Congo, for example, Chérie Rivers Ndaliko (2016, 157) discusses how tensions often arose during projects because international NGOs were singularly focused on addressing one problem. To correct this myopic approach, Ndaliko stresses the importance of being attentive to the web of issues that arise in the politics of producing arts-oriented projects. In a similar vein, Nomi Dave (2015) argues for paying greater attention to the methods and practices involved in music and human rights projects, placing emphasis on the political dimensions and real-world impacts of such initiatives. These kinds of evaluative approaches are crucial for analyzing the multiple, uneven, and wide-ranging impacts of arts-oriented humanitarianism. As the dispute during the Afrostars meeting demonstrates, the most pressing issue for many of its members was not generating peace through music. Their primary concern was with receiving payment for their labor.

When an NGO, especially an international one, does not offer sufficient pay, musicians can feel exploited, disrespected, and undervalued, which can in turn damage the credibility of the NGO (Ndaliko 2016, 152). When NGOs do pay musicians, however, allocating too much money can have adverse effects. Humanitarian projects are often ephemeral and conducted in economically disadvantaged areas. Overpaying musicians can create unsustainable conditions harmful to both a musician's career and the local cultural scene (Ndaliko 2016, 152). Additionally, donors and NGOs can use finances to exert control over musicians by paying them to circulate organizational messages that suppress local viewpoints and obfuscate oppressive forces (Ndaliko 2016, 142–155;

Dave 2015, 6–7). The issue of money and labor in arts-oriented aid projects is thus not only about setting the correct compensation levels but also about a range of factors concerning self-worth and autonomy, relationships between institutions and communities, and ideological and institutional control.

Many of these factors and issues surrounding money and labor applied to NGO music projects in the Kakuma camp. Indeed, the musicians who wanted to stop performing in NGO events felt exploited, disrespected, and under-valued by the aid agencies' refusal to pay them. They believed that the music they made was of professional grade and deserved fair compensation. And yet it was the aid agencies' music workshops and performance opportunities that enabled these musicians to develop their skills and confidence. So why were they not more grateful to the aid agencies and UNHCR for their charitable contributions? Answering this question requires delving more deeply into the kinds of relationships that exist between refugees and aid agencies, as well as the forms of ideological and institutional control that structured Kakuma's humanitarian labor economy.

The Inequality of Humanitarian Labor

To run its camp operation in Kakuma, the UNHCR contracted a host of na-tional and international NGOs. Typically, these agencies staffed their organi-zations with a small minority of foreign workers occupying managerial and volunteer or intern positions, a large minority of Kenyan nationals working across all levels (from managerial to custodial positions), and a large majority of refugees carrying out the bulk of the workload required to operate the camp. Refugees worked as teachers educating young people in primary and secondary schools administered through the LWF, NCCK, and Windle Trust; medical staff treating patients at the main hospital and clinics overseen by IRC; support staff distributing iron-sheet roofing through the NCCK; water technicians repairing taps and pipelines managed by the LWF and NRC; and musicians composing and performing songs for UNHCR social campaigns. Refugees also carried out senior and mid-level management duties by providing guidance and insights on best practices learned over many years spent living and working in the camp. Such knowledge was often passed down to new NGO employees, a process repeated frequently due to high turnover rates among international, and to a lesser extent, Kenyan national, staff.

And yet while many experienced refugees worked for the aid agencies, their pay rates were defined neither by their qualifications nor their work ethic but rather by their migratory status. In 1991, the Kenyan government shifted its

policy from providing refugees and asylum seekers with work permits to denying them the full employment rights outlined in the 1951 Refugee Convention
(Verdirame and Harrell-Bond 2005, 216). Under the new policy, the UNHCR
and NGOs were not allowed to formally hire refugees. Instead, the aid organizations labeled them *refugee incentive workers* and paid them a nominal fee for
working a full-time schedule. In 2015, the average incentive pay totaled about
$60 per month. To put this level of payment into perspective, a foreign resettle-
ment officer charged with determining whether or not a refugee deserved to
immigrate to a Western country received about $4500/month.

Troublingly, the institutional structure of Kakuma's humanitarian labor
sector operated in a similar fashion to the British colonial labor system. In
Kenya, colonized peoples played a major role running the colonial system,
working in diverse jobs ranging from manual labor to civil service. And yet,
like Kakuma's camp inhabitants, the colonized were not permitted to receive
the same wages and rise to the same level as the colonizers. Beyond noting the
resemblance between the two systems, it is important to consider how the current migratory regime in East Africa has been shaped by its colonial past. In
their historical study of labor and migration regimes in Kenya and Tanzania,
Hanno Brankamp and Patricia Daley argue that "a number of contemporary
laws and institutions that organize land, ethnic territoriality, migration, and
asylum in fact perpetuate colonial legacies of differential mobility, though often in modified form" (2020, 115). From this perspective, the different pay rates
applied to refugees and nonrefugees in the Kakuma camp have historical ties
to the migration regimes of British colonialism.

In another caveat to this issue, the inequality of humanitarian pay scales also
applied to nonrefugees. Agencies usually paid foreign nationals higher amounts
than Kenyan nationals for doing the same job. For the first two decades of the
camp's operation, agencies paid Kenyans from down-country areas such as
Nairobi more than local Kenyans from the surrounding area. The logic used to
justify both pay disparities was the same—higher salaries were needed to attract high-quality workers from wealthier areas who would not otherwise come
to an impoverished area. The unequal labor practices of Western-imported aid
thus became replicated within Kenya's borders. When I first came to Kakuma
in 2011, I learned that the difference in pay scales for Kenyan nationals had
recently ended after local protesters showed up with spears outside the LWF
compound, angrily demanding the same wages and salaries as their compatriots. The same compensation for refugees, however, never materialized.

In addition to denying refugees formal wages and salaries, Kakuma's camp
system enabled other exploitative labor practices. Part of understanding how

these practices functioned requires discussing humanitarianism's "innovation turn," a shift that became identifiable in 2009 (Betts, Bloom, and Weaver 2015, 4–5). According to researchers at Oxford's Refugee Studies Center, "United Nations agencies, NGOs, governments, businesses, and even the military have begun to engage with the idea of humanitarian innovation, creating special labs, funds, and partnerships to enable untapped ideas and solutions to be drawn upon" (Betts, Bloom, and Weaver 2015, 4–5). Tom Scott-Smith has argued that this new direction is indicative of an ideology of "humanitarian neophilia," a term he coined to convey how left- and right-wing politics have emphasized technology, markets, and self-reliant subjects rather than strong nation-states supporting substantive socioeconomic rights (2016, 2229).

A dubious case of note involves UNHCR-Kakuma's decision to allow a social enterprise from the United States to conduct a pit latrine project. Supporters of the project believed it would help solve the recurring problem of overflowing pit latrines. The agency's delivery model was designed to turn human waste into briquettes of cooking fuel, which were then collected and sold for profit and operational sustainability. In perhaps the ultimate form of biopolitical control, camp officials turned a captive population's excrement into capital through the premise of improving refugee health outcomes. Meanwhile, Kakuma's camp residents obtained few monetary benefits while their bodies enriched the social enterprise's bottom line. Or consider the uncompensated labor scheme of the UNHCR Youth Initiative Fund (YIF). United Drama Group (UDG), winner of the UNHCR YIF's global competition, was initially told that UNHCR-Geneva would provide $12,000 to run the group's proposed projects. However, UDG never received this money. Instead, the UNHCR-Kakuma and its contracting agency took control of the funds. When members from the group needed to buy costumes or supplies for performances, they had to invoice "the office." In the end, the camp administration used a significant amount of the $12,000 to fund salaries and operations, while UDG's members carried out the bulk of the work. Both of these projects may be characterized not as innovation but as innovative exploitation. Both were designed to find creative solutions to pressing social problems without addressing refugees' socioeconomic rights. Both enriched the budgets of aid organizations through discourses and logics of care that obfuscated inequality. And both made containing refugees more orderly and efficient. In a period of dwindling funds for maintaining Kenya's refugee camps, projects such as these were created with the intention of doing more with less in a manner that discriminated against refugees.

Some might contend that making music for NGO projects was voluntary and that musicians should not have felt obligated to participate. This rationale is expressed in the UNHCR *Global Appeal Update*, which states that "participation is encouraged, but not mandatory, to take account of possible financial constraints and the demands of work" (UNHCR 2015). This report, however, contradicts itself in the next line, stating that "the programme serves to strengthen social cohesion, communication, and understanding within and between groups, at no cost to the participants or to the community." On the one hand, the report recognizes refugees' financial pressures and work obligations. On the other hand, it suggests these projects will come at no cost to refugees. The underlying assumption of the latter idea is that the UNHCR is covering project expenses, ignoring the fact that refugees conceived, designed, and implemented the projects, contributing all these forms of unpaid labor.

It was within this context that some commercially minded musicians became upset with the UNHCR and its contracted agencies over the issue of unpaid labor. Recognizing the exploitative aspects of the humanitarian labor system turned feelings of gratitude toward the UNHCR and NGOs into feelings of resentment. Rather than begrudgingly accepting their subordinated economic statuses, however, select musicians voiced their discontent. So how did aid workers, many of whom dedicated their lives to helping others, operate within this system? More specifically, how did aid workers driven by sentiments of care and compassion justify not paying Kakuma's performing artists?

Altruistic Subordination

Most aid officials in the Kakuma camp disagreed with refugees' claims for payment, so much so that UNHCR and NGO managers often worked to silence musicians' requests. During an NGO meeting I attended with several performing artists, for example, I witnessed one manager explicitly forbid a group of agonistic musicians to express their desires for financial compensation during an upcoming donor meeting. On this occasion and others, I became privy to the types of discourses aid officials used to justify not paying Kakuma's musicians for their labor. Aid officials' persuasive approach may be aptly understood through what I refer to as altruistic subordination—a process of discourses and practices that, intentionally or not, operate on principles that connote selfless concern for the well-being of others while masking discrimination.

Noncompliant behavior had to be dealt with in a fashion that aligned with humanitarian values. Many UNHCR officials and aid workers attempted to convince performing artists in the Kakuma camp that their policy of nonpayment was valid for the following reasons:

1. Volunteers are more genuine and thus produce better work than financially motivated musicians.
2. Performing artists gain from intangible compensation such as leadership skills, fame, and musical development.
3. Aid agencies provide refugees with free services, and refugees should think of these services as their compensation.
4. Refugees are not members of the Kenyan state and thus do not deserve the same rights as Kenyan citizens.

Three out of these four reasons operate on principles of altruism that subordinate performing artists to aid agencies. The first morally discriminates against the economically minded musician on the grounds that financial motivation is selfish. Aid workers who suggest volunteers provide better responses to alleviating social problems code those seeking fair financial compensation as inauthentic providers of humanitarian assistance. The second and third justifications promote the aid agencies' selfless acts in providing support to needy performing artists, thus remedying any moral need to provide fair wages.

At first glance, such justifications may seem valid. On closer inspection, however, they are problematic. The idea that paid musicians would do inadequate work compared to volunteers is hypocritical if we recognize that most aid workers in the Kakuma camp earned salaries for their charitable work. A counterargument to this perspective might be that agencies often hired nonrefugee volunteers in exchange for developing their professional skills. In this sense, the volunteer intern was no different from the volunteer refugee-musician. The difference, however, was that volunteer interns typically worked for an agency for only a few weeks to a year, while refugee-musicians were required to offer their charitable services at no cost for years on end. And while NGO project planners always managed to find volunteer musicians, they often failed to see the hours of infighting between musicians over the issue of payment. With regard to the third point, refugees did indeed receive social services. However, I found that many refugees felt agency projects were more for the aid workers than for them. When I asked Smart his thoughts about NGO arts-based projects, he said:

> They have been training people in the community. After they have done with the training, they give them certificates. And after that, they call us artists to perform, and, well, we have our fans in the community in the camp. Oh, Musician A is going to perform. Musician B is going. Musician C is going to perform. They come. When they are there, they can also listen

to the message, learn more about the [project]. You know it is a kind of
politics. [The agencies] are calling musicians so that people can follow them
and get the message that they want to pass.[4]

Smart had developed a critical consciousness about his role as a performer in
the Kakuma camp. In his mind, the aid agencies used musicians to further their
own organizational agendas. "It's a business for the aid agencies," he explained.
"They are making money off us when they do their projects."[5] More than just
the viewpoint of one musician, this perception was common among many of
the refugees I knew.

This critical perspective of aid work raises another important issue involving payment for musical labor in a long-term refugee camp. If aid agencies are
indeed sponsoring music projects that advance their own agendas as well as
their donors', and if a main aim of these organizations is to manage a site designed to segregate, sort, and control forced migrants, then it is perhaps fair to
conclude that the practice of paying musicians to make music for NGO/donor
projects would reproduce this very system. Musicians would thus become part
of the business of aid. In this sense, the practice of NGOs paying musicians
would still function as a form of altruistic subordination. What exists, then, is
a system in which even seemingly just practices can reproduce inequality. As
Giorgio Agamben has argued, individuals who enter "the camp" move into a
paradoxical "zone of indistinction between outside and inside, exception and
rule, licit and illicit, in which the very concepts of subjective right and juridical
protection no longer made any sense" (1998, 170).

Verdirame and Harrell-Bond (2005) have argued that the duality of helping
and harming refugees is a common facet of camps designed to deny people
basic civil liberties. Indeed, the Kakuma camp's structural inequalities blurred
distinctions between the promise of music as aid and the perils of music for aid.
From the music as aid perspective, the UNHCR and its contracted agencies
activated music's therapeutic and didactic attributes to support and improve
the well-being of refugees. From the music for aid perspective, these projects
relegated refugees into subordinated positions. The repetition of aid-funded
music projects enabled aid officials to position themselves as custodians over
refugees made to reside in a site of segregated care. The power of this duality
lay in the capacity of the seemingly altruistic nature of NGO music projects to
obscure the violence of encampment. Musical aid, in this regard, operated as
a form of symbolic violence that both masked and reproduced an oppressive
system of migratory control. It was within this challenging context that professionally minded musicians strove to earn money from their music.

The Cost of Music-Making

As part of my research, I helped make a short video about the cost of musical labor in the Kakuma camp in collaboration with local filmmaker John Baraka, rapper King Moses, and the Afro-reggae group E-Squad. We made the video to educate the UNHCR and NGOs about the cost of making music so that they might reconsider their positions on not paying musicians for work in NGO social campaigns. Over the course of several weeks in July and August 2015, King Moses and E-Squad graciously invited us into their homes and communities to learn about the economics of music-making. King Moses brought us into his modest mud-brick home in Kakuma One, intent on describing the costs associated with his craft. He strove to emulate and particularize the images and sounds he saw in music videos. He wore shorts and a teal 76ers jersey with NBA star Allen Iverson's name inscribed on the back. Next to him laid a notebook filled with lyrical compositions and his smartphone, a device he used for making music, marketing his image, and organizing meetings and shows. With a single phone, he could download hip hop beats, develop his lyrical compositions, perform live and playback (lip-synched) shows, update his Facebook page, promote events on WhatsApp, and organize Afrostars meetings. After we asked King Moses why he required payment for his participation in NGO events, he said, "When I am performing, the money that I'm going to be paid is the money that is going to help me for buying credit, for buying my phone, for buying my clothes, my shoes."[6]

For many musicians, recording music in a studio is a central rite of passage. For this reason, some of Kakuma's rappers traveled to studios in Eldoret and Nairobi to record their music. Within the Kakuma camp, a select group of musicians were able to lay down tracks at no cost with producers from FAI and the Octopizzo Foundation in the studios located in Youth Center Two and the LWF compound. Others relied on the services of refugee-run media production shops. King Moses had a strong relationship with FAI, which provided him opportunities to record music with their producer free of charge. E-Squad did not. As such, they used a local business that charged 1500 KSH ($15) for recording an audio track and 2500 KSH ($25) for shooting a music video.

Many of the rappers living in the Kakuma camp desired to share and disseminate their music to fans and audiences. They watched popular musicians perform live concerts on TV and wanted to do the same. They understood that their professional legitimacy was tied to organizing shows. The partial fulfillment of this goal lay behind the doors of the camp's *hoteli*—Franco, Dynamics, and the Nile Hotel. In these places, they could entertain their fans. They could

hone their craft. They could even make some money, though this last objective was not a simple task. Before the first beat dropped in a set, artists had to
pay *kitu kidogo* (bribes) to the police in exchange for performance permits.
They had to spend money on posters and fliers for advertising and on renting
out public address systems and generators. And they bore fees for securing
event space in the *hoteli*. One of E-Squad's members explained some of these
expenses: "It is costly. We used to hire system, sound with 2500 [KSH]. So we
have to rent a hall with 4000 [KSH]. Then also we need to print the posters—
design and print the posters. It is really something which is very costly. Yeah.
We really struggle to get those money in order to ensure that our activities are
conducted."[7] Musicians often charged between 75 KSH ($0.75) and 350 KSH
($3.50) as entry fees, though after covering organizing costs, returns were mar-
ginal. Additionally, the police mandated that all public shows in the camp area
should end at 7:00 p.m. This policy prevented any possibility of establishing a
nighttime music scene, a staple of urban music entertainment throughout many
areas of the globe.

Rappers residing in the Kakuma camp needed other options. In Kenya,
a viable opportunity existed in Lodwar, a city 120 kilometers from Kakuma,
where entertainment companies Turktribe and Turkland periodically organized popular music events. These companies would hire some of the Kakuma
camp's most established musicians to perform, and pay them between twenty
and thirty US dollars for their participation. To make it to Lodwar, these musicians would follow a difficult route. They would take the Dayah Express bus
service or cram into a private taxi, colloquially referred to as a "ProBox," named
after the car's make. If they were caught leaving the Kakuma camp without a
travel permit, they would pay bribes to police officers parked along the roadside just outside the town of Kakuma. They would arrive in Lodwar, perform
all night, sleep in accommodations provided to them, and return to Kakuma
the next day. They made these trips believing that their performances as paid
musicians brought them one step closer to professional legitimacy.

After hitting a ceiling in his advancement as a professional musician in the
Kakuma camp, Smart began traveling to Nairobi to better establish himself in
the East African music industry. In Nairobi, he could access the music studios,
radio stations, and media facilities required to hone his craft and advance his
goal of becoming a professional musician. In addition to having music infrastructures, Nairobi has long served as the main cultural hub for urban music
in Kenya (Eisenberg 2012, 559). In his study on rappers of the Swahili coast
in Mombasa, Andrew Eisenberg (2012) documents the challenges rappers
faced in constituting "cultural citizenship" in the context of their peripheral

positionalities in relation to the dominance of the hip hop industry in Nairobi. If it was challenging for rappers in Mombasa—a place often considered Kenya's second major city—to gain musical and cultural legitimacy, then for musicians in a refugee camp in Turkana County, the obstacles were even more immense. And yet Smart was undeterred.

Over the years, Smart worked tirelessly to become a successful musician. His relentless drive to rise in the music industry bolstered his will to establish himself as a professional musician in the face of multiple challenges. In 2018, he signed with the recording company Gifted Music Group, based in Kampala, Uganda, through which he put out the Afro-dancehall track and music video for "Show Dem Love," an upbeat song that calls for love to be shown to African women. In 2019, he produced a music video for a slow dancehall track called "She Want" through his company Born Town Creations. His song "She Want," much like his previous work, garnered the attention of both fans and mainstream media outlets in Kenya. In an interview for the Kenyan newspaper the *Standard*, Smart spoke about why he took control over his own music video productions: "They would stay with the video for long. Others were displeased whenever I gave another concept contrary to what they had in mind of how the video should look like. I like to control the ideas in my videos. I decided to shoot my own music videos with the little that I have."[8]

This brief look at what is required of some professional musicians with refugee status in Kenya provides another perspective on why some musicians felt resentment toward the NGOs in the Kakuma camp when they did not receive payment for their labor. They did not just fantasize about being musicians. They put time, effort, and money into developing their craft. Musical fulfillment required not only the normal demands of composing a song, buying equipment, and hiring external services but also the added demands of paying bribes for performance permits and travel passes as well as operating without a nighttime music scene. An understanding of musicians' struggles in the informal sector helps make clear why some musicians felt frustrated with and exploited by the humanitarian labor system and the numerous barriers that refugees faced in Kenya.

Musical Solidarity

While it seems fine and good to pay musicians and all refugees involved in NGO programming, it is crucial to recognize the tensions involved with doing so. Many aid workers, UNHCR officials, and Kenyan citizens believe refugees do not have a right to equal employment. They believe this entitlement would encourage refugees to stay in Kenya and that paying Kenyan citizens market-based salaries is a minor compensation for bearing the burden of refugees. A popular perception holds that aid workers join humanitarian organizations out of an ethical responsibility to care for vulnerable people. In reality, many of the aid workers I knew in Kakuma joined for economic reasons, while others joined for both. With few jobs available in Kenya, a country with a GDP per capita of about $1500 per year in 2015, Kakuma's humanitarian labor economy provided attractive options for work. If refugees received the same payment as Kenyan citizens, this practice would reduce the number of already scarce job opportunities.

This perspective is important when it comes to understanding why a differentiated pay structure existed in Kakuma's aid economy. However, it is not the only one. Part of understanding political engagement in the public sphere requires turning attention toward "expressions and formations of underground cultures, lyrical dissidence, radical care, and civic generosity, and the ways in which people drive forward a critical disruption onto dominant orders through strategies and practices born from the depths of life" (LaBelle 2018, 5–6). Indeed, critical attention to the lived experiences of the Kakuma camp's underground musicians elucidates how a musical solidarity manifested in the actions of performing artists struggling against the discriminatory logics and practices of the aid economy. Listening to the complex and interwoven lives of these musicians offers a crucial counterperspective to narratives that pit refugees, citizens, and aid workers against each other.

During my research, I learned that performing artists from both the refugee and local Kenyan populations in Kakuma failed to receive formal payment for participation in NGO social campaigns. This finding could be used to support the idea that the UNHCR and NGOs did not in fact discriminate against refugee-musicians. The fallacy of this thinking is that humanitarian organizations have long subjugated Kenyan-Turkana citizens in Kakuma. As stated earlier, it took over twenty years for the UNHCR and NGOs to compensate Kenyan-Turkana with the same wages as their compatriots from other parts of Kenya. This unequal arrangement allowed foreign and down-country Kenyan musicians, producers, and project managers to fund (if they chose to accept payment) their involvement in charity music programs while denying refugees and Kenyan-Turkana the same levels of financial compensation. Under this unequal system, several rappers I knew from refugee and Kenyan-Turkana populations felt resentment toward the aid agencies because of their inability to receive payment for the music they made for NGO social campaigns. Their shared economic subordination, in conjunction with a mutual respect for the labor and costs required to develop their musical craft, prompted both groups to voice their desires for greater labor rights during UNHCR and NGO meetings. Their shared senses of belonging to the norms of the commercial music industry, coupled with their mutual marginalization within the aid system, manifested in a musical solidarity aimed at disrupting the legal distinctions separating refugees from Kenyan citizens.

In general, I found that many of the refugee-musicians I knew resented the aid workers who ran music projects in the Kakuma camp because of the wealth disparities that existed between the two groups. One aid worker, however, rarely, if ever, faced any criticism. Robert was a FilmAid International staff member held in very high regard among all the popular musicians I met. He was a musician and a music producer from Nairobi who had relocated to the Kakuma camp for a job as FAI's main music producer. Robert could often be found recording the songs of local musicians in the shipping container turned makeshift studio in the LWF compound. As a musician, he empathetically understood the desires and goals of musicians, regardless of their legal status, to make careers out of their artistic craft. As such, he recorded music free of charge and often lobbied for artists to receive higher wages during administrative meetings. His acts of musical solidarity came in the forms of vocal support and music-making activities going beyond his organization's programming requirements. Even though Robert lived in the NGO compound and earned an income that exceeded those of the refugees he recorded, many musicians living in the Kakuma camp appreciated his concerted efforts to negotiate and challenge the inequities of the aid economy. His actions highlight how musical solidarity required the participation of allies from across the camp system.

Radical Edutainment

In recent years, many theater for development groups in Africa's Great Lakes region have adopted the radical elements of the theater-action methodology developed in Augusto Boal's *Theater of the Oppressed* without incorporating its revolutionary potential (Le Lay 2020). A similar outcome has occurred in the Kakuma camp, despite Kenya having its own radical theater tradition. Renowned playwright and political activist Ngũgĩ wa Thiong'o helped create politically charged productions with the *Kamĩrĩĩthũ* Popular Theater Experiment, productions that faced censure from both Kenyatta's and Moi's postcolonial regimes. It is worth noting that Thiong'o placed great importance on songs and dances in his decolonial approach to African theater (Thiong'o 2005 [1986], 45). In his musical play *Maitũ Njugĩra*, for example, he deploys specific songs and dances to expose and oppose the exploitative and hegemonic effects of British colonialism (Ndīgīrīgī 2017). In the Kakuma camp, TfD shows rarely, if ever, included revolutionary messages. Instead, TfD groups typically adopted the model of mutual education through fluid and dynamic performer-audience interactions to address UNHCR- and NGO-identified social problems—conflict and violence, HIV and AIDS, alcohol and drug abuse, just to name a few. The audibility of nonradical TfD performances, and edutainment activities more broadly, is indicative of how the UNHCR and NGOs announced their commitment to supporting participatory and bottom-up initiatives while simultaneously using these projects to obfuscate the oppressive forces constituting humanitarian encampment.

In the absence of institutionally approved opportunities for making radical forms of art, some performing artists in the Kakuma camp made their voices heard through other means. If the process of claiming rights involves the struggle for recognition of particular social groups within a larger political system, then dissonance and disruption can make audible subjectivities that fail to comply with the status quo. Musicking can serve as a powerful medium for meeting these goals, as evidenced by the public protest of select hip hop, R&B, and dancehall musicians I described at the outset of this chapter. In this case, the performing artists reconfigured the NGO social campaign through their staged protest in a manner that made visible the economic inequality that undergirded the refugee regime, subjugating forces hidden by the seemingly sensical logics of humanitarian altruism. Oftentimes, aid officials dismissed musicians' claims for financial compensation as nonsensical noise because of their perceptions of what constituted a right or good refugee: a subject of humanitarian aid who (1) should be grateful for the care and support they receive in exile and (2) should not expect the same economic rights as formally recognized citizens of democratic states. Buoyed by their senses of belonging to the popular music industry in East Africa, the protesting artists leveraged their craft to elucidate the fallacies of the humanitarian labor economy.

Their public act of refusing cheap mobile phones for their work in an NGO social campaign compels a rethinking and reconfiguring of the dividing lines that separate refugees and citizens. For the organizing agency, the event was aimed at educating refugees about the wrongful effects of sexual and gendered based violence. This objective was important, and the organizers should be commended for their hard work in addressing this issue. At the same time, it is important to recognize that this edutainment event was just one of many UNHCR-sponsored events that highlighted refugees' behavioral and social problems. From this perspective, these kinds of shows legitimized the aid agencies' control over the refugee subject as an object of care. In countering this dominant arrangement, the musicians' performance-oriented protest made it known that it was the camp system, not the refugees, that required fixing. It was the aid official who failed to understand the injustice of obtaining payment for aid work when people with refugee statuses did not. It was the UNHCR and Kenyan state that failed to uphold the basic principle of the right to employment.

If the musicians' initial performance for the aid agency's social campaign was a form of edutainment because of its focus on addressing a social problem *within* the camp, their refusal to play the role of the appreciative refugee transformed the event into a form of radical edutainment that addressed the social problem *of* the camp. In this sense, the dissonance the musicians created through disruptive actions infused the event with the kind of revolutionary potential of earlier politically engaged theater productions in Brazil and Kenya.

From Labor Restrictions to Labor Rights

The rappers and singers I met between July and August 2013, and again between October 2014 and August 2015, exhibited gratitude, ambivalence, and an unwillingness to participate in the aid system's preferred roles. Some of them performed in NGO shows, proud and confident, because it was through pride in music that they felt a sense of power. They would grab the mic, pace the stage, and spit rhymes in front of crowds of aid workers, refugees, and local Kenyans. Over time, their music developed, their confidence grew, and their fame increased, but their economic position remained stagnant. To survive in a refugee camp, they needed an income, and music was their job. State policies, however, denied refugees the right to receive formal employment. So, they spoke out. They organized. They provoked.

Forced migration is commonly viewed as an exceptional circumstance requiring a humanitarian response to meet basic subsistence needs for survival. The provision of equitable labor conditions is often absent from this globally oriented response due to a dominant belief that refugees are and should be distinct from economic migrants. This chapter's case study on professional and aspiring professional musicians in Kakuma, however, elucidates why the issue of paid labor within a long-term refugee camp is of paramount importance to people striving to improve their living conditions. For select members of Afrostars Entertainment, a shared sense of belonging to a hip hop music industry largely made up of African and African American musicians catalyzed desires for greater economic well-being. These artists drew on performance skills and social networks cultivated through participation in popular music scenes to garner greater economic well-being in a place of precarity and uncertainty. Their endeavors were similar to those of performing artists in other social contexts across the globe who use performance for economic gain through participation in transnational and transregional social networks (Reed 2016; Perullo 2011). Over time, several musicians who regularly performed in UNHCR and NGO social campaigns witnessed the material wealth of aid workers increase while they continued to perform for "broken biscuits and juice." This noticeable disparity compelled musicians to protest for cash payments and to refuse to make music for the aid agencies. This phenomenon shows that forced migrants require more than relief; they require opportunities for dignified and equitable economic livelihoods.

In 2022, Smart Djaba left Kenya for Germany through the resettlement process. And yet his efforts, along with those of King Moses, E-Squad, and countless other musicians and professional workers who have fought for greater labor rights for refugees in Kenya, have had an enduring effect. Crucially, ideas about refugees and labor rights are not static. Indeed, the idea that refugees in Kenya should not have full employment rights was an ideological shift that began in the early 1990s. Three decades later, another major shift in economic policies involving refugees occurred. In February 2022, Kenyan state officials put into law a revised Refugee Act aimed at improving refugee labor conditions. The new act states that refugees "shall have the right to engage individually or in a group, in gainful employment or enterprise or to practice a profession or trade where he holds qualifications recognized by competent authorities in Kenya."[9] It also states that refugees from the East African Community (EAC), a regional intergovernmental organization consisting of Burundi, Rwanda, South Sudan, Tanzania, Uganda, and the Democratic Republic of the Congo, can give up refugee status and become citizens of the EAC. Doing so affords EAC refugees the right to live and work in Kenya, provided they have a work permit. Crucially, they do not need a movement permit. This new policy is a positive step forward, though it still has limitations.[10] To obtain recognition of their employment qualification, refugees need to pay for travel costs and provide official documentation, which may prove difficult for economically disadvantaged individuals. The new act also indicates that while refugees can obtain jobs when their qualifications have been recognized, they must still reside in what are referred to as "designated areas," a measure that places limits on their freedom of movement. Furthermore, the labor rights afforded to EAC members do not apply to Somali refugees, who account for almost 60 percent of refugees in Kenya. Despite these very real challenges that must still be addressed, it is important to acknowledge that Kenyan officials have made concerted efforts in recent years to rethink an existing policy that failed to provide refugees with adequate protections for upholding labor rights—rights that Kakuma's musicians and other working professionals have long struggled to achieve.

Notes

1. Article 23 of the UN Universal Declaration of Human Rights states that "everyone, without any discrimination, has the right to equal pay for equal work." Articles 17 and 18 of the 1951 Convention state that refugees should be allowed to engage in wage-earning employment.

2. Smart Djaba revised my initial translation of this song to more accurately reflect the intended meanings and phrasings of his lyrics.

3. Members of Afrostars Entertainment, personal observation, April 2014, Kakuma Refugee Camp, Kenya.

4. Smart Djaba, interview with the author, October 30, 2014, Kakuma Refugee Camp, Kenya.

5. Smart Djaba, interview with the author, October 30, 2014, Kakuma Refugee Camp, Kenya.

6. King Moses, interview with the author, June 2015, Kakuma Refugee Camp, Kenya.

7. E-Squad member, interview with the author, June 2015, Kakuma Refugee Camp, Kenya.

8. Anjellah Owino, "How Political Clashes Separated Me from Half My Family," *The Standard*, October 4, 2019, https://www.standardmedia.co.ke/entertainment/features/2001344331/how-political-clashes-separated-me-from-half-of-my-family.

9. Izza Leghtas and David Kitenge, "What Does Kenya's New Refugee Act Mean for Economic Inclusion?," *Refugees International*, May 4, 2022.

10. Leghtas and Kitenge, "What Does Kenya's New Refugee Act Mean for Economic Inclusion?"

FOR
PROTECTION

4

~~

IMMOBILITY

Culture and Containment

"We don't want to lose our culture," Kuol stated, "because our culture is very important."[1] An avid participant in the Dinka weekly dances, Kuol shared his perspective on why he and his community members gathered each week to dance together in the Kakuma Refugee Camp. We held our conversation among a small crowd of children under the shade of trees growing on the perimeter of the dirt-covered Dinka-Bor (South) dancing field. This field was located near the entry road to the Hong Kong market in Kakuma One. Kuol and Mark, two Dinka-Bor community leaders, graciously invited me to their weekly dance in July 2013 so that I could better understand and share the significance of this social practice as well as the challenges of living in a refugee camp. Over the roaring and sonorous timbre of communal singing, Kuol continued, "Every Sunday we come here and practice our dancing all the time because we need our small children to grow up and to know what the culture of Dinka is. So that is why we come here today to maintain our culture."[2]

I left the Kakuma camp about a month later. However, the Dinka dances made such an impression on me that when I returned fourteen months later, I reconnected with Kuol to continue studying their significance. To my surprise, he informed me that camp officials had halted the dances in June 2014, having attributed the deaths of three young Dinka men to the dances. Supporters of the ban believed the weekly dances caused Dinka men to behave violently and needed to be halted indefinitely. Others believed the dances were unfairly linked to fighting. They felt the ban should be lifted in order to enable participants to practice important aspects of their already marginalized cultural traditions.

Unlike members of social groups in the Kakuma camp that hailed from cities, many Dinka refugees came from rural parts of South Sudan. Individuals from pastoralist areas, in particular, faced the added challenge of establishing senses of belonging in a site where camp policies denied refugees freedom of movement and access to grazing lands and cattle. And yet despite these obstacles, Dinka refugees managed to maintain linkages to their herding traditions through songs and dances. Their social resilience, however, was further tested in 2014 when the camp administration halted their main dancing activity. In this chapter, I examine the social significance of the Dinka weekly dances and the campaign to reinstate them. In doing so, I discuss how Dinka community members sounded out their claims to belonging in a heavily regulated environment.

Restricted mobility is a defining feature of the refugee camp (Verdirame and Harrell-Bond 2005; Schmidt 2003). Tracing financial inflows from international organizations in Geneva, Switzerland to war zones and refugee camps in the Horn of Africa, Jennifer Hyndman argues that borders are more porous to humanitarian aid than to the people for whom this aid is intended (2000, 38–60).[3] This disparity, she suggests, can be attributed to an "institutional culture of containment in camps" (2000, 60). For three decades, refugee policies in Kenya have mandated that most forced migrants reside in camps until they can legally achieve one of three "durable solutions"—repatriation, resettlement, or local integration. These outcomes have proven difficult to achieve, leaving many forced migrants to reside in Kenya's refugee camps for years or even decades. And while forced migrants move in and out of the camps for various reasons, their mobility is highly regulated. Travel passes are elusive. Police checks are frequent, and releases from detention are expensive. For individuals eligible for resettlement, the process is extremely cumbersome and only a viable option for a small percentage of refugees. Scholars critical of the restriction of refugees' freedom of movement have discussed how the encampment model violates basic civil liberties; reduces economic opportunities; increases vulnerability to attack from warring enemies; and enables abuse from so-called security personnel (see Brankamp 2019; Verdirame and Harrell-Bond 2005; Crisp 2000). These findings offer important counternarratives to the dominant idea of the refugee camp as a site of protection by exposing how limits on mobility violate the rights of refugees and hinder their well-being.

Building on these analyses, I discuss the experiences of Dinka weekly dance participants within the context of institutional constraints on the mobility of refugees. While music and dance are often associated with circulation and movement, it is important to recognize their relation to immobility (Steingo 2015). In the Kakuma camp, the Dinka dances became enmeshed within an urbanized environment of regulated immobility consisting of social segregation, nightly curfews, and official restrictions on social gatherings. How did restricting the mobility of refugees affect Dinka pastoralist livelihoods? What role did the mobile aspects of Dinka dancing play in negotiating and contesting regulated immobility? How were the Dinka dances entangled with a wider politics of immobility? The stories and perspectives of social actors involved in the spreading and halting of the Dinka weekly dances elucidates the resiliency of pastoralist communities while denaturalizing the linkages between expressive culture and the refugee regime's culture of containment.

From Cattle Camp to Refugee Camp

In many ways, the pastoralist is the antirefugee. Herders require movement and access to natural resources. Their mobility is essential for locating grazing fields, adjusting to weather patterns, and navigating difficult terrains. People in "closed" refugee camps, on the other hand, are compelled to maintain more sedentary lifestyles because of state mandates and centralized aid programs. These contradictory modes of living indicate that cattle herders do not belong in refugee camps. And yet tens of thousands of Kakuma's camp inhabitants hailed from herding communities.

Over the last several decades, politics and war in Sudan and South Sudan have forced millions of cattle herders away from their lands. Between 1983 and 2005, cattle herders fled their homes and fields as a consequence of the Second Sudanese Civil War. The Comprehensive Peace Agreement in 2005 and South Sudan's independence in 2011 failed to create stability in the ensuing years. By 2013, a struggle for political control between President Salva Kiir's administration and ousted Vice President Riek Machar catalyzed what has become known as the South Sudanese Civil War. According to a 2015 report published by the Food and Agriculture Organization of the United Nations (FAO), conflict zones exacerbated the propensity for cattle raiding as pastoralists fled their homesteads for already occupied areas (FAO 2015). Decades of ongoing conflict and instability compelled pastoralists in South Sudan to exchange the cattle camp for the internally displaced persons (IDP) camp and the refugee camp.

In Kenya's Kakuma Refugee Camp, people of Dinka descent made up a major social group with a strong attachment to pastoralist lifeways. Cattle, in particular, have historically played a central role in Dinka social life (see Cormack

2014; Impey 2013a and 2013b; Deng 2010; Deng 1973 and 1976; Lienhardt 1961; Evans-Pritchard 1934). "Their [cattle's] significance," notes security and development studies scholar Luka Biong Deng, "goes beyond their economic value, as they are used to maintain social relations, religious values, and political institutions" (2010, 237). Anthropologist Godfrey Lienhardt, for instance, observes in his ethnographic study on Dinka religion in Bahr el Ghazal how the transfer of cattle through dedication and sacrifice regulated relationships between humans and the divine (1961, 24). Noted Dinka scholar and son of a Dinka chief Francis Mading Deng emphasizes the depth of this strong identification with cattle when he states, "the profundity with which the Dinka identify with cattle in general and oxen in particular and the degree to which they find pride and dignity in such identification cannot be overemphasized" (Deng 1976, 2).

Silencing Nomadic Life

Over time, the more I learned about the role of cattle in Dinka social life, the more I heard the silence of nomadic life in the Kakuma camp. The common practice of young men proudly singing to their "personality oxen" while leading herds to pasture was nonexistent (Deng 1976, 2). The voices of historically influential Dinka religious leaders known as "masters of the fishing spear" became largely muted (Lienhardt 1961, 105, 137). Ritualistic practices ranging from front-teeth extraction and circumcision to scarification were greatly diminished. What happened? Why were the social practices of such a large group in the Kakuma camp so marginalized? What roles have the refugee camp and wider political systems played in delegitimizing nomadic lifeways in East Africa?

During my conversation with Kuol and Mark in July 2013 at the Dinka-Bor dancing field, we discussed some of the challenges that came with reestablishing pastoralist ways of life.

"In Kakuma, can you have cows—can you have cattle?" I asked.
"No, we don't have cows here," replied Kuol, "because this place is not for the cow. [This] place is very dry, and we left the cow there in South Sudan—and we are refugees here."
"What about the host community?" I responded.
"Yeah, actually, that is the right question you have asked," replied Mark.
"When people came in 1992, some guys, they tried to buy goat, sheep, and also some cow. But I heard that there was a time, the host . . . people, ehhh . . . the host community, they came. They took the cattle,

so it discouraged the others from having cattle here . . . So that is why, you see, these refugees, they are just living without goat or without cow. Because they know the moment they will have cows, I mean goats or cattle here, they will have problems with the host community."[4]

Kuol and Mark's explanations highlight two main reasons why refugees in Kakuma did not own cattle: poor environmental conditions and conflict disputes. Indeed, the often drought-stricken semiarid desert was not an ideal place for locating grazing fields and watering holes. Nevertheless, some herders in Turkana County still brought their animals to pasture. In an area with limited resources, conflicts arose early in Kakuma's history when refugees attempted to reestablish pastoralist practices. Stopping this conflict was a main justification for the camp administration's decision to ban all refugees from owning and herding cattle.

Like most cases involving prohibitions, however, there is more to this story than the practicality of preventing conflict. Bans are political. They do not merely mitigate divisive behavior—they can also reproduce systems of social control. In the case of the Kakuma camp, prohibiting pastoralist livelihoods had the effect of normalizing refugee containment. The ban on cattle herding reinforced divisions between refugees and Kenyan citizens. Social conflict between people categorized as "Kenyan-Turkana" and "refugee" provided support for the idea that Kenyans were the rightful owners of land and cattle in the region and in Kenya as a whole.[5] This idea, in turn, reaffirmed the state's mandate of limiting refugee mobility to the camp area. Furthermore, the situation created by forbidding pastoralist livelihoods made humanitarian encampment seem not only practical but also just. Similar to cattle herding, firewood collection stoked conflict between refugees and local residents. Camp administrators responded to the situation by restricting all refugees from collecting firewood. The UNHCR then contracted the German agency GTZ to provide refugees with aid in the form of solar-powered cooking stoves and bundles of firewood. These projects operated through an affective politics of fear and care. Consider how the UNHCR understood the role and potential of the solar cooker program in an article entitled "Solar Cooker Offers Ray of Hope for Refugee Environment."[6] The article reads as follows: "The agency hopes that the stove project can lessen the impact of refugee influxes on the environment, and protect women who risk assault when they forage for firewood." This statement frames the potential impact of the solar cooker through connotative powers of care and common sense. For proponents of this technology of aid, the solar cooker provides care for at-risk women, care for the natural world, and care for local Kenyans. At the same time, this view perceives mobile forms of rurality as a threat and danger to both environmental sustainability and social stability.

Such perspectives provided legitimacy to both the UNHCR's aid programs and the Kenyan state's containment policy, simultaneously marginalizing pastoralist ways of living. The following conversation I had with an aid worker in the LWF compound provides a typical account of how the value of cattle herding often fell on deaf ears among agency staff. "It's so frustrating," the aid worker said with an exasperated tone.

"I'm sorry—what happened?" I replied.

"Well, we need to get this project done, but our workers just aren't very skilled," she explained. "So there is this new guy we hired from the camp—I mean, he can't even type. He's from a rural area in South Sudan, and he just doesn't have a lot of education."[7] This account typifies the disqualifying remarks I heard aid workers routinely make about refugees and Kenyans who hailed from rural areas. Such narratives are problematic because they falsely conflate education with urbanized skills while ignoring the high level of intellect required to raise cattle, especially within difficult environmental conditions. These narratives are part of a wider hegemonic system that privileges and depends on urban over rural life skills. The UNHCR/NGOs required the refugee incentive workers they hired in the Kakuma camp to run schools, hospitals and clinics, and water and sanitation systems, just to name a few. In this sense, the wide-scale proliferation of pastoralism would have posed an existential threat to operating the encampment system.

To more fully comprehend the delegitimization of pastoralism in this region, it is crucial to recognize that this phenomenon is not a recent development but rather one that is closely linked to the violence of British colonialism (see McCabe 2011, 50–52). The British occupation and plundering of present-day Turkana County began in 1888. The British colonial administration of Uganda and the Ethiopian Empire under King Menelik fought against each other for colonial domination over the Turkana pastoralists. While the Ethiopians traded with the pastoralists and supplied them with rifles to fight the British and competing pastoralist tribes, the British engaged in brutal forms of punishment that included massive confiscations of livestock and the killing of individuals who resisted. The great Turkana war leader Ebei responded by amassing large armies to fight against the British and other pastoral tribes. Fearing for the safety and stability of white settlers' ranches and farms, the British responded by forming a military force called the Labur Patrol. This armed group eventually broke the military strength of the Turkana, causing thousands of people to die of starvation and disease and hundreds of thousands of cattle to be lost.

In 1924, Ebei was killed in an attack by the Dassanetch of southern Ethiopia. His death marked the end of large-scale raiding and further enabled the British colonizers to consolidate power in the region. The British reintroduced a civil administration in 1926 and a taxation system in 1928. Never fully able to pacify and incorporate Turkana peoples into their colonial system, the British labeled the Turkana region a "closed district." By the 1960s, one mission and two primary schools had been built in this area. In 1963, the British colonial administration ended with the start of Kenyan independence.

Since then, the Kenyan government has incorporated pastoralists living in this region into the state system, with the UHNCR refugee camp operating as one of its main tools for achieving this goal. A strong selling point for deploying the UNHCR camp was that it could be used to so call develop and modernize Kenya's hinterlands by attracting and compelling Kenya's pastoralists to take up urban and agricultural livelihoods. This shift has occurred at such a significant rate that Jansen has referred to individuals involved in this process as "drop-out pastoralists" (2018, 132). In a similar vein, a widely circulated narrative among refugees and aid workers was that many South Sudanese refugees hailing from rural areas migrated to the Kakuma camp not only to escape conflict but also to obtain education, find urban jobs, and help build the newly formed nation of South Sudan on their return. Moreover, dominant ideas in the camp linked education and employment, beyond economic pursuits, to wider notions of modernity. According to Katarzyna Grabska's (2014, 66) study of Nuer repatriation to southern Sudan, new ideas and identities of modernity were constituted in the Kakuma camp at three levels: (1) camp management structures, (2) global communication, technology, and resettlement, and (3) gender and age. Grabska found that the young Nuer refugees she met were often influenced by these levels and used English terms such as "modern" and "civilized" to distinguish their identities and behaviors from those of their peers still living in rural Nuerland areas of South Sudan (2014, 67). The subject-making effects of the Kakuma camp thus had a tremendous impact on transforming and delegitimizing pastoralist subjectivities.

From poor environmental conditions and conflict to prohibitive bans and humanitarian interventions to British colonialism and current state-making agendas, many factors support Mark's statement that the Kakuma camp "is not for the cow." Indeed, it was not only Dinkas who faced this issue but rather all refugees hailing from pastoralist areas. Almost everyone I met from Dinka, Nuer, Nubian, and Shilluk communities—social groups with long histories of nomadic traditions—told me that pastoralism was either not viable or not desirable within the refugee camp. And yet the more I opened my ears to the

Kakuma camp's soundscape, the more it became clear that in the absence of cattle, elements of nomadic life persisted.

The Portability of Cattle Culture

In contrast to ownership of cattle herds, the capacity to store and recall songs and dances from corporeal and mental archives makes them difficult to dispossess. As embodied forms of expression, songs and dances can be transported, accessed, recalled, and performed even in the most isolating conditions. In the Dinka compound where I stayed from April to August 2015, young and middle-aged men sang out loud or under their breath, pondering their next moves while playing cards, checkers, and dominoes under the cool shade of the few trees that grew in the dirt-covered courtyards. Women sang to themselves as they mixed batches of batter for *kisra*, a crepe-like dish common in South Sudan. Ox songs emanated from mobile phones laid next to young men resting in their houses during the day's hottest hours. Many Dinkas listened to and shared recordings of cattle songs and Dinka dances through cassettes, CDs, MP3s, and videos. Cattle songs filled the air during communal events ranging from marriage ceremonies and Dinka weekly dances to UNHCR-organized performances and patriotic South Sudanese celebrations. While herding was nonexistent among Dinka refugees in Kakuma, a culture tied to cattle was still very much present.

Cattle have historically played a prominent role in Dinka song traditions (Impey 2013a and 2013b; Deng 1973, 80). According to Francis Mading Deng (1973, 80), main Dinka song themes include cattle disputes, suffering from herding, reflecting on cattle, admiring cattle, and having family pride in cattle wealth. Angela Impey's (2013b, 66) study of the testimonial qualities of Dinka songs notes how some of the core thematic conventions of Dinka songs are connected with cattle. The use of ox names, for example, functions to name particular clan members, leaders, and places, reaffirming senses of belonging to specific clans and cultural identities (2013b, 66). Additionally, tensions between the individual and collective are often expressed in songs through references to cattle and nature.

As it turns out, cultural expressions have served as important resources for forced migrants facing the material loss of cattle. Lowell Brower, for example, discusses how Congolese Kinyarwanda-speaking residents in the UNHCR-administered Mukarwego Refugee Camp in Rwanda maintained a strong "herder identity" despite living in a "cow-less camp" (2020, 291–294). Even without cattle, they composed poems and told folktales about cows, engaged in debates about cows, and recited their former cows' names. Singing and discussing these songs was part of a wider capacity to draw on artistic practices and performances to endure the ill effects of violence and exile (2020, 283). Similarly, Angela Impey writes about the ways members of the Dinka diaspora in the United Kingdom have responded to dislocation from consecutive civil wars by accessing personal songs as "audio-letters" via cassettes (2013a, 198). These recordings have played an important role in fostering real and imagined interactions between clan members and their homelands, blending cultural forms and technologies with new geographic areas and issues of concern. Impey notes that "the global connectivity between Dinka clan members is not only supported by the exchanging of audio-letters as information, but that the corporeality of songs and their sensuous invocations of time and place draws listeners into tangible, iterative associations with clan, home space, and cultural identities" (2013a, 206).

The portability of cattle culture has thus enabled migrants who no longer have physical access to cattle camps to maintain meaningful attachments to their pastoralist lifeways and to each other. One of the more impactful ways in which many Dinkas living in the Kakuma camp forged social and spatial belonging in the face of dislocation and dispossession was through gathering at their dancing fields.

Dinka Weekly Dances

On a Sunday evening in July 2013, Kuol invited me to Block Eight. I came to witness how members from the Dinka-Bor (South) community prepared for their weekly dances. We sat in a modest mud-brick house under a roof fashioned out of discarded food ration tins. Kuol explained to me that Dinkas all across the Kakuma camp were preparing for the evening's dance in their respective neighborhoods. For the occasion, he and his friends, relatives, and neighbors donned outfits and accoutrements imbued with pastoralist aesthetics. They wore synthetic wraps with leopard print designs in place of real animal hides. They spread maize-meal flour and wood ash over their bodies and faces instead of dung ash. They carried bare wooden staffs (sing. *lëc*, pronounced "lech"; pl. *läc*) taken from the branches of local trees. Long, thin *läc* were commonly used by herders to direct cattle movements across pastures, while the shorter, thicker *läc* were used to pound stakes into the ground for the purpose of tethering cattle. The refashioning of local materials into outfits and instruments demonstrates how former pastoralists creatively reconstituted their cultural knowledge using local means.

Around 6:00 p.m., Kuol and members from his community left Block Eight on foot, side by side, moving their legs and arms in rhythm as they made their way to the Dinka-Bor (South) dancing field near the Hong Kong market. Lined up shoulder to shoulder, the members of each group sang songs about their clans and cattle in a call-and-response form as they moved through neighborhoods and turned onto the main dirt road. They engaged in a communal practice, similar to jogging, when arriving or leaving important social events. Joseph, a Dinka youth leader for the LWF, believed that the ways Dinkas bobbed their heads and shoulders up and down while moving in collective formation mimicked the mannerisms of cattle herds. In this fashion, Kuol and his friends processed across the sanitation field, turned onto the main road, and jogged past IRC's main hospital. Their feet and voices announced the presence of Dinka people in the camp as they carved out sound paths linking public and private places. When they passed the Zone 3A Dinka Episcopal church just before reaching the Hong Kong market, they turned right down a dirt path and entered the dancing field. Atop this small field—nestled between the often dried-out banks of the Tarach River, a Dinka Episcopal church, and a host of overhanging trees—pastoralist social life manifested in collective singing and dancing.

Small groups of Dinka men in their teens, twenties, and thirties warmed up for the evening's event. At the center of the dancing field, two drummers organized the event's flow by continuously beating out interlocking rhythms using wooden sticks against a double-headed drum (bul) fashioned out of wood and cowskin hides. The person in charge of the drum, whom my interlocutors referred to as the "controller-of-the-drum," had transported this instrument to the Kakuma camp from a rural area in the southern region of Jonglei State in South Sudan. A few participants played makeshift wind instruments called tung, which when blown, produce a bellowing sound. These instruments are traditionally constructed from the horns of bulls, though in the Kakuma camp, musicians made them with water bottles and plastic tubing. Small male groups surrounded the drummers and sang songs about cattle camps, bulls, and wrestling. While they sang, they raised their arms above their heads. These were not random hand motions. Rather, their hands mimicked specific horn shapes of bulls, displaying the dancers' relationships to specific prized animals that belonged to them or their clans in South Sudan. Each of the small male groups engaged in deregel, a dance style widely popular among Dinka-Bor communities that involves jumping up and down in unison while raising the arms to the side or above the head.[8] In a separate performative move, a few young men showed off their physicality by jumping into the air with their feet tucked to their bottoms and their arms prostrated outward as they glided to the ground. As more groups of young men and women arrived, spectators took places along the field's edges while others continued dancing around the drummers.

In the face of dispossession, the weekly dances provided Dinkas with a way to lay claim to cattle through symbolic means. Dancers, singers, and musicians enacted and displayed a symbolic constellation of Dinka pastoralist expressions through song lyrics, syncopated beats, horn playing, and hand gestures. The materiality of cattle herding appeared in the form of cowskin-covered drumheads, performative displays of wooden staffs, and bullhorn instruments refashioned with plastic bottles and tubes. Communal participation in *deregel* dancing and the repetitive beats of the *bul*, the double-headed drum, created cohesion. The weekly dance practices helped Dinkas without access to cattle and traditional grazing areas in South Sudan maintain possession of a deeply important connection to their revered bulls and oxen.

By the time I left Kakuma in August 2015, six main Dinka dancing fields were in operation. All except one were in Kakuma One, with four out of five located in close proximity to the Hong Kong market. These dancing fields were largely separated by regional affiliations in South Sudan, with each of these regions producing culturally distinct dance forms. Dinkas from the Padang region in South Sudan held their dances in Kakuma Three and on a field behind Dinka housing compounds on the eastern side of the Hong Kong market in Kakuma One. Dinkas from Bahr el Ghazal held their dances atop a dried-out riverbed near former Group Forty-Seven. This area was located on the western side of the same market. Dinka-Bor (South) conducted their dances near the Dinka housing compounds located at the entrance to the Hong Kong market, while Dinka-Bor (Twic) held their dances in two locations—the field next to the Luol Deng basketball court near the turnoff to the Don Bosco compound and the courtyard of the Torit primary school.

Dancers and spectators met once a week during the school term, strictly on weekends to accommodate the schedules of school-going youths. During breaks in the semester, many Dinkas studying in other parts of Kenya would return to the Kakuma camp to visit family and friends. The dancing fields would swell during this period as many sought to reconnect with their Dinka cultural traditions through engagement in the weekly dance practices. For this reason, members from the Dinka-Bor (South) and Dinka-Bor (Twic) regions held dancing practices every Thursday and once either on Saturday or Sunday between the hours of 5:30 p.m. and 7:30 p.m. Why did members of the various Dinka communities make their way to the dancing fields week in and week out? What made these dances so popular?

Courting without Cattle

Part of understanding why the Dinka weekly dances were so well attended requires a better understanding of their unique social functions. Without access to cattle and with limited employment opportunities, many young Dinka men, especially those raised in the Kakuma camp, lacked the socioeconomic capacity to attract marriage partners through the accrual of wealth. My interlocutors told me that this outcome had led to a reduction in formal marriage ceremonies, arguably one of the most important rites of passage for many Dinka individuals and families in East Africa and other areas of the globe. Undeterred by this predicament, many Dinkas relied on other means for supporting the continuity of marriage, one of the most salient of which was the weekly dances.

The dance format enabled young, unmarried Dinka men to court potential partners even if they did not personally own any cattle. In the words of one young Dinka-Bor dancing participant, "OK, I am saying the main purpose of the dance, or the main item of which we consider as the Dinka community. We have to consider that what we have to [do] is to maybe to find girls. That is the main one. We have to look for girls here. Because it is very hard to get a girl at the place that she comes. You might not know. But after coming here, and you accompany her, you are going to know her."[9]

The Dinka-Bor dance practices were similar to practices in nightclubs in Nairobi but with their own Dinka appeal. Some young men suited up in trousers, fitted dress shirts, and closed-toe shoes; others wore knee-length tunics or went shirtless, their bodies covered in ash and an ostrich feather fixed atop their heads. Still others wore the football jerseys of their favorite international club team or the local team on which they played. Men often carried symbols of strength and bravery in the form of a *lëc*, or less commonly, a wooden model of an AK-47 encased in thin black rubber strips. Women typically wore long, formfitting dresses woven out of multicolored fabrics, outfits they often wore to church services and formal wedding ceremonies. The care with which dancing participants selected their outfits demonstrates how the dances were places to see and be seen among young Dinkas looking to identify suitable partners.

After several weeks of observing the weekly dances, my Dinka teacher Alier suggested that I actually participate in the dances with him and my friend Manyang in order to better understand how the courtship process worked. Manyang was in his early twenties and had attended school in Kenya's urban areas—Nairobi and Nakuru. When I met him, he had recently relocated to the Kakuma camp to complete his studies. We spent many evenings and nights in Block Eight conversing about a range of topics from music and education to dating and marriage. Our friendship made him an ideal dancing mate. We positioned ourselves next to other small groups that surrounded the drummers in the center of the dancing field. We then collectively sang cattle songs that Alier had learned in Jonglei State and taught me. When the drummers stopped playing, all of the male dancers ceased singing and began fanning out across the field in search of female dancing partners. According to Dinka tradition, women served as the primary judges of the beauty and skillful articulation of male singers (Deng 1973, 98). We approached several young ladies from the crowd of women, children, and men standing along the field's perimeter. Alier stood between Manyang and me, facing the woman of his choice. With each of our *läc* in hand, we sang an ox song that was typical of the kinds of songs Dinka men used to attract potential dancing partners. Through this song, we sang praises and admiration for the Malou cattle camp located in Baidit, a small town in Jonglei State, South Sudan where Manyang and Alier's family and relatives resided. Thus, while Alier's access to cattle was nonexistent in Kakuma, he was still able to draw on the symbolic power of ox songs to evoke a sense of cattle wealth to court a potential dancing partner. It is important to note that although Alier was the focus of attention, Manyang and I sang in unison with him. This common practice reinforced the idea that courtship and marriage were not merely between a single man and a single woman but also between their respective clans, families, and relatives (see Deng 1973, 18). As for the outcome of our attempts at communal courtship, we were unsuccessful in convincing the first young woman to dance with us. The next person we approached, however, happily agreed.

We moved into formation around the drummers with the other male groups and their dancing partners. Once we were all in place, each woman took a position in front of her chosen male group with her back turned to them and her front facing the moving circle. All at once, the entire dancing circle, numbering well over one hundred people, broke into collective singing in unison and call-and-response form while dancing *deregel*. The dancers moved incrementally in a counterclockwise direction as they jumped up and down to the repetitive rhythmic beats of the drum. I was often told that good dancing required moving in sync with the entire group. Clinking sounds reverberated from dancers who had wrapped "jingles" made from soda bottle caps to their ankles.[10] Each time their legs hit the ground, the clang of metal created a "dense texture," a sonic aesthetic conducive for participatory music and dance (Turino 2008, 45). Communal singing and the consonant thumping of hundreds of feet jumping up and down together created social cohesion.

Over the course of an hour or so, the process of locating a dance partner and joining in the large dancing circle was repeated several times, providing participants with multiple opportunities to match with different individuals. The weekly dances always ended by 7:00 p.m. due to evening curfew restrictions. While dancing stopped, however, the courtship process continued. On the walk back home, men and women met on the roads. Some had danced together in the dancing circle. Others had noticed each other in the crowd or in other areas of the camp. If things went well, a couple might schedule a date for the man to make a formal visit to the woman's compound, continuing the courtship process. The weekly dances thus served as a potent means for many Dinkas to negotiate the camp-wide ban on cattle herding and the subsequent rupture to their traditional marriage practices. Their resiliency, however, was further put to the test after the camp administration halted the dances, citing reasons of insecurity.

The Halt on Dinka Dancing

In June 2014, members of the Dinka-Bor (Twic) community gathered at their dancing field to practice for their upcoming performance at the annual World Refugee Day event. Per the usual routine, a young man tried to persuade a young woman from another subclan to dance. She refused his advances, but rather than accept her decision, he became resentful. After the dancing practice ended, a fight broke out along the road, leaving the young woman badly injured. Several Dinka elders ordered the aggrieved parties to meet with them the following day. Instead, members from both sides fought again in the dried-out riverbank, and three young men tragically lost their lives. Officials from the LWF's Peace Building Unit coordinated two meetings with the police and representatives from the two Dinka subclans involved in the fights. After hearing what happened, the officials decided to suspend all Dinka weekly dances for an indefinite period of time.

"Dancing is the main source of the problem," explained a security officer with almost two decades of work experience in the Kakuma camp.[11] We sat in his office in one of the gated administrative compounds, joined by his colleague, a high-ranking security official who began working in the camp in 2013. I asked the veteran official to describe his understanding of Dinka dancing dating back to the 1990s. Cultural dances were most common at wedding ceremonies, he explained. Sometimes, small conflicts would occur; other times, big fights would break out.

"If I want a lady, I want a lady by force," he continued, explaining how
   Dinka gendered relations operated at the dances. "Since this man is
   taking the lady, I will again take the lady by force."
"I have talked to them [South Sudanese people]," remarked his colleague.
   "Their country is lawless. Killing is not a big deal to them." He went
   on to contrast the South Sudanese to his own ethnic group, which he
   claimed would expel a community member responsible for killing
   someone rather than condone violence.
Later in our conversation, I suggested a possible policy for allowing the
   dances. "What if you asked them to dance between these times [5:00
   p.m. and 7:00 p.m.] with no alcohol, no weapons, and no fighting?"
"Sudanese will never understand," the veteran official responded. "If you
   compare them to the Ethiopians, the Somalis, the Ugandans, Rwan-
   dese, Burundian, they will take the advice. With the Sudanese it is not
   easy."[12]

Camp security officials were not the only individuals in support of halting
the Dinka dances. "Even me myself, I am supporting what the police say,"
stated Bol, a Dinka elder and community leader with whom I met in a café in
the Ethiopian market to discuss this issue.[13] He arrived to the Kakuma camp
as a young Dinka man from a cattle camp in Sudan in the mid-1990s. Though
he was an active dancing participant in his youth, he stopped dancing at the
practices in his older age. He explained that people seeking revenge could use
the dances to target another person. Referring back to the incident in June
2014, he remarked that "if the dancing are not brought out . . . no three people
can be killed."[14] He explained that in 2012, when the UNHCR had switched
to a political system based on electing refugee representatives from zones and
blocks rather than based on ethnic affiliation, Dinka elders had lost control over
their youths' deviant behaviors.
   The above perspectives suggest that the Dinka dances incited violence, but
for different reasons. Bol believed the camp's reorganization into a zonal/block
system in 2012 had reduced the ability of Dinka leaders to control their youths.
The security officials, on the other hand, argued that Dinka men as a whole
were inherently prone to violence and to treating Dinka women as objects
to be fought over. Whereas the former view found fault in the UNHCR's dis-
empowering governing structure and the deviance of young Dinka men, the
latter invoked xenophobic attitudes toward Dinka men and paternalistic views
of Dinka women. Overall, both groups focused on protecting human life by

positioning young Dinka males as perpetrators of violence and infantile beings unable to protect themselves from themselves.

Other individuals with knowledge of the situation held opposing views. My Dinka teacher Alier believed that the ban's supporters were taking a "shallow" view of the incident.[15] Instead of blaming the dances, he thought a deeper examination of historical grievances between the conflicting parties was necessary. Nyibol and Abuk, two young Dinka women I met in Block Eight after finishing my Dinka language lessons, were also opposed to the police's ban. They were attending high school in Nakuru and had recently returned to the Kakuma camp to celebrate Christmas and New Year's with their families and friends. As a student in Nakuru, Nyibol explained that "we do not have many opportunities to connect with our Dinka culture through dancing."[16] For Nyibol and Abuk, the weekly dances served as an important social space to reconnect with Dinka-Bor communities and traditions. Motivated by similar perspectives, other Dinka community members favored reinstating the dances. Several months after the initial ban, select Dinka elders and youths from the Bahr el Ghazal region of South Sudan delivered formal statements to the Department of Refugee Affairs (DRA) requesting that the administration review its decision. Their weekly dances, they explained, were different from the Dinka-Bor (Twic) and should not be stopped. After waiting for a response that never came, they sent another statement with the same request, to no avail.

Campaigning for "Cultural Freedom"

Between February and April 2015, I met with representative leaders from the Dinka-Bor (South), Dinka-Bor (Twic and Dukeen), Dinka-Bahr el Ghazal, and Dinka-Padang in the tree-shaded courtyard area of Youth Center One to discuss the halting of the weekly dances. During our conversations, the youth leaders decided the most potent strategy for reinstating the dances would be to engage in a collaborative campaign. Working together, they crafted and submitted formal statements to the camp administration outlining reasons why their dances should be reinstated. Below are excerpts of some of the main arguments from their letters.

***

The Dinka Twic and Dukeen representatives highlighted how the incident in June 2014 should have been attributed not to the dances but to external political tensions in South Sudan.

We are saying in the voice of all Twic and Dukeen youth in Kakuma that
our cultural dance was closed down last year because of fighting between
two subclans of Twic, and it was a conflict that started in South Sudan over
a disputed land in a town shared by these two subclans. The Kenyan police
and the LWF security have said that the cultural dance is the source of creating conflict in the camp. It is not. The source of the conflict in the camp was
caused by external conflict. (Dinka Twic and Dukeen youth representatives,
Statement to Camp Manager, March 16, 2015, Kakuma Refugee Camp)

The Dinka Tonj representatives drew on the language of rights and the law to
make their case.

We, the Tonj community members, would like to bring to your attention
the restriction of our cultural dance. Since June 2014, we have been robbed
the right to practice our cultural dance which we think is illegal under the
Kenyan constitution and the international law. (Dinka Tonj youth representatives, Statement to Camp Manager, March 16, 2015, Kakuma Refugee
Camp)

The Bor representatives highlighted the cultural importance of the dances and
the exploitative treatment of the police.

These dances are part of our lives, and we cannot afford to be separated
from them. Every young person would want to identify himself or herself
with their cultural practices when going beyond refugees [*sic*]. (Dinka-Bor
youth representatives, Statement to Camp Manager, March 16, 2015, Kakuma
Refugee Camp)

At times, arrests are made by the police, and only after money is paid will
those arrested be released. For example, in August 2014, we paid sixteen
thousand shillings when the person who controls the drum, two other
leaders, and our drum were put in a "lodge," a phrase used by the police to
refer to a "cell." The drums are like the engines of the dance. Without drums,
the dances cannot start. Without drums, the dances stop . . . The essence
for payment is what we fail to comprehend. We only see exploitation at the
expense of our cultural freedom. Something is really amiss! (Dinka-Bor youth
representatives, Statement to Camp Manager, March 16, 2015, Kakuma
Refugee Camp)

***

The Dinka youth leaders' collective action eventually shifted the camp administration's position on the dances. Their letters prompted the manager of

the LWF's cultural programming arm to craft his own statement of support for the Dinka youths. He also officially registered each of the cultural dance groups with the LWF. In turn, the Dinka youth leaders agreed that if fighting were to occur at future dances, the parties involved would be held accountable and the dances of the specific cultural group could be subject to suspension. In April 2015, ten months after the ban, the police reversed their decision and allowed all Dinka communities to resume their weekly dance practices. The Dinka youth leaders no longer had to pay bribes, and guidelines were put in place to prevent future bans on all Dinka dances. In August 2015, another fight broke out at a Dinka-Bor Twic dance. Several influential Dinka elders suspended dancing for this group. However, the other Dinka cultural groups were able to continue dancing without interference from the police or the administration.

The ten-month suspension of the Dinka weekly dances provides a salient example of the culture of containment in the Kakuma camp. The police and LWF security program responded to a conflict by restricting all Dinka communities from attending their respective weekly dance practices. The police also detained any organizers caught violating the ban and even confiscated one group's engine of the dance—the drum. Some members of the police then used the detention of dance organizers to extract fees for personal financial gain. Through their campaign, the Dinka youth leaders eventually managed to overturn the ban. In doing so, they demonstrated a keen capacity to maneuver around the restrictions imposed by humanitarian government. And yet a deeper understanding of how the Dinka dances operated within the wider encampment system reveals how they were still enmeshed with forces of immobility.

Dance, Subject-Making, and Immobility

Up to this point, I have largely discussed the resiliency of Dinka communities in negotiating the effects of containment on nomadic livelihoods by drawing on music and dance. It is crucial, however, to understand how the Dinka weekly dances were interwoven with the subject-making effects of refugee containment. Regulating human movement in northwestern Kenya required more than just prohibitive measures. As Michel Foucault (1976) argues, power is not only a repressive force but also a productive force that operates through normative practices and dominant discourses. Social activities were perhaps more effective than prohibitions when it came to administering the encampment project because refugees often willfully engaged in them.

For many Dinkas, the weekly dances functioned as "place-making activities" that established meaningful senses of belonging to specific areas of Kakuma (see Kaiser 2008, 379; also see Novak 2007; Turton 2005). The dances' potency lay in the idea that places are not only physically formed but also sensorially constituted through movement. As Steven Feld argues, "because motion can draw upon the kinesthetic interplay of tactile, sonic, and visual senses, emplacement always implicates the intertwined nature of sensual bodily presence and perceptual engagement" (1996, 94). Participants in the weekly dances jogged across the Kakuma camp's dirt roads in rhythm with each other and onto specified dancing areas where they subsequently moved their bodies in communal formations. The thumping of hundreds of feet hitting the ground at the same time, the unison singing of ox songs and wrestling songs, and the collective display of shared visual signs—from herding sticks to smeared ash—had the effect of emplacing Dinka-Bor in both their dancing field and the wider Dinka spaces in the camp area. And yet as beneficial as the dances were for reconstituting culturally specific forms of social and spatial belonging within an unfamiliar bureaucratic environment of zones and blocks, the dances were still inseparable from the politics of immobility. Singing and dancing in the same fields each week emplaced Dinka refugees within the officially designated spaces of the UNHCR-administered camp. In this sense, the weekly dances operated as a disciplinary force that reproduced the boundaries of encampment.

Additionally, the weekly dances' place-making and subject-making effects extended to the wider ethno-national political system within which the refugee camp materialized. As signifiers of Dinkaness, the weekly dances reproduced ethnic subjectivities. Specifically, they shaped essentialized ideas of Dinka-Bor, Dinka-Bahr el Ghazal, and Dinka-Padang. The campaign to reinstate the regionally specific dances also resulted in the formation of a wider Pan-Dinka alliance. Moreover, organizing the dances mimicked and reaffirmed governmental structures and subjectivities. Each of the main Dinka social groups in the Kakuma camp selected a head of sport and culture. This person was in charge of scheduling the dances and conferring with camp officials and, in particular, the LWF's office of cultural programming. The head of sport and culture was akin to South Sudan's minister of culture, youth, and sports, and Kenya's minister of sports, culture, and heritage. The dances' capacity to constitute ethno-national subjectivities thus had the effect of normalizing the kinds of socio-spatial politics that justified using the refugee camp.

Another striking feature of the weekly dances was how they aligned with the humanitarianized dimensions of encampment. Participants often told me that dancing helped ameliorate the stresses of everyday life in a refugee camp. NGO managers held this same idea. In fact, the LWF cited this aspect of cultural dancing as a main reason for opposing the police's ban on the Dinka weekly dances. As substitutions for pastoralist livelihoods, ox songs allowed Dinka men to court potential marriage partners despite not having access to land or cattle in Kakuma. The weekly dances thus functioned similarly to the solar cooker and firewood programs, each of which enabled refugees to maintain linkages to rural livelihoods without violating official restrictions on consuming local resources outside the camp area. Consider also how the temporality of the dances aligned with the camp's urbanized operations. Organizers scheduled the dances toward the end of the week during evening hours, and they increased the number of dances during school break periods. These scheduling formats accommodated the demands of both school-going individuals and refugee incentive workers, the kinds of economic subjectivities required to run the camp system.

Furthermore, the process of organizing the dances enculturated refugees into the bureaucratic norms, lexicons, and values of a UN-run refugee camp. The Dinka leaders who campaigned to reinstate the weekly dances, for example, communicated in a manner that appealed to the sensibilities of the Kenyan police administration, DRA, LWF, and UNHCR. Through their statements, they made legible counterpoints through appeals for UN forms of human rights. Their statements aligned with the primary mode of communication recognized by humanitarian bureaucracy—the written word. For their campaign, the Dinka youth leaders drew on affective forces of fear and care, two kinds of emotions that played a large role in governing the refugee camp. They highlighted their fear of the police and the responsibility of LWF's Youth Protection Office to care for their cultural, physical, and financial well-being. The way they conveyed their social groups as organized and aligned units with existing leadership structures appealed to camp officials' hierarchical dispositions. Thus, the continuity of the dances depended, in large part, on the youth leaders' skills in reproducing fundamental principles and practices of a humanitarian government tasked with containing forced migrants.

Finally, the subject-making effects of the Dinka weekly dances extended into the realm of UNHCR-sponsored staged performances. The UNHCR/ NGOs typically incorporated ethno-national dances during annual events such as World Refugee Day. As one of the earliest and largest groups in the Kakuma camp, Dinka performances became mainstreamed into these cultural programming initiatives. Some Dinkas believed that showcasing their cultural dances at UNHCR/NGO events was important for generating cultural pride and enhancing the visibility of Dinka refugees in an extremely diverse social environment. Others believed that these performances were more for the UNHCR/NGOs to demonstrate to donors and journalists how they were promoting and supporting refugees' cultural practices and well-being, while ignoring how the camp system actually subjugated refugees to a system of inequality. For example, Thon, a Dinka-Bahr el Ghazal community leader who was instrumental in the campaign to reinstate the weekly Dinka dances, pointed out to me how UNHCR/NGO officials praised the creativity of the Dinka-Padang cultural performance during the 2015 WRD, even awarding it a prize for best performance. Meanwhile, these same officials failed to make any mention to the donors and journalists in attendance about the police's halting and exploitation of the Dinka weekly dances, the very dances from which the staged UN performances were derived. From this perspective, the audibility of the Dinka cultural performance at the WRD event obfuscated the marginalizing effects of a camp built on regulating and constraining refugees' physical and cultural mobility.

Beyond a Culture of Containment

As in other refugee camp contexts, restricted mobility has been a defining feature of the Kakuma camp. During my research, I found that this practice acutely affected refugees with pastoralist backgrounds because of their inherent need to move to fulfill their livelihood needs. Rather than acknowledge the value of cattle herding, camp officials banned it, citing reasons of insecurity and protection. In confronting these challenges, music and dance served as main resources through which former herders could retain linkages to their revered bulls and oxen. And yet these cultural practices were not just performed on stages and in fields—they were woven into the encampment system. In the face of dispossession, the weekly dances fostered Dinka social belonging. At the same time, their enactment required conforming to the norms, values, and ideologies that undergirded a humanitarian government mandated to regulate and constrain refugees' movements. What are the implications of a heightened awareness of the Kakuma camp's institutional culture of containment and its relationship with Dinka dancing?

Recognizing the co-constitutive relationship between the Dinka dances and refugee containment elucidates the dangers of the UNHCR and its contracted agencies instrumentalizing narratives about refugees' creative resiliency in ways that normalize encampment. Proponents of confining migrants in camps may view the Dinka weekly dances similarly to the UNHCR's distribution of solar cooking stoves and firewood bundles. They may suggest that the ability of former pastoralists to conduct their dancing traditions demonstrates how the camp enables cultural continuity in the face of rupture and loss. They may contend that dancing serves as a suitable replacement for land and cattle, which if refugees were permitted to obtain, would stoke conflict between refugees and local pastoralists. Moreover, these kinds of obfuscating narratives may apply to other music and dance practices that have manifested from the politics of immobility governing the Kakuma camp. Attention to the interwoven relationship between cultural activities and the culture of containment can thus compel institutional actors to go further than merely supporting activities that reproduce a system of inequality.

Crucially, a better understanding of the value of Dinka pastoralist traditions can contribute to and open up new discussions about the benefits of supporting rather than co-opting and delegitimizing pastoralist ways of living. Recognizing the importance of nomadic lifeways challenges policy makers and NGO workers to collaborate with pastoralists to develop ideas and practices for supporting rather than devaluing their lifeways. If humanitarian agencies are indeed in the business of helping forced migrants reconstitute the social fabric of lives ripped and torn by violent upheaval, then greater focus on the livelihood practices of such a large portion of Kakuma's camp population may help inform decisions to better enable forced migrants from pastoralist backgrounds to rebuild their lives. Achieving this goal requires rethinking colonialist mentalities toward nomadic peoples and resisting the domestication of encampment.

More than just an isolated case, the impingement of the refugee regime's institutional culture of containment on the Dinka weekly dances raises concerns and questions about other kinds of cultural activities negatively affected by this system. Researching this issue, I learned that the police often infringed on the capacity of different social groups to engage in nighttime social activities as part of enforcing curfews that confined Kakuma's camp residents to designated neighborhoods after sundown. As stated in the previous two chapters, popular musicians were unable to establish a viable nighttime entertainment scene due to the curfew restrictions, simultaneously being subjected to police exploitation and abuse. Several community leaders from a social group from the Equatoria region of South Sudan recounted one night when police officers encroached on their communal event by halting it, burning cultural artifacts used in the event, and detaining the event's organizers. In a system where institutional practices of curfews, detentions, bans, and travel passes were common facets of controlling refugees, what other cultural activities were marginalized by this culture of containment? Exposing and redressing these kinds of situations requires critical attention to music, dance, and the politics of immobility governing the Kakuma camp and other similar sites.

While the Dinka weekly dances were not always free from conflict, most of the time, they were social events during which Dinkas sang together, remembered together, and came together. Recognizing these benefits, members of Bor, Bahr el Ghazal, and Padang campaigned to reinstate them. Several youth leaders even formed a new Pan-Dinka collective. The logo they created for their group consists of three stones and a black cooking pot. The stones represent the regions of Bor, Bahr el Ghazal, and Padang, emphasizing the diversity of Dinka social life. The color black signifies pride in their dark skin color. And the cooking pot signifies a shared sense of Dinkaness. This logo serves as a vivid reminder of the role expressive culture played in feeding their communities' social lives. Music and dance were food. The weekly dances satisfied not only a cultural taste but also a cultural hunger for leading productive, healthy, and meaningful lives. While food rations might have kept Dinka refugees from starving, their songs and dances made many of them feel alive.

Notes

1. Kuol, community-organized video interview recorded for author during meeting at Dinka dancing field, July 28, 2013, Kakuma Refugee Camp, Kenya.

2. Kuol, community-organized video interview recorded for author during meeting at Dinka dancing field, July 28, 2013, Kakuma Refugee Camp, Kenya.

3. While Africans constituted 36 percent of all refugees worldwide in 1994, not a single refugee-receiving country came close to setting a proportion of resettlement quotas for refugees from Africa matching this figure. For 1994–95, the allocation of resettlement quotas for refugees from Africa among Western countries was as follows: Australia allocated 800 out of 13,000 spots; Canada allocated 1,520 out of 7,300 spots; and the United States allocated 7,000 out of 110,000 spots. In 1992, however, UNHCR-Geneva paid for more NGOs to offer humanitarian services in Africa than any other continent (35 percent of the NGO total) (Hyndman 2000, 56–57).

4. Kuol and Mark, community-organized video interview recorded for author during meeting at Dinka dancing field, July 28, 2013, Kakuma Refugee Camp, Kenya.

5. This line of thinking is ironic because the Kenyan government has long treated Turkana pastoralists as markedly distinct from dominant members of Kenyan society.

6. Jennifer Clark, "Solar Cooker Offers Ray of Hope for Refugee Environment," UNHCR, June 4, 2004.

7. Agency staff, personal communication, October 29, 2014, Kakuma Refugee Camp, Kenya.

8. "Deregel is a traditional type of dance. It is originally from Deregel sub-tribe of Mundari. This type of traditional dance is now spread to Aliab and Atuot Dinka of Yirol and almost all of Bor Dinka, with Gok and Athooc adopting it as the leading form of drum dance" (Guarak 2011, 639).

9. Youth representative, community-organized video interview, July 28, 2013, Kakuma Refugee Camp, Kenya.

10. My Dinka interlocutors referred to this instrument as "jingles" because of the jingling sounds it made when played.

11. Security personnel, interview with the author, November 2014, Kakuma Refugee Camp, Kenya.

12. Security personnel, interview with the author, November 2014, Kakuma Refugee Camp, Kenya.

13. Bol, interview with the author, February 21, 2015, Kakuma Refugee Camp, Kenya.

14. Bol, interview with the author, February 21, 2015, Kakuma Refugee Camp, Kenya.

15. Alier Jok, interview with the author, November 21, 2014, Kakuma Refugee Camp, Kenya.

16. Nyibol, interview with the author, December 2014, Kakuma Refugee Camp, Kenya.

5

SECURITY

The Ban on Christian Worship

This was God's country. Past the gold-domed Ethiopian Orthodox church in the town of Kakuma, past the Christian aid agencies' faded signs clustered near the entry road to the camp area, past the lone Jewish synagogue in Kakuma One, past the Qur'anic bookshop and sacred mosques in the teeming Somali market, up the main dirt road opposite the Jebel Mara and Bahr el Nam primary schools, over one hundred Episcopalians of Dinka descent gathered on a parched dirt field on December 12, 2014. They came to celebrate the first of four *mathira* scheduled for the Christmas and New Year's holiday period.[1] *Mathira*, a religious ceremonial procession, has become a common way to celebrate holy days in the Episcopal Church of the Sudan (ECS). Every year in the Kakuma camp, church members spent countless hours preparing for it. Choir groups composed and rehearsed songs. Marchers procured matching outfits. Organizers demarcated appropriate routes. For many ECS members, *mathira* was a much-anticipated ceremonial event for Christian worship. In 2014, however, members of Kakuma's Administration Police (AP) did not share their enthusiasm.

Following a period of civil unrest in the Kakuma camp during the months of October and November 2014, police officials prohibited ECS members from conducting the remaining three *mathira* and upcoming midnight church services, believing that these activities posed a real threat to Kakuma's overall stability. What makes this case study so compelling is not that the police suspended an important ritual per se, but that they targeted a Christian ceremony, during Christmastime, in one of the world's most Christian countries, in a refugee camp predominantly run by Christian agencies. The Lutheran World Federation, the National Council of Churches of Kenya, the Jesuit Refugee Services, and Don Bosco Kakuma ran services ranging from water and housing to education and mental health counseling. All the primary and secondary schools offered courses in Christian religious education. Every NGO-organized meeting opened and closed with the solemn utterance of a Christian or Islamic prayer. If certain pursuits resonated with the administration's values, *mathira* and nighttime worship surely counted among them. And yet in 2014, the police put a halt to these activities, citing security concerns. Why? What does the practice and suspension of *mathira* elucidate about the ways in which security was constituted in the Kakuma camp?

Security can mean different things to different people, and these different meanings can produce different outcomes. A dominant viewpoint posits that real threats exist in the world. This perspective supports removing security threats in order to ensure a population's safety. From a more critical angle, scholars from the Copenhagen School have argued that this realist approach may be more accurately understood as a process of "securitization" consisting of "speech acts" that authorized actors use to construct a shared understanding of an issue as a danger and threat, a process that in turn enables such actors to take extraordinary political measures (Buzan, Wæver, and de Wilde 1998, 26). Other scholars of securitization have infused this discursive approach with greater emphasis on the roles and effects of unequal relations of power, institutional interests, and bureaucratic practices (see Hammerstad 2014, 4).[2] In this chapter, I draw on these critical approaches while adding a focus on security that delves into refugees' responses to insecurity through religious music. This study builds on anthropological approaches that examine ideas, experiences, and practices of security not only at the level of state institutions and authorized actors but also of individuals, communities, and social groups at more oft-neglected levels (Marriage 2020; Goldstein 2010; Horst 2006). The high degree of securitization in the Kakuma camp is central to my analysis of the police's halting of *mathira* and midnight church services. However, just as important are the diverse ways select Dinka Christians addressed the insecurities they faced using sacred songs and ceremonies.

The conjoining of religion and music can have a profound effect on the ways in which people experience, constitute, and grapple with their lives. Jean Ngoya Kidula argues that music and religion serve as resources through which members "inscribe, crystallize, and document social identity" (2013, 1). Robin Sylvan argues that music has a synergistic capacity to affect people at different levels— physiological, psychological, sociocultural, semiological, virtual, ritual, and spiritual—in a manner that integrates each of these levels into a larger whole (2002, 21, 42–43). This aspect of music makes it a particularly useful vehicle for religion, which is itself a multidimensional phenomenon that functions at different levels (2002, 21). Taking a similarly integrated view of music and religion, Daniel Kodzo Avorgbedor suggests that "religious encounters engage the affective and emotional core of the human psyche; they bear also great implications for the quality and continuity of life, especially when they are integrated with sound, gesture, movement, and ritual performance" (2003, 16). In the context of the Kakuma camp, Dinka Christians constituted spiritual and social belonging through engagement with the affective and synergistic capacities of religious music and sacred ceremonies, a process that enabled them to cope with the insecurities of humanitarian encampment.

As state security apparatuses designed to control population have proliferated across the globe, music has served multiple purposes. Japanese Americans have used music to alleviate trauma and pain in US internment camps (Waseda 2005). Palestinians have incorporated oppressive experiences with Israeli checkpoints and prison cells into oppositional performance frames (McDonald 2009). US military personnel have wielded music to inflict physical and psychological harm on people detained in torture cells in Guantanamo Bay and Iraq (Cusick 2008). These studies demonstrate music's capacity to function as a mode of violence, resistance, and healing within securitized situations of inequality. In what follows, I extend the conversation on music and state security by examining the diverse ways in which Christian religious music responded to, reproduced, resisted, and reconfigured the securitization of refugees in Kenya. The stories and experiences of Dinka Christians residing in the Kakuma Refugee Camp offers crucial insights on long-standing debates about security during a period when the refugee figure has become marked as a defining symbol of national insecurity in households and governments across the globe.

The Insecurities of Protection

Refugee camps are often thought of as places where forced migrants can obtain protection. And to some extent, they can. Many individuals living in Kenya's refugee camps have been able to escape violence and political persecution. Aid agencies in Kenya have provided economic security for forced migrants lacking sufficient income and community support (Horst 2006, 78). And yet a critical understanding of Kenya's camp operations and the wider refugee regime elucidates how the process of protecting refugees has also generated insecurities.

Over the years, scholars of Kenya's Kakuma and Dadaab camps have documented a host of insecurities plaguing camp inhabitants and surrounding residents. Physical insecurity has included violence at domestic and community levels; sexual abuse among refugees and between camp officials and refugees; armed robbery and criminality; fighting within and between ethno-national refugee groups and between refugees and Kenyan nationals; police abuse; and vulnerability to forced repatriation (see Brankamp 2019; Horst 2006; Crisp 2000). Economic insecurity has manifested in degraded and unstable food ration delivery along with limited economic opportunities (Horst 2006, 81). Physical and economic insecurity have also been linked. Women and girls in Dadaab, for example, have been vulnerable to rape when collecting firewood in surrounding areas (Horst 2006, 86–87; Crisp 2000, 604–607). These conditions, combined with the brutal effects of protracted conflicts, have generated social and psychological insecurities (Crisp 2000, 624). Medical and social service workers in the Kakuma and Dadaab camps have reported refugees' mental states as being characterized by "nervous depression and dependency," "traumatized," "aggressive," "highly stressed," and "suffering from emotional and behavioral problems" (2000, 624). Why would a place designed and operated to provide refugees protection from harm suffer from so many insecurities?

A common rationale among many of the aid workers and security personnel I met was that refugees' insecurities were directly tied to the insecurities of the countries they had fled. Violent conflicts and forced exile, they often explained, produce trauma and social tension, which in turn induce some individuals to behave violently in homes, bars, and distribution centers. By locating refugees as the primary sources of insecurity, this viewpoint helps explain why a place designed to protect refugees would still suffer from insecurities. Refugees' problems were simply difficult for the UNHCR/NGOs to resolve. And yet while this claim does have some validity, more to this story exists than the problems refugees brought with them to the camp.

A more critical understanding requires unpacking the securitizing forces that extend across and beyond Kenya's encampments. Cindy Horst (2006, 107) has argued that the security of refugees in Dadaab has been affected by the nature of interests of different parties constituting the refugee regime—governments, implementing agencies, and donors. The UNHCR has been constrained by "a compromised position" wherein it must confront states on politically tense protection issues while depending on these same states for operational funding and voluntary support (2006, 109). The UNHCR's capacity to fight for refugee rights and well-being has thus been impeded by its dependency on the very institutions it is supposed to confront. Meanwhile, many states, both donor and receiving, have justified using refugee camps not to protect refugee security interests but rather to protect national security interests. By the early 2000s, the UNHCR had abandoned its decade-long attempt at using an inclusive language of security based on the mutual interests of donors, host governments, and displaced persons because of the stubbornness with which the concept of security reverts to common tropes of national security (Hammerstad 2014, 273–274).

In the Kenyan context, the precedence that national security interests have taken over refugee security interests is evident in the location and operation of the refugee camps in Kenya. The refugee regime established the Kakuma and Dadaab camps in relatively remote, impoverished areas far from major metropolitan centers and fertile lands, which has contributed to refugees' economic insecurity as well as social tensions between refugees and local residents. The camps' accessible locations to refugees' countries of origin, coupled with their function as catchall sites for forced migrants in the region, place competing factions in close proximity and create conditions for conflict. The neglect of refugee security interests can also be seen in a weak judicial system that rarely holds perpetrators accountable (Horst 2006, 86; Crisp 2000, 619–622). In recent years, Kenyan officials have threatened to close the Kakuma and Dadaab camps on the grounds that they pose a threat to national security, further contributing to refugees' uncertainty and fears of forced repatriation.

From a different perspective, Bram Jansen (2018, 82) has found that the Kakuma camp experienced a reduction in violent conflict during the mid-2000s. In his study, a UNHCR security officer referred to this period as a "security revolution." The officer attributed the reduction in animosity between the refugee and Turkana populations to greater institutional efforts made to include the latter in assistance programs. Relatedly, some refugees suggested that the decrease in violent conflict resulted from social development processes that included people learning more about each other, as well as institutional initiatives such as the Peace Education Programs and peace and security committees (2018, 82). Jansen (2018, 146–148) also notes that previous studies on the high levels of sexual violence in the Kakuma camp may have failed to consider the host of false stories reported by refugees seeking to obtain resettlement. A UNHCR protection officer in Nairobi, for example, estimated in 2006 that only 1–2 percent of insecurity claims were true. Kakuma's chief of police cited specific examples of refugees' fictitious attempts at proving violent rape, recounting cases of a woman shoving mashed spaghetti in her vagina to simulate sperm, a mother cutting her daughter's vagina with a razor, and women applying chili peppers to their vaginas so they would swell up. While these performative acts of self-harm are concerning, Jansen's findings do point to a more secure environment than previous studies have shown.

And yet there is more to consider when it comes to this issue. Elizabeth Wirtz has argued that women facing SGBV in the Kakuma camp underwent further abuse within a humanitarian system where staff were often shaped by a "culture of disbelief" and "culture of victim blaming" (2017, 118–120). And while she does not deny the existence of false claims, Wirtz argues for the necessity of relying not only on the accounts of aid workers and security personnel but also on the voices of women affected by both sexual violence and the structural violence of the humanitarian system (Wirtz 2017, 117). As for the issue of Kakuma's overall stability, I found that some refugees and aid workers attributed the improved conditions to the camp's capacity to foster social interaction between new groups and to the establishment of peace and security programs. However, I also met many refugees who took issue with the abusive tactics of the camp's security arms. These individuals were angry and resentful of members of the very group responsible for protecting refugees—the police. They told me countless stories of police officers harassing, abusing, and exploiting refugees. This pattern of police brutality may be viewed as part of the Kakuma camp's transformation into what Hanno Brankamp (2019) has termed an "occupied enclave"—a military-style occupation consisting of four domains: an architectural system of roadblocks, patrol bases, and compounds; a bureaucratic system consisting of permission documents and curfews; the recurring use of physical force through incarceration and collective punishment; and the material exploitation of refugees through bribes.

This heavily securitized environment greatly affected camp inhabitants' social lives. The bureaucratic practice of requiring performance permits for holding nighttime events—weddings, birthday parties, rituals, and commercial music shows—made organizers vulnerable to economic exploitation by police officers who charged unofficial fees for what were supposed to be free permits. Failure to abide by nightly curfews or obtain performance permits subjected organizers to police roundups, detention, and release fees. At times, police-mandated bans prevented refugees from engaging in social activities deemed a threat to safety and security. Securitization thus not only limited refugees' capacities to constitute social lives but also furthered economic, physical, and psychological insecurities in an already precarious circumstance. Within this environment, even normative and benign social practices faced censure and subjugation, including, in 2014, the ECS's annual Christmas and New Year's holiday marches.

Mathira

During the first *mathira* of the 2014 Christmas holiday season, representatives from *Jɔl Wɔ Liec* (See Us, God), the pedagogical section of the ECS, positioned the parade of marchers into five sections grouped in rows of three. Teachers stood in front, followed by the young adult section, the Mothers' Union, the instrumental choir, and the children's section. *Jɔl Wɔ Liec* members' green sashes distinguished them as lead organizers, while the young adults' red sashes indicated their general role in the church. Both groups wore white button-down shirts, with the men in black trousers and black closed-toe shoes and the women in black skirts and open-toe sandals. I likened *mathira* to a long hike and put on black sneakers, which must have seemed excessive to the young girls and mothers dressed in flip-flops for the four-hour procession. The Mothers' Union carried small wooden crosses and dressed in white headscarves and long, pristine white dresses cinched at the waist. The instrumental choir displayed the most pomp and pageantry. They draped white sashes over their yellow shirts and black bottoms, and all the ladies sported red headscarves. Once we were in position, Pastor Joseph Garang opened the march with a prayer.

After the group recited a collective "amen," Chol, a choir teacher and one of the tallest members of Parish One, led the procession. He affixed a towering wooden cross to the left side of his lanky frame, swinging his right arm back and forth and striding forward with his long legs. Behind him, a young man and woman from *Jɔl Wɔ Liec* carried a large white banner emblazoned with the words "Episcopal Church of the Sudan—Diocese of Bor—Zone One Parish." We marched and sang to the repetitive rhythms of the instrumental choir as we headed in the direction of the Hong Kong market, the area with the densest population of Dinkas in the Kakuma camp. Children as young as five marched at the back. They moved with less order and stamina than the adults and sometimes clumsily bumped into each other, yet they never retired from the pace of the march.

As we tramped down the main road, a person holding a cross, followed closely by two baton twirlers, headed the choir. Behind them, two young men carried a large wooden drum by its side handles while one player pounded out a repetitive, thumping beat on the cow-skin drumhead with a wooden stick. The other musicians used their sticks to beat smaller drums hung to their stomachs in a similar fashion to Euro-American military drum lines. A cowbell player struck his instrument in sync with the central drumbeat and contributed a clanging tone to the choir's orchestration. Young girls comprised the largest section of instrumentalists. The synchronized manner in which they shook

small rectangular metal shakers made from old food ration tins added a volu-
minous sound to the marchers' sacred sound path.

Everyone sang. The high-pitched voices of five-year-old children mixed
with the lower tonalities of their adult counterparts. All the songs were composed with few lyrics and a simple, repetitive melody, making them conducive for participatory music-making. We repeated each song for fifteen to
twenty minutes in unison and call-and-response styles at a moderately slow
pace and in a tempo suitable for several hours of marching. Majok, one of my
Dinka language teachers and a member of *Jɔl Wɔ Liec*, sang in a deep, rich
baritone as he moved past me. His role was to inspect and correct the carol-
ers' form and audibility. The teachers selected the song list and encouraged
the marchers to sing with confidence. Some used bullhorns, while others
simply sang louder.

Left arm, right leg, forward! Right arm, left leg, forward! I thought to myself while practicing the proper order of swings and steps. As I got the hang of
it, I noticed my own body and the marchers around me. I felt the beat of the
bass drum, and at times, it seemed like my heartbeat pulsated in rhythm with
my legs and arms. When I looked around, everyone's movements were synchronized. When I made mistakes, one of the marchers or audience members
immediately corrected me, like when a young boy no older than ten pointed
out that my arms and legs were alternating in the wrong directions. I quickly
calibrated my movements and rejoined community.

In the moment of *mathira*, a Christian God's dominion emanated from the
marchers' voices. They performed all the songs in Dinka language, though
some lines articulated universal Christian words in lyrics, such as "*Lëcku
Aleluya, Aleluya Wën de Rën*," which translates to "Thank you, Hallelujah,
Hallelujah, Son of Man." Most of the songs they sang evoked and honored
the birth of Christ. The hymn below is a typical carol from the Christmas
repertoire:

Original Version	Translated Version[3]
Xɛn bë tit. Xɛn bë tit.	I will wait. I will wait.
Agut bine Bëny bën,	Until the Chief will come.
Ku ba loor,	And will welcome,
Yakke wël piɛth.	His good words.
Gam ku bak ya luɔk ci rap.	Accept and will ripen like cereal crops.
Wël ke Bëny dït.	Words of the Big Chief.
Anɔŋ piir athɛɛr.	Has eternal life.
Aköl ben bën.	The day will come.

Interestingly, the word used to denote God in this song is "*Bëny*," which in English means "Chief." While the Kenyan government and the UNHCR held official jurisdiction over the Kakuma camp, this song served as a lyrical reminder that for many Dinka Christians, the ultimate commander in chief was neither the president of Kenya nor the secretary general of the United Nations—it was their Christian God.

In addition to Parish One, six other parishes marched across Kakuma One. They demarcated their affiliations with banners and respective instrumental choirs' pink, orange, and blue uniforms. At times, the roads became so congested that we had to stop and give way to other groups. These moments allowed us to rest and admire each group's artistry. Thousands of spectators across multiple generations lined the roadside and followed along with the procession from the front, back, and sides. Young Dinkas with smartphones and tablets stood between the rows of marchers, seeking to capture an inside view of the singers' facial expressions and movements. The spectators and marchers stuffed the main road, which sometimes created a nuisance for motorcyclists, who blared their horns in discontent. The teachers responsible for policing street traffic waved batons and short, whip-like branches as they cleared paths for the marchers and provided a level of order for the day's event.

When we arrived at the Hong Kong market, we turned right off the main road and paraded along the walls of different Dinka neighborhoods. Kicking up clouds of dust around our stamping feet, we passed Clinic Two, then entered and left the market again. We marched by the police station and Wau Primary School. After a brief rest, we turned around and swung back up the main road. At 7:00 p.m., as the sun began to dip, we marched across the dirt field and passed through the gates of the Parish One compound. We encircled the mud-walled church's exterior, still singing. Just before the sun made its exit, we convened in the courtyard. As we gathered, Pastor Garang gave a short speech and closed the sacred event with a prayer.

The pageantry with which the ECS conducted *mathira* produced pride, dignity, and pleasure in the bodies and minds of performers and spectators. The marchers' tailored and pristine sashes, shirts, and dresses were meaningfully donned with care. Their uniforms required not only planning but also financial expenditures, a matter of great significance in a precarious situation. Alier, for example, purchased a brand-new pair of black dress shoes for the event and wore them with great satisfaction as he marched with his fellow parishioners. Young audience members documented the day's festivities with their tablets and smartphones as they sought to digitally archive a memorable and meaningful event in their lives. The crowds in attendance moved alongside the marchers, cheering and delighting in their fellow parishioners' achievements.

As a communal activity, *mathira* stitched together the social fabric of Dinka Episcopalians in a situation of displacement. This sacred ceremony was a microcosm of the ECS and Dinka Christian social life. Each parish that participated in the parade belonged to the Diocese of Bor, South Sudan/Sudan, the Episcopal Church, and a wider Christian faith. *Mathira* was thus a ceremonial event that constituted multiscalar forms of belonging at local, state, regional, and cosmological levels. The visible nuisance *mathira* created for taxi drivers and non-ECS members demonstrates how a culturally organized religious ceremony established inclusion through exclusion. This event brought together parish leaders, Jɔl Wɔ Liec, the Mothers' Union, the Sunday school choir, and general members of the congregation. The aggregation of songs, outfits, instruments, and marches united multiple generations, from children to elders. The voices singing together, legs locking in step formation, and arms swinging in synchronic fashion generated group cohesion. The ECS's gathering around the Hong Kong market area was not an arbitrary decision. The crisscrossing of marchers from all six parishes in this Dinka-populated area reinforced sociospatial belonging to a shared locality and social group.

Crucially, for many ECS members, the spiritual and synergistic dimensions of *mathira* enhanced their capacity to grapple and cope with precarity. The ceremonial display of crosses linked *mathira* to a wider Christian faith. The marchers' segmentation into three lines signified Christianity's Holy Trinity—God, Jesus Christ, and the Holy Spirit. When I asked my Dinka interlocutors about the form and practice of *mathira*, most believed it was tied to military marching. From this perspective, the marchers were like soldiers enlisted in God's army, dedicated to saving lost souls. Instead of guns, bombs, and spears, they used drums, songs, and crosses. They promoted their faith, in part, because of their belief in God's righteousness and benevolence. With each lyrical line, they praised, glorified, and celebrated their faith in God—a divine sovereign to whom they looked for guidance and protection. Through song, they called out to Bëny and believed that through faith, their lives would "ripen like cereal crops." They gave thanks and praise to Jesus because they trusted in God's will to offer them assurances amid uncertainty. The movement of hundreds of legs stepping forward at the same time, in the same tempo, and in the same direction reinforced the idea that the participants of *mathira* were in it together, as members of the same Dinka community and faith, striving to cope with life in a difficult environment, an environment wherein just a couple of months earlier widespread conflict had broken out.

"There Is Fighting!"

Several young Somali boys cautioned me not to walk any further.
"Why not?" I asked. "What happened?" I responded.
"There is fighting!" exclaimed a young boy.

At first, I did not see anything out of the ordinary. And then, suddenly, several young Dinka men carrying staffs of wood in their hands jogged past me, down the narrow dirt pathway and in the direction of the dried-out riverbed just thirty meters or so from where I was standing in Kakuma One. I stopped one of the young teenage men jogging in my direction. He had an anxious look in his eyes.

"What is going on?" I asked.
"We are defending ourselves from an attack by the Nuer."
"Are you going to fight?"
"No," he replied.[4]

He probably thought I was a camp official. So instead of heading toward the potential conflict, he stood next to me as we watched several other tall, lanky young men jog past. Each carried a wooden staff or spear in his hands. I was hyperalert but not frightened. I had initially come to meet with Kuol to converse more about the importance of Dinka song and dance traditions. I called him, but he did not pick up. I texted him, but I still did not receive an answer. I thought about heading down to the riverbank. Instead, I turned around to leave. On my way out, Kuol rang my phone and told me to turn around and wait for him. When we greeted each other, he was out of breath and sweating profusely through his white button-down shirt. He had gone to the riverbank to help defend his community from attack, but the assailants never came. Given the circumstances, I suggested we meet another time. He assured me that it was fine to sit down to talk.

He led me through the gated entrance of Block Eight, across the dirt courtyard, past several mud-brick houses, and toward an area where a host of women, children, and babies were sitting on reed mats under a large acacia tree. They had gathered there to ensure that everyone in the community would be accounted for if their compound was attacked. Several of the women held babies in their arms, while toddlers and small children rested anxiously beside them. The scene resembled common newscasts of people in war-torn countries, except that these people were in a place designed to provide refuge. These families were displaced in displacement.

I arrived in the Kakuma camp on October 28, 2014, during one of the more violent periods in residents' recent memory. Weeks earlier, fighting had broken out between Nuer and Dinka communities over the alleged defilement of a young girl. Soon after, another conflict broke out between members from the Nuer and Great Lakes region of East Africa. Several Nuers from Kakuma Four claimed a motorcyclist from Burundi had run over a young child from their community. Angered by this unfortunate occurrence, they retaliated by attacking Burundians and Congolese because they could not tell the two nationalities apart. Fearful of attack, hundreds of people who felt targeted left their homes and relocated to the courtyards outside the main police station and the Department of Refugee Affairs (DRA). They constructed makeshift shelters using plastic sheeting and empty maize-meal sacks. They brought mattresses, food rations, and cookery for their daily needs.

As Kuol and I talked about the most recent conflicts in South Sudan, he took out his phone and showed me a BBC newscast that graphically depicted gunfire exchanges between South Sudanese military forces and rebels in South Sudan in December 2013. The fighting captured in the video clip and the recent outbreak of conflict were powerful reminders of how regional violence and everyday life in the Kakuma camp were linked. Ethnic tensions manifested into physical fights, while memories and acts of violence were reenacted and circulated on digital screens. While the defilement case served as a catalyst for interethnic conflict, many Dinkas, Nuers, and aid workers attributed the violent fallout to the outbreak of civil war in South Sudan.

Several weeks later, I headed back to the LWF compound from the town of Kakuma and watched lines of refugees carrying mattresses on their heads and pots in their arms as they slowly walked across the main road. The UNHCR and police had ordered everyone to return to their designated housing plots. The police had fired gunshots into the air and forcibly removed refugees from the DRA's premises. According to UNHCR's official press release, a total of eight people were killed—several at the hands of the police—while the *Sudan Tribune* put the number as high as twenty.[5]

I hesitated to include this description of civil unrest in Kakuma. Each time I read it, I wonder if I am merely reproducing tired, cliched, and sensationalist representations of the African refugee; tragic stories that sell books, movies, and ad revenue for TV newscasts; conflict narratives that reaffirm and reproduce the logics and norms of the aid industry and the wider refugee regime. A recurring theme in this book is a focus on the ordinary, mundane, and everyday aspects of life in a refugee camp. These kinds of stories are crucial for fostering a recognition of our shared humanity within a discursive regime that operates through the representation of forced migrants as exceptional subjects requiring discriminatory treatment. After much reflection, however, I decided to keep this vignette in this chapter because it offers concrete evidence of the violence of encampment. Media depictions of the refugee figure tend to focus on conflict in the countries from which forced migrants have fled and on their subsequent relocation to relief camps where they can obtain safety and protection. In contrast, the story I have told depicts the negative consequences of using a refugee camp as a catchall site for controlling forced migrants from competing political factions.

During my research, I found that state officials and aid workers often cited these kinds of violent episodes to legitimize disciplinary schemes of segregating refugees and securitizing the camp. This finding supports Jansen's (2018, 78) understanding of the Kakuma camp as operating through a "warscape," a concept he uses to discuss the role different understandings of violence play within the camp environment in connection with wartime dynamics. Specifically, Jansen argues that the dynamics of "war-related imageries and various forms of past, present, and symbolic violence translate into forms of spatial and social ordering" (2018, 78). This framework is useful for denaturalizing the idea of the violent refugee and for recognizing the ways imaginaries of violence are wielded within the realm of humanitarian government.

It was in this context that the police forbade Dinka Christians from engaging in *mathira* and nighttime worship service during Christmas and New Year's. They believed these activities would lead to further escalation of violence and conflict. As agents responsible for the safety and well-being of the Kenyan and refugee populations, the police believed reducing public gatherings was necessary for security in Kakuma. A closer examination of the police's rationale for halting the Dinka Christian ceremonies, however, reveals that there was more to their decision than merely upholding security.

"Why Do You Exaggerate God?"

For the worshippers I knew, *mathira* strengthened group cohesion, faith, and protective support from a divine Christian sovereign. This is why they gathered each year to march across the Kakuma camp's dusty dirt roads in the sweltering heat. It is why they spent significant time tailoring outfits, rehearsing songs, and planning parade routes. What is more, these practices were not all that different in intent from why Christian relief workers attended weekly choir sessions in the LWF compound, why the Kenyan Ministry of Education offers Christian courses in the school curriculum, and why families across the globe gather in churches and chapels on Christmas Day. Yet when it came to Dinka refugees in the Kakuma camp, Christian traditions were rendered unintelligible to the police. Why?

A few days after the police announced the suspension of *mathira*, Achol, a middle-aged Dinka woman, came to the doorway of the mud-brick house in Block Eight where Alier and I were doing our daily Dinka language lesson. Alier was a prominent leader in this Dinka-Bor community due to his proficiency in English and his deft ability to navigate the humanitarian system. Achol came to update him about a recent meeting between Dinka church leaders and a high-ranking police official. "Why do you exaggerate God?" she said,[6] was the police officer's response to the church leaders when they asked why he chose to suspend *mathira*. Both Achol and Alier became visibly upset with the officer's view of their sacred rituals as superfluous Christian practices.

Following my lesson, I walked to the police station located at the turnoff point to the LWF compound. I wanted to find out more about why the police halted Dinka Christian rituals. One of the station's officers was kind enough to chat with me. When I asked him why Dinkas could not attend midnight worship service on Christmas and New Year's Eve, he informed me that the police had recently received intel indicating Dinkas and Nuers were using church meetings to plan attacks against each other. Churches in the Kakuma camp were often used to discuss community issues, though I was skeptical of their role in planning military attacks. Furthermore, if Dinkas and Nuers really were using church gatherings for this purpose, why did the police not forbid Sunday morning services?

For the ban's supporters, it did not matter whether Dinka Christian practices had more foreign or familiar elements. Christian police officers justified their suspension of *mathira* as not only a threat to security but also an unnecessary form of Christianity in excess of their own normative beliefs. The police allowed their understanding of Dinka refugees as violent beings to haunt their perceptions of *mathira* and midnight service, reacting in a manner that did little to address any real, objective threat. This interpretation elucidates the police officers' perception of Dinka refugees and their Christian practices. However, a fuller understanding of this situation entails interrogating why the police could enact a ban in the first place.

Social Abjection and Humanitarian Security

Threatening, dangerous, violent, misogynistic, mentally deficient, socially different—these were some of the ways high-ranking security personnel in

Kakuma described South Sudanese men. As such, the Administration Police (AP) often relied on prohibitive and punitive measures—curfews, bans, and detention—to control and regulate refugees. Such perceptions and practices may be understood as manifestations of what Imogen Tyler has termed "social abjection": a lived social process wherein individuals repeatedly find themselves as the "object of other's violent objectifying disgust" (Tyler 2013, 4). In recognizing the political dimensions of abjection, Tyler (2013) approaches the process as a mode of governmentality sociohistorically constituted through exclusionary neoliberal practices of state power. Drawing on these ideas, I apply the concept of social abjection to the securitizing forces of Kakuma's humanitarian governmentality.

According to Tyler (2013, 25), a main aspect of social abjection is constituted through "aversive emotions" aimed at shaping negative perceptions toward specific persons or groups. Indeed, camp security officials invoked such emotions when they explained to me with disdain why the security team could not reinstate the Dinka weekly dances in 2014 (see chap. 4). One officer described South Sudan as "lawless" and the act of killing as "not a big deal" to South Sudanese. He contrasted his perception of the violent nature of South Sudanese people to his view of his own ethnic group, which he perceived as more morally just and thus would not "merely condone violence." During the same conversation, a more senior security official made a remark about the mental inability of Sudanese to "understand" that they should not drink and fight at their dances. More than just stereotypes about one dance activity or one nationality, wider xenophobic attitudes toward all refugees existed among supporters of Kenya's refugee containment policies. Supporters of encampment believed refugees posed a threat to national sovereignty, cultural integrity, economic stability, and social well-being.

These xenophobic attitudes toward refugees materialized into a heavily securitized camp operation in Kakuma with a "military-style occupation" (Brankamp 2019, 67). Refugees were not permitted to travel outside the camp area without oft-elusive permits. By 6:00 p.m., all aid workers and nonrefugees had to vacate the camp premises, and all refugees had to exit the UN and NGO compounds. All transportation activities were prohibited, and all nighttime public rituals and performances could only be carried out with official permission. Furthermore, UN officials and aid workers self-segregated in gated compounds lined with barbed wire fencing and staffed with armed G4S security guards. These practices normalized imaginaries of violence that positioned refugees as dangers to themselves, aid workers, and the stability of Kakuma and Kenya more broadly.

Another main aspect of social abjection in Kakuma was that camp inhabitants were expected to adopt modest lifestyles to justify their presence in a UNHCR site governed through the principles of care and maintenance. My discussions with camp officials about the administration's halting of nighttime cultural dances associated with different South Sudanese groups in 2014 are instructive for elucidating this facet of camp life. When I asked a DRA official why the dances could not be reinstated, he responded that "refugees did not come here to dance."[7] He meant that refugees' main purpose for coming to a UNHCR camp was to escape political persecution and conflict, not to have a good time through nighttime dancing activities. Underlying assumptions behind this official's comment presume that refugees neither needed nor deserved to dance. Nighttime dancing was seen not only as dangerous to social stability but also as in excess of what it meant to be a refugee. That is, a fundamental aspect of human social life was deemed irrelevant within the space of encampment.

In another caveat to this issue, the hierarchy of the humanitarian system produced social distance between refugees and aid officials/workers. The camp-wide policy on sexual misconduct offers a striking example of how a basic aspect of personhood was rendered unintelligible in this system. Paradoxically, aid workers were deemed both protectors of and threats to refugee well-being. All UN/NGO staff in the Kakuma camp signed pledges stating that they would not engage in sexual or romantic relations with refugees. This policy was put in place because a gross pattern of sexual abuse and exploitation of refugees had long plagued the Kakuma camp and other humanitarian situations. In 2003, the UN enacted stricter rules on sexual misconduct for organizations entering into cooperative arrangements with it. It did so following revelations in 2002 of a chronic pattern of sexual abuse and exploitation of refugee children by aid workers in Liberia, Guinea, and Sierra Leone and a more expansive study by the Inter-Agency Standing Committee that found sexual abuse to be a widespread problem (UNHCR and Save the Children UK 2002). The differential power relations inherent in humanitarian work thus turned the Kakuma camp and similar sites into places where fundamental elements of personhood—sexuality and intimacy—no longer applied to refugees in the imagination of their humanitarian custodians.

It was within this securitized system of social abjection that innocuous Christian activities could be viewed as an exaggerated form of Christianity and subsequently halted during Christmastime in a largely Christian-run camp. The police marginalized Dinka Christian forms of worship because refugees as a whole were treated as abject subjects of a wider nation-state system. *Mathira* and midnight worship were made illegible and unrecognizable within a securitized system that perceived and treated refugees as dangerous, deviant, downtrodden, and socially separate from their humanitarian benefactors. It was in this context that Christian forms of worship could be transformed from sonorous sacred practices into noisy threats. It was within this context that the ECS leadership engaged in another facet of social abjection—resistance (see Tyler 2013, 4).

Campaigning for Christianity

Following the police ban on *mathira*, Alier and several leading Dinka religious leaders from the Episcopal churches in the Kakuma camp invited me to meet to discuss this issue in more depth. We met in the courtyard of the main church in the neighborhood where I had my Dinka language classes with Alier. Of the leaders seated in plastic chairs arranged in a circle, Archdeacon Deng was one of the first to speak:

> It is a wonder for me. Why it is only the church's services to be blocked? For example, like, like, distribution center, people do go to all of them—Dinkas and even Nuer, then there is no fighting. And even here in schools, they are mixed, and nothing happens, the same to the hospitals or clinics. People do go there, and I think, even in the market, like now with the Somali and Ethiopians, people, they are just mixed, and nothing happens. They are supposed to do, just to provide the security. That is the option, not to block the activities. This one cannot bring peace at all. It is not a solution.[8]

To be fair, Archdeacon Deng's analysis of the ban painted an overly rosy picture of the harmonious operations of food distribution centers and market areas, places where fights most frequently occurred in the camp. Popular market areas in Kakuma One were nicknamed "Hong Kong" and "Baghdad" because of their reputation as conflict-prone areas. According to popularly circulated narratives, the former was named after kung fu movies, while the latter was named after the US-led war in Iraq. Archdeacon Deng's critique of the police's discrimination against Dinka Christian practices, however, was sound.

After over two decades in operation, the Kakuma camp developed its own normative policies and practices. Many of its residents internalized their marginalized positions to the governing authority. They accepted degraded food rations and restrictions on movement without much protest. Contrastingly, the police had never banned *mathira* or nighttime church services since the opening of the Kakuma camp in 1992. In this sense, this prohibition served as an exception to the norm, a sort of "state of exception" within a state of exception (Agamben 2005).

The unexpected nature of the suspension—and the importance of the sacred practices—compelled the ECS leadership to challenge the police's decision. "We cannot do without these religious activities. We believe these Christmas activities help in bringing about peaceful coexistence among refugees at the local, national and global level," wrote the church leaders in a letter to select members of the camp administration on December 22, 2014. The authors included Alier, a *Jɔl Wɔ Liec* teacher, and four of the Dinka Episcopal Church's main leaders: the Venerable Archdeacon Deng and Reverends Kur Majok, Joseph Garang, and Andrew Makur. The leaders delivered copies of the letter to the DRA, UNHCR, AP, and Christian aid agencies to garner institutional support for their cause. In an act of good faith, the camp manager wrote a letter of support for the ECS campaign. Alier delivered this letter to the police station, but the top brass were still adamant in their decision to uphold the ban.

When the church leaders asked me how I could support their cause, I promised to seek advice from influential members of the administration. I first met with a lawyer at the UNHCR. He personally did not believe the ECS events would cause conflict, yet he doubted the UNHCR or any agency could challenge the police's decision on legal grounds, especially because it was tied to issues of security. The lawyer's reaction to the ban was not one of surprise but of familiarity with a governing system designed to rule through prohibition. In this sense, the police's ban was not as an exception to the norm, but rather a norm of the exception. Following this meeting, I sought the advice of Timothy Mwangi, a Kenyan program manager at the LWF's Youth Protection and Development Office. Mwangi was a devout Christian; he would sometimes arrive a few minutes late to work because his Bible study ran over. For him, security and freedom of worship were intertwined. He believed the police ban had the potential to alienate church leaders from participation in LWF's peacebuilding initiatives. Like a pressure cooker, too many restrictions could cause the aggrieved to shift from docile to defiant subjects. As such, he arranged for the Dinka church leaders to attend the upcoming security meeting at the Don Bosco compound.

The next morning, the pastors and I arrived first, followed by block and zonal leaders from the refugee population. Two hours later, white and olive-colored sport utility vehicles carrying officials from the UNHCR, DRA, and AP pulled into the courtyard. After we sat and introduced ourselves, the police laid out their mandates for the holiday season. One of their more glaring decisions mandated that all bars and restaurants in the camp close by 8:00 p.m. on Christmas and New Year's Eve, while the same establishments in town could stay open until 2:00 a.m. In contrast to their perception of the capacity of local Kenyans to drink responsibly, the Kenyan police stereotyped all refugees as incapable of drinking alcohol without resorting to violence. Common imaginaries of festive drinking during New Year's Eve celebrations were replaced by chaotic visions of violent brawls. This police initiative was yet another instance of how the social abjection of Kakuma's camp inhabitants manifested in discriminatory valuations of social activities at the bureaucratic level.

Over the course of four hours, the attendees discussed several issues, none of which dealt with the ban. Shortly after the meeting commenced, Alier handed the panel of security personnel the ECS letter, the camp manager's letter, and the police's rejection letter. We watched the officer in charge of the police department (OCPD) read them without comment. Each time the pastors raised their hands, the moderator called on another attendee. Just before the meeting closed, the OCPD stood up and turned to the Dinka church leaders. I held my breath. The following day was Christmas Eve, and his decision would determine the holiday season's outcome for thousands of people. He paused . . . eyed the attendees . . . and with a measured tone in his voice, announced that the ECS pastors would receive official permits for their holiday rituals. He explained that the original ban was excessive and that all refugees should have the right to worship their faith. I turned to the Dinka church leaders. Our faces lit up with smiles. At the OCPD's behest, Archdeacon Deng rose and closed the meeting with a prayer.

Coping through Sacred Ceremonies

The next morning around 6:30 a.m., I awoke to the sounds of collective song permeating through the small mesh-wired window of my cement-block room in the LWF compound. I dressed quickly and rushed out the entrance gate. In the near distance, a line of people in white and purple attire sang in unison as they marched past the walls of the World Food Program's compound. They moved past me and headed toward the path near the dried-out riverbed that ran parallel to the Turkana cafeteria. I knew the Dinkas in the Episcopal Church had planned to do *mathira* that day, but they had scheduled it for the late afternoon. I soon learned that this group was one of several Nuer and Nubian Christian parishes that also celebrated Christmas by marching. The success of the Dinka Christian leaders' campaign had a ripple effect, allowing not only their community but also other ethnically organized Christian parishes to engage in meaningful religious worship.

On Christmas Day, I participated in *mathira* as a spectator. Although congestion often made it necessary for one parish to give way to another, overcrowding was not the reason for the longest stall of the day. A white vehicle emblazoned with the UNHCR logo on its doors and hood sat parked on the roadside near the turnoff to the Don Bosco compound. Beside the vehicle, UNHCR-Kakuma's acting head of suboffice stood and admired the marchers' pageantry. Members of a Mothers' Union section surrounded her while they sang and waved their crosses. She smiled appreciatively and snapped photos while her colleague did the same with his iPad. I was amazed that *mathira*, banned for security purposes just two days prior, was by Christmas Day a public event photographed in a touristic fashion by the UNHCR's highest-ranking official in Kakuma.

Later that night, hundreds of Dinka community members packed the Parish One church. They gathered to watch a reenactment of the Massacre of the Innocents, a biblical story about Herod's plan to protect his throne from the newborn King of the Jews through the murder of all first-born males. Shiny, frilly, multicolored metallic streamers hung from the church's wooden rafters. Drawings of Jesus and the three wise men were etched on the church's front walls. Their depiction as white men signified the consequences of European colonization and missionization and the problematic racialization of Christianity in the region. Long, slender banners with the words "Merry Christmas" hung on the sidewalls, and two small plastic evergreen trees dressed in lights stood by the altar. Soldiers were prominently displayed in the drama. They wore berets and sunglasses on their heads and faces, affixed water bottles and leafy branches to their waists, and carried machetes, sticks, and wooden guns in their hands. The Herod character wore a suit and tie and stuffed his belly with a pillow. He transformed himself into the stereotypical image of the African big man. The play ended with the death of Herod, his body carried away by the soldiers. In the end, the police were correct. The Dinka parish members technically did use their nighttime gathering at church to mobilize "military" personnel.

This performance was indicative of how select Dinka Christians used cultural signs to come to grips with a long history of violence. Parish One's parishioners used the Christmas story in a performative way to critique and make sense of the ill effects of war and conflict in South Sudan. The death of the Herod figure, dressed as a corrupt African big man, signified the ousting of a long line of despotic politicians in their country's history. In his place, baby Jesus figuratively and cosmologically remained as a progenitor of promise and hope for a better future.

***

On December 31, members of the Dinka and Equatoria communities in Zone Two brought in the new year at 7:30 p.m. They pounded the metal sheeting on their rooftops, generating a jolting and thunderous sound. The nighttime church service was more subdued by comparison. The congregation sang many of the same songs they had performed during *mathira*, except that during the service, a young male keyboardist accompanied the congregation. He played the hymns' melody lines on a Yamaha connected to a speaker system and powered by a petrol generator. While I thought of New Year's as a secular holiday, for members of the ECS it was important to acknowledge and praise God's role in supporting them in both the outgoing and incoming years. This idea was expressed in the following song, sung by Parish One during *mathira* and the New Year's Eve service.[9]

Our God, Our God, Eternal King,
You, we appreciate Father.
(You) helped in the year that has passed.
We came in the New Year.
We lay down ourselves to you.
(You) will help us in the year ahead.

Francis Mading Deng's analysis of Dinka religious songs notes that hymns can reflect appeals to God, spirits, and ancestors for assistance (1973, 238). Alier expressed a similar idea to me about why Dinka Christians participated in *mathira* in the Kakuma camp, saying, "We ask protection from God because no one of us can say that I've had very good food yesterday, that's why I'm healthy, but it is the protection from God, so in those activities we are asking the protection from God."[10] For Alier, singing to God during *mathira* and midnight worship offered him and his community protection from the economic insecurity that plagued camp inhabitants. Historically, UNHCR-Kakuma's approach to refugee protection prioritized the provision of safety from physical violence and political persecution over the advancement of economic wealth. Bland biweekly food rations, for example, only met the minimum caloric intake required for human biological survival. Refugees thus had to supplement their diets through other sources, such as the informal economy and remittances. Most of the daily meals eaten in Alier's Dinka-Bor compound were meager, consisting of small portions of *kisra*, maize meal, and beans. During the rare times when meat was served at dinners, each individual typically received only one to two pebble-sized morsels at the end of the meal. Singing to God for protection was thus vital for Alier and other members of his congregation to cope with the difficulties of economic insecurity.

Crucially, special occasions such as Christian holiday ceremonies offered ECS members the opportunity to create a richer quality of life. On the morning of New Year's Day, members of Parish One collectively purchased an ox from the cattle market across the Arupe Center in Kakuma One. They herded it into the church courtyard and tied it under a tree. Just after midnight, several men roped the ox's legs and held it down while Kuol slit its throat. The Dinka men spent the next three hours skinning and chopping up the carcass with machetes and axes. When they finished, they were rewarded with hot cups of sugary tea. The men then handed the meat in large metal tins to a group of women responsible for cooking the meat and other side dishes. The next morning, leading church members from different South Sudanese ethnic groups arrived at the Parish One church compound for a feast consisting of soda, macaroni, okra soup, cabbage, *kisra*, and beef.

After finishing their meals, members of Parish One gathered in church for the closing gala. Christian religious leaders from multiple ethnic groups from South Sudan also attended. Representatives from Nuer, Nubian, Dinka, and various ethnic groups from the Equatoria region of South Sudan marked the occasion with speeches. Song and dance performances were prominently displayed by members of *Jɔl Wɔ Liec*, the Mothers' Union, and the Sunday school choir. Each group dressed in different uniforms and was allotted time to perform choreographed song and dance routines. The dances consisted of repeatedly jumping up and down in unison in a line formation from the back to the front of the church. As they jumped, dancers raised both arms in the air, brought their hands inward toward their heart, and bowed down toward the ground. These gestures were done to honor and praise God.

The church dances were adaptations of traditional Dinka-Bor dances— *deregel* and *liengjieng*—often performed at Dinka life cycle events and weekly practices. As such, they were inextricably tied to the identities of Dinkas from the Bor region of South Sudan. To dance *deregel* and *liengjieng* signified pastoralist lifeways. Song texts were also primarily sung in Dinka language as a means of further indigenizing a European religion. The reconfiguration of traditional Dinka dances into Christian dance forms and the composition of Christian hymns in Dinka language generated new performance styles imbued with sociohistorical forces signifying Dinkaness and Christian spirituality.

Dinka Christians' Christmas and New Year's holiday activities reflected and demonstrated how performance, music, dance, and prayer served as potent expressive practices for coping with insecurity. The reenactment of the

Massacre of the Innocents provided a creative and spiritual means through which to interpret and process the ill effects of conflict and political instability in South Sudan. New Year's hymns offered individuals a means to feel hope and attain assurances of spiritual protection in the face of economic insecurity. The Christmas and New Year's period provided Dinka Christians with special social occasions to indulge in and share sumptuous meals in ways that enhanced their quality of life. Moreover, singing and dancing activities provided Dinka worshippers with the capacity to make associative connections between pastoral lifeways, Christianity, and shared social lives.

Rethinking Security

When it comes to refugees, state security is inextricably linked to issues of political-economy, nationalism, and morality. In 2015, Kenyan president Uhuru Kenyatta threatened to shut down the Dadaab Refugee Complex in eastern Kenya in the name of national security following El-Shabaab's horrific attack at Garissa University. Kenyatta walked back his statement after US secretary of state John Kerry flew to Nairobi and offered $45 million to enhance Kenya's security operations. A year later, Kenyatta once again demanded Dadaab's closure shortly after European donors pledged four billion euros to the Turkish government to prevent Syrian refugees from reaching European soil. Some critics condemned Kenyatta's actions for using refugees as bargaining chips to exact monetary gains.[11] Others argued that his actions shamed Western donors for their long neglect of refugees in eastern Africa when they clearly had the finances to help. Still others suggested that if Kenyatta closed Dadaab, Kenya's refugees should be provided with something better.[12]

I suggest that part of creating something better requires rethinking what constitutes effective security. Important lessons can be learned from the role *mathira* and nighttime church services played in fostering security among practitioners. The cooperative efforts of Kakuma's camp officials and the ECS leaders provide keen insights about the logics and sentiments necessary to transcend bifurcated distinctions between self/other and citizen/refugee. Serious consideration of the aims and commitments of camp officials can lead to a greater understanding of how to transform humanitarianized security from one of abjection into a more anti-oppressive environment grounded in an inclusive approach to difference. The story of *mathira* reveals that what constituted security for many Dinka Episcopalians had little to do with police monitoring, nightly curfews, and bans on religious activities. During the conflict in 2014 and its aftermath, Dinka Christians required, perhaps more than ever, opportunities to engage in social belonging through sacred practices. If praying, singing, dancing, and marching were indeed crucial means through which to achieve the needs and demands of security, dignity, and spirituality, then it seems reasonable to conclude that banning these activities furthered insecurity.

With the reversal of the ban, the police's social valuation of *mathira* and nighttime worship shifted from one of excess, noise, and instability to a necessary, sonorous, and stability-inducing sacred practice. This shift came about, in part, not because of a sense of belonging to a shared polity but rather because of a shared recognition in a common God. The police's violent imaginaries of *mathira* as an exaggeration of Christianity and of midnight church services as a planning station for military-style attacks transformed into respect for significant and legible forms of worship. Bodies of violence became members of society with similar needs and Christian worldviews, a sentiment Reverend Garang expressed in our campaign meeting when he said, "We are all from Adam and Eve. So when we come together in the church, there is no tribe, there is no nation; we are all children of God. It is here on the earth—that's where we are alien, but if we go to heaven, we are children of God. There is no Kenya. There is no southern Sudan. There is no USA."[13]

And yet appreciation of the police's eventual realization of their shared Christian faith with Kakuma's refugee population should be tempered by recognition that their reinstatement of Dinka Christian practices failed to usurp the practice of encampment as a technology of state security. The ban's reversal merely augmented relations of power between the police and aid agencies without radically altering the structural conditions of segregated care. In this regard, the ECS's subsequent celebration of *mathira* and midnight church services performatively reinforced and reified their submission to the powers that be. By giving the police what they wanted, Dinka worshippers actually solidified the consensus under which they were governed.

Furthermore, it is crucial to be mindful of the idea that Christianity privileges certain types of subjectivities over others. I was reminded of this point when I saw what appeared to be two transgender Dinkas at a *mathira* event dressed in makeup, long wigs, sunglasses, and dresses.[14] Moving in the opposite direction of the marchers, they walked against the physical and ideological tides of the ECS parishes. Learning that the pastors deemed this an offensive act challenged my certainty in advocating for the proliferation of Christian lifeways, ways of being and thinking that have historically supported gender and sex-based discrimination toward anyone who does not ascribe solely to heteronormative behaviors. In this sense, the Dinka Christians' contestation of the police's halting of *mathira* contributed to the subjugation of Dinkas with nonheteronormative identities. The two individuals' decision to protest by marching against *mathira* is indicative of their social strength as well as the work still required to transform marginalized perceptions of people with nonnormative sexual orientations in Kakuma, East Africa, and Christian circles more broadly.

However, instead of being discouraged by the vexing nature of totalizing power and domination, there is much to learn from moments of shared recognition. The relative success of the ECS campaign served as an emergent politics of possibility for composing new ways to relate to migrants of all backgrounds. All too often, high-ranking officials claimed the UNHCR and NGOs were unable to intervene in matters of security. The reinstatement of *mathira* and nighttime worship demonstrated the collective capacity of the UNHCR, DRA, aid agencies, refugees, and activists to overturn policies that undermined the dignity of refugees—even during periods of conflict and mounting pressure to securitize the Kakuma camp. The invalidated became validated; the unintelligible became legible, and the inaudible became heard by public officials. This shift in perception of Dinka Christian activities occurred through the empathetic recognition of a shared personhood and respect for difference, which in turn advanced political will to reinstate *mathira* and nighttime church services. In other words, procedural changes and social changes require recognition, empathy, respect for difference, and political will. These kinds of logics and sentiments are crucial for transforming xenophobic attitudes, be they against people with different sexual orientations or sociopolitical backgrounds. These are the humanistic resources required to turn a refugee regime predicated on abjection into one that fosters shared senses of belonging and togetherness.

Most books and films about the so-called Lost Boys of South Sudan portray Dinka youths walking long distances to escape violence and war. Relatedly, many Dinkas I met in the Kakuma camp remarked proudly about their walking ability, an attribute tied to a long history of pastoralist livelihoods. However, on days of *mathira*, instead of walking as a consequence of war, hundreds of Dinka Christians stamped their feet across the camp's dusty roads, celebrating the importance of their religious beliefs and practices and acknowledging the literal continuation of life into the next year.

Notes

1. My Dinka interlocutors told me that the name of this event can be spelled *mathira* or *masira*. I have elected to use *mathira* throughout this book.

2. Securitization has been productively understood through Foucault's concept of biopolitics, which emphasizes "the role of power relations, bureaucratic politics, and institutional interests in determining who or what becomes securitized, and

what sort of security practices are promoted to deal with 'threats'" (see Hammer-stad 2014, 4).

3. After the author provided an initial translation of this song, Alier Manyang Jok revised it to better reflect the intended meanings and phrasings of the lyrics.

4. Personal observation, December 17, 2014, Kakuma Refugee Camp, Kenya.

5. "20 Killed in Renewed Clashes in Kenya's Kakuma Refugee Camp," *Sudan Tribune*, November 1, 2014, https://sudantribune.com/article51615/.

6. Personal observation, December 17, 2014, Kakuma Refugee Camp, Kenya.

7. DRA official, personal communication, November 24, 2014, Kakuma Refugee Camp, Kenya.

8. Archdeacon Deng, personal communication, December 20, 2014, Kakuma Refugee Camp, Kenya.

9. This version is Alier Manyang Jok's English translation of the original song composed in Dinka language.

10. Alier, personal communication, December 24, 2014, Kakuma Refugee Camp, Kenya.

11. Ben Rawlence, "Refugees Shouldn't Be Bargaining Chips," *New York Times*, May 17, 2016, https://www.nytimes.com/2016/05/17/opinion/refugees-shouldnt -be-bargaining-chips.html.

12. Conor Gaffey and Gidda Mirren, "David Miliband: Dadaab Camps Must Be Replaced with Something Better," *Newsweek*, November 17, 2016, http://www.news week.com/dadaab-camps-must-be-replaced-something-better-david-miliband -522282.

13. Reverend Garang, meeting with the author, December 20, 2014, Kakuma Refugee Camp, Kenya.

14. I have used the term "transgender" to describe the two individuals protesting during *mathira*. However, I am not certain that they would use this term to describe themselves because I did not speak with them directly.

6

——— ∿ ———

PEACE

The Loudness of Peace

Expressions of peace resounded loudly in the Kakuma Refugee Camp—loud in audibility, loud in forcefulness, loud in urgency. Musicians emphasized peace in their music, music that pumped through the aid agencies' speaker systems during UNHCR-sponsored programs. Police and security personnel demanded refugees maintain peaceful coexistence, especially during times of social instability. The International Organization for Migration (IOM) constructed a multipurpose facility near the Kalemchuch Hill and named it the IOM Peace Centre. Japanese donors funded an educational site in Kakuma Four and called it Peace Primary School. The LWF ran a Peacebuilding Unit, staffed with peacebuilding project officers, and provided support to a youth-led Peace Parliament. During his visit to the Kakuma camp in 2018, UNHCR high commissioner Filippo Grandi responded to rising conflict in South Sudan by saying that "political leaders must assume their responsibility and deliver peace, these are their people—they want peace."[1]

Why did songs, signs, and speeches about peace circulate so widely in Kenya's Kakuma Refugee Camp? What did politicians, aid workers, and performing artists hope to accomplish through the amplified promotion of peace? Most importantly, perhaps, what did the loudness of peace distort and obscure about governing cross-border migration?

Part of understanding why music and the arts seem right for advancing peace in the lives of refugees requires elucidating some of the main assumptions behind how refugee camps work. A study on the strategic use of the arts for peacebuilding by Michael Shank (from George Mason University's

Institute for Conflict Analysis and Resolution) and Lisa Schirch (from East-ern Mennonite University's Center for Justice and Peacebuilding) is helpful for elucidating some of the dominant assumptions about the role of refugee camps in addressing conflict. Shank and Schirch argue that refugee camps are able to "interrupt the cycle of violence and lay the foundation for further peacebuilding in three ways: preventing victimization, restraining offenders, and creating safe space for other approaches" (2008, 223). They offer unique insight on how the arts function in similar ways to refugee camps in terms of fostering peacebuilding. In particular, they suggest that "artists working to reduce direct violence can interrupt the cycle of emotional, spiritual, physical, and/or psychological violence, through visual, literary, performance, and/or movement art forms. Artists can also use the artistic medium as a safe place for victims to find respite and security from ongoing racial, political, or eco-nomic conflict" (2008, 223). From this perspective, artistic expressions and refugee camps work in compatible ways for ameliorating violence. Indeed, there is much validity to this perspective. Many forced migrants come to refugee camps for safety and security from conflict and persecution, and music and the arts can have positive therapeutic and transformative effects. It thus makes sense for aid agencies to organize arts-based peace projects in refugee camps. An issue with this perspective, however, is that it ignores how both refugee camps and the arts function within wider systems of power and inequality.

In this chapter, I offer a counternarrative to dominant ideas of music and the arts as wholly positive mediums for building peace in refugee camps. From a theoretical perspective, I consider music for peace projects as part of a wider peace discourse, a socially constructed assemblage of words, music, and sounds relationally constituted within wider systems of power. This analytical orienta-tion shifts attention away from questions of whether or not music can generate peace by ameliorating trauma or resolving local conflicts. Instead, it considers why some individuals or groups require peace over others, who decides why they need peace, and what peace means to different individuals and groups. With these ideas in mind, I argue that the recurring and patterned ways certain forms of peace were made audible over others in the Kakuma camp had a seg-regating effect. In one sense, camp inhabitants were compelled to need peace within the wider architecture of the nation-state system. In another, they were compelled to follow the logics, norms, and ethics that came with maintaining nonviolence in a demarcated territory. More than compliant subjects, however, they also engaged in oppositional acts through creative negotiation, protest, and public critique.

It is crucial to note that my aim in this chapter is not to contest the importance of ending conflict and war. Rather, my interests lie in examining the
effects of the peace discourse, an oft-neglected topic in forced migration studies. From the uneven power relations fundamental to humanitarianism to the
inherent discrimination of refugee containment, scholars most notably in the
fields of anthropology, political science, and geography have long interrogated
the ways physical and imagined violence have shaped the governance of refugee camps (e.g., Jansen 2018; Hyndman 2000; Crisp 2000; Agier 2002; Malkki
1995a). Of lesser concern in the literature are studies of peace, both empirically
and conceptually. In keeping with the foundational idea that peace is inextricably tied to violence (e.g., Galtung 1969), this chapter extends the conversation
on violence and encampment by turning a critical ear toward peace.

In recent years, music scholars have offered keen insight to peace and conflict
studies (see Sandoval 2016; Urbain 2008). Much of their work has demonstrated
how and why music can contribute to varied forms of peace at physiological,
psychological, and sociopolitical levels. Recent scholarship elucidates how music can address trauma (Gilman 2016; Pilzer 2014; O'Connell 2011; Kartomi
2010; Bergh and Sloboda 2010), reduce discrimination (O'Connell 2011; Brinner 2009; Hemetek 2010), narrate the sufferings of war (Wadiru 2012), and
reconcile conflict (Pinto García 2014; Impey 2013b; Cohen 2008; Ritter 2012).
From a different perspective, some of these scholars and others have provided
a more cautionary outlook on music's relationship to peace (Willson 2011 and
2013; Pinto García 2014; Sugarman 2010). As Pinto García (2014) explains,
songs can both foster reconciliation efforts and reproduce and incite conflicts
and discriminatory beliefs. In this chapter, I bridge these literatures by attuning to the ways music and sound, within a wider peace discourse, constitute
political subjectivities made to fit within a discriminatory system of migratory
control. In doing so, I join an increasing number of scholars intent on listening
to and analyzing music's relationship to both peace and violence (Sandoval
2016; Ndaliko 2016; Pinto García 2014; Willson 2011 and 2013; Sugarman 2010;
Johnson and Cloonan 2013).

Many forced migrants are subjected to war and conflict, and when they
make calls for peace, they are responding to real problems. Indeed, Kakuma's
camp inhabitants conversed about politics and conflict on a daily basis. Community leaders quelled retaliatory attacks by holding long and tense meetings
with aggrieved parties. The work of musicians, dancers, and actors who use
creative skills to ameliorate suffering from violence should garner respect. I
seek not to disregard peace projects. Rather, I elucidate their limits so as to
contribute to ongoing discussions about music and peace in ways that prove

useful for activists, administrators, and academics interested in redressing the violence of encampment and the refugee regime.

Beyond the Application of Music for Peace

Aid agencies in the Kakuma camp evaluated music for peace projects in several patterned ways. Project evaluators typically collected qualitative data on the number of participants as well as the number of individuals reached through the program. Managers then used these data sets to assess levels of social outreach. They also gathered qualitative data that examined the degree to which music-making fostered social collaboration, aroused positive feelings, and created greater cultural understanding. These evaluative metrics were apt for assessing the extent to which music for peace projects could alleviate trauma and generate social harmony among different population groups.

When it comes to the refugee regime, however, it is crucially important to consider more than the application of the arts for generating peaceful minds and peaceful groups in a site of migratory control. Sociologist Johan Galtung's (1969; 1990) work on the relationship between peace and violence has become central to my understanding of how the peace discourse normalized the marginalization of Kakuma's camp inhabitants. "Negative peace," he argues, constitutes an absence of violence (1969, 190). Such peace can occur through actions like UN troops separating disputing parties or state governments enforcing citywide curfews. The rationale behind these interventions suggests that with direct violence abated, steps toward conflict resolution can be made to produce long-term situations of social harmony. When it comes to state violence and war, however, this shift is complicated, taking years (and more often, decades) to materialize. In the case of the Kakuma camp, the maintenance of negative peace has resulted in the prolongation of institutionally constituted violence, a situation whereby a network of organizations, both state and humanitarian, have legitimized precarity and inequality within a demarcated territory.

Galtung's theoretical framework on violence includes an important cultural dimension, useful for critiquing the peace discourse. The manifestation of direct violence and the reproduction of structural violence, he argues, are tied to what he calls "cultural violence" (Galtung 1990, 291). This type of violence uses symbolic means—in the realms of religion, ideology, language, art, and science—to justify and legitimize direct and structural violence (1990, 291). There is an opacity to cultural violence that "makes direct and structural violence look, even feel, right—or at least not wrong" (1990, 291). By scrutinizing the seemingly right role of arts-oriented peace projects, this chapter makes

audible the cultural violence of the peace discourse in the Kakuma camp. By listening beyond the stated functions of music to foster peaceful minds and peaceful relations, I illustrate how music and sound constituted subjectivities that
legitimized and reproduced the systematic violence of long-term encampment.

Where most evaluations of music for peace projects in the Kakuma camp
fell short was in their tendency to ignore wider systems of power and social
control. They ignored the ways refugees were denied basic civil liberties, the
conditions of planned precarity, and the ways artistic expressions distorted
and reproduced social hierarchies. Contrastingly, a critical approach toward
evaluating music for peace projects in an encampment situation attunes to the
intersecting forces of creativity and violence involved in processes of refugee
making. As Ndaliko and Anderson suggest in their study of arts interventions
in emergency contexts in Africa, "the thin line between representational and
real violence reminds us that creativity can itself be a form of violence, and one
that is always double-edged" (2020, 20).

With heightened attention to the violence and distorting power of music
and the arts, I suggest the peace discourse in the Kakuma camp can be ben-
eficially understood by recontextualizing Jennifer Lynn Stoever's (2016) research on sound and the cultural politics of race. Drawing on W. E. B. Du
Bois's theories about the segregating effects of visual and auditory perceptions
of race, Stoever elucidates the advantages of thinking about racial differences
through an aural epistemology. "The sonic color line," Stoever explains, "is
both a hermeneutics of race and a marker of its im/material presence. It enables
listeners to construct and discern racial identities based on voices, sounds,
and particular soundscapes" (2016, 43). To better understand how racial lines
are constituted through aurality, she offers the "listening ear," a concept she
defines as a "socially constructed ideological system producing but also regulating ideas about sound" (2016, 50). "The listening ear," she suggests, "enables
the key dichotomies of the sonic color line" (2016, 50). Stoever's framework
advances useful analytics for understanding the historically contingent and
socially constructed relationship between sound and racialized subjectivities
within a hierarchized system of white supremacy.

While Stoever's theoretical ideas emerge from racial politics in the United
States, they are highly useful for critically examining the cultural politics of
peace in the Kakuma camp. In what follows, I unpack how and why the listening ears of social actors and institutions that make up the refugee regime have
become conditioned to hear refugee subjectivities in particular and patterned
ways when it comes to ideas of peace. My analysis of the difference-making
effects of the peace discourse suggests that the formation of subjectivities in

Kakuma may be aptly understood by thinking in terms of the segregating sounds of peace. This analytical orientation shifts attention away from questions of whether or not music can generate peace by ameliorating trauma or resolving local conflicts and toward questions of how sound and music structure belonging within a wider political system of nation-states.

Attention to the segregating sounds of peace considers the degrees to which different types of sound circulate within a wider political-economy of encampment. This approach examines how uneven power relations dictate what types of performances should be amplified in public programming and what types should be silenced from the public sphere. Such focus attends to how certain sounds become associated with certain groups in ways that align with dominant social, political, and moral orders. It also places heightened attention on how and why certain sounds are heard as peaceful music while others are heard as unpeaceful noise. When hearing that some individuals or groups need peace, it is crucial to consider why they need peace, who is deciding they need peace, and what is meant by peace.

Aural Imaginaries of Peace

In the Kakuma camp, the discourse of peace functioned as more than mere promotion for an ideal outcome. It also produced stereotypical imaginations of the refugee figure. From UNHCR officials and aid workers to foreign volunteers and refugees themselves, the listening ear expected musicians to compose songs about their experience with war and their desire for peace. In what follows, I demonstrate how music and sound aurally marked performing artists in ways that made them audible within the wider refugee regime.

A conversation I had with a rapper and singer about his musical interactions with a white Australian music producer exemplifies the dominant tendency to hear refugees in this manner.[2] Sitting in his modest mud-brick home, I listened as he recounted how the producer had spent a few days recording the songs of several rappers and singers using mobile recording equipment in her van. He went on to explain that after the musicians had performed their personal compositions, the producer had asked if they had composed any songs about war. They had not. However, they fulfilled her request by improvising lyrics for what would become the song and music video "Life Is a War."[3] Through her request, the foreign producer satisfied her "fixed sonic desires" of what a young musician in a refugee camp should sound like (Stoever 2016, 89). In the track itself, rappers take turns poetically describing their struggles in daily life. The somber quality of their lyrical topic is complemented by sustained piano tones played in a minor key and a slow hip hop beat composed of hi-hat and snare. After each verse, the chorus line—"life is a war"—is sung in a plaintive voice. Heavy reverb and echo effects applied to the vocal lines add an eerie and somber affect.

This song materialized from the filter of a listening ear that heard refugees as subjects of war within a wider nation-state system. More than the imagination of one foreign music producer, popular perception holds that an ideal refugee escapes war and seeks peace for themselves, their family, and their homeland. This story is told and retold in movies and novels, newscasts and charity campaigns. From gunfire and bombs to crumbling buildings and fleeing bodies, images of war reaffirm and reproduce the imagination of the war-torn refugee. Adding to these visual orientations, aural imagery shapes ideas about the normative refugee subject. Sound enables refugees to not only be heard but also felt by audiences. From the grief-stricken timbre of crying children to the mournful tone of songs recounting the ills of war and the search for peace, sounds and lyrical imagery make forced migrants audible and tangible to the wider refugee regime.

My own position as a foreign researcher from the United States made me acutely aware of the aural effects of the peace discourse in the Kakuma camp. Many of the popular musicians I met assumed that my interest in their artistry had to do with their prowess in composing "serious music," music dealing with topics such as peace and conflict. They had become accustomed to the UNHCR, LWF, and FilmAid International's recurring requests for them to promote peace through music. They were used to interacting with volunteer music producers and musicians from Western countries interested in recording and composing songs about war and peace. Moreover, they, like millions of forced migrants across the globe, were often compelled to recount their grim flight stories to justify their claims for refugee status determination and resettlement.

More than just passive actors, performing artists were acutely aware of what the listening ear expected of them. Whereas some musicians wholeheartedly produced music for the purposes of advancing peace, other musicians performed in peace shows not to promote peace per se, but rather to showcase their popular music personas. From 2011 to 2015, I attended several of these shows at local youth centers. I was struck by how the musicians and dancers rarely (if ever) mentioned peace in their performances. I later learned from show organizers that one of the only ways refugees could obtain access to LWF and FAI's public address systems was by framing their performances around a humanitarian issue. The topic of peace allowed them to sing and rap their songs without making any lyrical changes. Conversely, if the show was about malaria or HIV, for example, the performers would feel obligated to perform songs that specifically mentioned these topics. Such micro forms of resistance, however, did little to reconfigure the subjectification of the peace discourse and its role in normalizing and legitimizing state and humanitarian social control.

"Peace Starts with Me"

In keeping with the participatory approach common to aid work, the UNHCR and its contracted agencies deployed the Kakuma camp's performing artists as advocates of peace. They did so by providing institutional support for musicians, actors, and dancers to leverage their chosen art form's communicative dimension. FAI facilitated media production projects in the form of recorded songs and music videos carrying messages of peace. The LWF provided transport and equipment for peace shows organized by grassroots organizations United Drama Group (UDG), Youth Education Programme Development (YEPD), and the Kakuma Youth Peace Ambassadors (KYPA). Using the arts to build peace, organizers reasoned, had the dual effects of advancing social stability and empowering refugees.

A UNHCR press release on the work of a local theater for development group highlights the UNHCR's commitment to and support for such projects:

> United Drama for Peace, a group of refugee youth drawn together by their love for theatre and drama has taken in Kakuma Camp by storm. The youth who come from various nationalities started the drama club in 2013 to promote peaceful coexistence in the camp through community theatre. They have been holding live performances in the various communities across the camp and spreading peace messages through theater arts, music and dance every weekend. Earlier in the year, the group was recognized by the Global UNHCR Youth Initiative Fund for submitting a winning proposal on how to tackle protection concerns through community theatre. They are now using their unique and laudable initiative to bring the more than 15 communities living in the camp together and promote peace in the camp and with the local Turkana host community. "Peace starts with me— Join us to promote peace!"[4]

The work of UDG and other grassroots organizations should receive praise for their interventions. The production of a high-quality peace show takes time, energy, dedication, and a nuanced understanding of conflict in and around the Kakuma camp's complex, heterogeneous social environment. Indeed, it is not the artists' work I scrutinize but rather their social location within a wider system of encampment.

Listening beyond the laudatory rhetoric of the UNHCR press release makes audible a more problematic feature of the peace discourse. The phrase "peace starts with me" has the seemingly positive connotation of promoting empowerment. However, if one recognizes that the goal of UDG was to "promote peaceful coexistence in the camp," as stated in the press release, a more critical understanding of these projects' refugee-making functions becomes clear. The term "peaceful coexistence" was a dominant moral ideology circulated at security meetings and UNHCR public events. The basic idea was that refugees and local Kenyans should refrain from violent conflict in exchange for protection and aid. The recurring narrative of peaceful coexistence manifested, in part, from a common tendency among many aid workers, police, and UNHCR officials to locate refugees and Kenyan-Turkana as sources of conflict in Kakuma. New arrivals, they reasoned, were fresh from war and thus prone to fighting.[5] Long-standing animosity between political factions, they suggested, fueled violent outbreaks. As some refugees improved their economic conditions in an impoverished region, crime levels increased. Documented incidents of sexual violence and domestic abuse, politically charged fights between refugees, and conflict between Kenyan-Turkana and refugees provided proof of the violence-prone subjects inhabiting the Kakuma camp and its surrounding areas. When understood from this perspective, the celebratory promotion of refugees and Kenyan-Turkana as advocates of peace may be understood as a hidden call for violators of peace to take personal responsibility for the conflict they have brought on themselves.

From a different angle, some governing officials and refugees in support of peaceful coexistence recognized conflict as stemming from wider structural conditions of the camp system. They pointed out the Kakuma camp's close proximity to war-torn South Sudan. They highlighted the government's policy of using the camp as a site to cater to refugees from warring factions. They identified social tensions, fights, and crime as symptoms of the limited job and educational opportunities available to refugees and Kenyan-Turkana. Those who recognized these structural factors disabused the idea that refugees should be blamed for violence and conflict. And yet, they still believed refugees should make do with their situation and maintain a commitment to upholding nonviolence. In other words, peace still started with refugees.

In another caveat to this issue, the audibility of the peace discourse was uneven in its designation. Here, critical attention to the silences that composed the soundscape of peace in the Kakuma camp makes audible the social hierarchies of the wider refugee regime. Between 2011 and 2015, I never heard show organizers or performing artists make calls for the camp's largest financial backer, the US government and its citizens, to become more peaceful. Former US president Jimmy Carter recently noted that the United States has only been at peace for 16 of its 242 years as a nation, making it "the most warlike nation in the history of the world."[6] The International Institute for Strategic Studies estimates that in 2015, the US military budget—$598 billion—was almost as much as those of the next fourteen countries combined. This expenditure accounted for 54 percent of all US federal discretionary spending. Aid agencies working in the Kakuma camp could have educated their sponsoring government and its citizens, with their multiple military operations across Africa and the Middle East, on the ills of war and the need for peace, and in particular on the role of the US government in exacerbating forced migration in East Africa through military interventions in Somalia and Ethiopia. Instead, this narrative of peace was largely inaudible. US citizens were held to a different standard than Kakuma's camp residents because of the camp system's dependency on US financial backing. It was the African refugee, instead, who became the primary subject linked to violence and instability.

Multicultural Exclusion

The idea that music and musicians have a unique capacity to transcend borders and barriers is common in the wider peace discourse. Proponents of this view believe music can foster shared interests and evoke positive emotions. Such attributes of music, they believe, can break down social divisions in ways that generate cultural understanding and social harmony among individuals and groups from different backgrounds. These assumptions about music undergird a common approach to so-called peacebuilding efforts in the Kakuma camp, assumptions that operate through what Elaine Chang Sandoval has termed "musical multiculturalism." These types of projects, Sandoval has explained, "emphasize the value of cultural diversity as a way to build peace" (2016, 205).

Here, I complicate the efficacy of musical multiculturalism by taking up another dominant aspect of music: its boundary-making effects. Ethnomusicologists have long noted how music not only breaks down divisions but also erects both physical and symbolic boundaries, especially when it comes to ethno-national formations (see Stokes 1994). In what follows, I examine the ways peace performances, framed in terms of multicultural inclusion, reaffirmed the encampment project. For those who sought to uphold a separation between population groups, it was not enough to construct border walls and checkpoints. It was also necessary to create symbolically constructed socio-political boundaries. In the Kakuma camp, multicultural approaches to peace did more than celebrate diversity and advance cultural understanding; they legitimized and normalized which population groups required peace and, in turn, segregation and administration under the UNHCR and the Kenyan state.

In June 2015, I attended a week-long program of multicultural activities that the UNHCR organized in observance of World Refugee Day (WRD). During what was billed as the "cultural dance competition," audiences heard the rich sounds of Kakuma's diverse population at the Napata Fairgrounds, a communal meeting space nestled between bushes and trees growing along the Tarach Riverbank in Kakuma One. Staff members from the UNHCR, Kenyan government, and aid agencies as well as refugees and Kenyan-Turkana gathered in a rectangular formation around the performance area, leaving just enough room for performing groups to enter the dirt-covered courtyard. Following a Kenyan flag raising ceremony and the performance of the Kenyan national anthem, the UNHCR welcomed attendees and opened the competition to an array of sights, sounds, and choreographies. The metal jingles wrapped around the legs of Nubian dancers chimed loudly as they stomped up dust and sang pastoralist songs. The high-pitched and powerful voices of the Congolese Mamas sang in time with the rhythmic thumping of a large wooden drum. The robust communal singing of over twenty Dinka-Padang men filled all corners of the courtyard as their female counterparts lifted wooden staffs over their heads, bobbing their waists in perfect unison. The metallic clang of Nuer-Phow State shields resounded each time the performers thrust them on the ground and brushed wooden spears along the shields' surfaces. Joyous voices emanated from the joint male and female Turkana Secondary School choir as they bobbed their heads and bounced their bodies in sync to the rhythmic flow of their pastoralist music tradition. After the day's final performing group, the UNHCR-appointed judges selected three winners for inclusion in the culminating ceremony at the IOM Peace Centre.

Days later, before the sun's rays reached peak temperature, diplomats, journalists, aid workers, and refugees arrived at the IOM's Peace Centre Fairground. They began the day by walking around a tented exhibition area replete with cultural artifacts ranging from multicolor beaded jewelry and worn calabash bowls to wooden hand drums and cooked food dishes. Representatives stood and sat by their displays amid banners demarcating their affiliated national community—South Sudanese, Ethiopian, Rwandan, Somali, Ugandan, and Congolese. The visitors mingled among the crowd, taking in the cultural displays before moving to the main performance space, situated under a professionally installed tented awning the UNHCR had ordered for the event. News cameras perched atop tripods peered above the visitor seating area. To cater to the large number of attendees, event organizers had installed a speaker system and rows of flat screen TVs in the aisles. Each of these performative infrastructures worked to legitimize the legibility and audibility of the event's invited performers and speakers.

Throughout the morning and into the early afternoon, a host of performing groups took to the stage. Musicians from Octopizzo's "Artists for Refugees" project performed three hip hop sets with rappers and singers exchanging ciphers in Swahili, English, Somali, and Nuer languages. The three winners of the dance competition performed their routines. Dressed in purple, green, and yellow with wooden staffs in hand, Dinka-Padang carried out their recontextualization of courtship songs and dances. Nuer-Phow State enacted their tightly choreographed war ballet with painted shields and wooden staffs. Decked out in brightly colored orange and white uniforms, members of Turkana Secondary School sang their traditional songs in choral formation.

The public display of Nuer and Dinka cultural dances on the same stage was symbolically significant. Just seven months prior to the event, members from both groups had been embroiled in violent conflicts in the Kakuma camp that resulted in social upheaval and displacement. The choice of a Turkana group was also noteworthy because in 2015, the UNHCR and the World Bank strove to convince the Kenyan state and aid agencies to accept construction of a new type of refugee camp in northwestern Kenya. Site planners envisioned Kalobeyei as a settlement with a more integrated economy between refugees and local Kenyans. This shift in programming at the state level was made clear during governor of Turkana County H. E. Josphat Koli Nanok's speech at the IOM Peace Centre when he stated: "My government is ready and open to partnerships and in the implementation of programmes that support both the refugees and the host community. There is need to encourage sharing and interaction of the refugees and the host communities in order to create a strong bond that shall serve to remove suspicion, build trust, and encourage peaceful coexistence for development."[7]

The diverse array of multicultural performances at the WRD events was supposed to demonstrate the Kakuma camp's standing as more than just a place of interethnic conflicts. The performances were supposed to remind residents and visitors that respect for cultural differences could and did take place. They were supposed to not only reflect but also reproduce collaboration and social interaction. A powerful aspect of the multicultural approach to peace was that performers and audiences alike took great pride in their displays. Forced displacement can generate a strong desire for cultural preservation in a foreign land. For some, the public display of traditional dances produced the dual effects of cultural continuity and social cohesion. Recognition of these positive aspects is important. However, so is understanding how these projects became implicated within wider sociopolitical orders.

More than just celebrations of cultural diversity, the WRD events normalized the nation-state system. The singing of the Kenyan national anthem at the outset of both the cultural dance competition and the culminating event reminded audiences that the Kakuma camp was first and foremost built on Kenyan sovereign territory. The inclusion of diverse cultural dances from the refugee population was framed in a manner that reaffirmed the sociopolitical boundaries separating refugees from Kenyan citizens. Songs, dances, and dishes affiliated with refugees erected symbolic boundaries in ways that justified the very construction of the Kakuma camp and the wider refugee regime.

Interestingly, the inclusion of a Kenyan-Turkana cultural group during the WRD events is indicative of another boundary-making effect in Kakuma. When it comes to humanitarian governance, ethno-national boundaries are defined not only by state belonging but also by the intersectionality of class and culture. Governing officials heard Kenyan-Turkana as impoverished and prone to violence due to their subjectivity as pastoralists and their history of disputes with refugees over limited resources. The cultural displays at the 2015 WRD event grouped refugees and Turkana together as subjects requiring peaceful coexistence—and thus, administrative oversight.

If the ethno-national cultural dances did indeed reproduce sociopolitical boundaries that legitimized the encampment of forced migrants, how might popular music styles offer correctives for advancing peace in ways that transcend the contemporary political system? Here, I consider this question through an analysis of the cultural aesthetics of a music video project that exemplifies the musical multicultural approach often deployed in the Kakuma camp.

In June 2014, Emmanuel Jal, a South Sudanese Canadian artist and activist, traveled to the Kakuma camp to conduct a music for peace project. With the support of the UNHCR and FAI, he created a multicultural song project as part of the annual WRD events. Jal's project drew on the camp's cultural diversity for the purposes of generating peaceful relations among its residents.

One of the main outcomes of this project was the music video "Kakuma Rocks."[8] The casting of a diverse group of musicians from South Sudan and the Great Lakes region and their collective engagement through song was intended to both signify and enable cultural understanding and social harmony.

A traditional Nuer song served as the main melody line over an up-tempo, digitally produced Afrobeat. The song's backing track provided danceable rhythms for not only the performers but also the crowd of young children that gathered for the video shoot. "Kakuma Rocks" signifies multicultural harmony through lyrics about peace and unity sung in an array of languages including Swahili, Sheng, French, Lingala, and Nuer. Throughout the song, shots alternate between images of the artists and views of audience members watching and singing along. The video closes with the 2014 WRD slogan: "1 family torn apart by war is too many."

A common facet of music for peace projects in the Kakuma camp was their propensity to reinforce the physical boundaries of encampment through symbolic means. This patterned practice is evident in "Kakuma Rocks." At first glance, it would appear that this song transcends ethno-national borders through aesthetics that constitute a hip hop cosmopolitan formation (see Turino 2000). Lyrically, however, this song frames war as a distinctly African problem, naming South Africa, North Africa, West Africa, and East Africa as primary areas requiring peace. It makes sense that musicians living in a refugee camp in East Africa would make calls for peace on the African continent. This dominant narrative in the camp, however, placed the onus on resolving conflict and crisis with Africans and African refugees. In this sense, the Pan-Africanist and cosmopolitan aesthetics in "Kakuma Rocks" succumb to a listening ear that hears Africa as a refugee-producing region requiring refugee camps.

What if the musicians in "Kakuma Rocks" simply edited out the lyrics demarcating Africa as the main source of war? Would this turn their music video project into a multicultural performance that transcends political boundaries? I contend that it would not. The problem with the way musical multiculturalism was done in the Kakuma camp was not merely a linguistic concern. It was a structural one. The production of "Kakuma Rocks" functioned under the same governing logics that undergirded the UNHCR's inclusion of multicultural music for peace projects. The UNHCR and its contracted agencies supported these types of projects for two main reasons. First, they tended to believe refugees required socialization to transition from violent to peaceful subjects. Second, they tended to assume such projects reinforced the propriety of peaceful coexistence. Both objectives reaffirmed a listening ear that heard refugees as subjects requiring rehabilitation and social control within a demarcated territory.

To further illustrate these primary agendas of the refugee regime, it is useful to examine what happens when camp residents strive to reshape existing sociopolitical boundaries. What can listening to noise, disruption, and dissent elucidate about the workings of humanitarian government? A politically charged incident that occurred at the IOM Peace Centre in 2014 offers keen insights on this issue.

Noise and the Politics of Peace

At the 2014 WRD ceremony, Oromo nationalists made culture expressly political by setting up a tent that showcased a distinct Oromo nation in the UNHCR-funded cultural exhibition area in the IOM Peace Centre Fairground. They wore long, white traditional garb, sang traditional songs, and engaged in communal dances in ways that expressed a sense of Oromo identity. They proudly displayed Oromo flags in the tented area. The sights and sounds emanating from the Oromo tent signified political self-determination and annexation from the Ethiopian state. Some foreign visitors were surprised to hear about this "new" country and inquired further into its location.[9]

This artful protest stoked conflict between supporters and detractors of Oromo nationalism. Opposing sides yelled and fought near the booth. Counterprotesters attempted to pull down the Oromo flags. When the police arrived, they arrested and detained Oromo leaders on charges of inciting violence and civil unrest. In subsequent days, fights persisted in the Ethiopian market in Kakuma One. Some individuals even hurled stones at Ethiopian and Oromo-run restaurants. In preparation for WRD events the following year, the UNHCR made it a point to meet with community leaders involved in the prior year's protest to ensure no such acts would occur again. None did.

This case study demonstrates the ways socially acceptable expressions of peace were contingent on maintaining suitable positions within established moral and political orders. Furthermore, the audibility of the scope, boundaries, and limits of such ordering processes becomes amplified through listening to the production of perceived noise—"sound that does not belong, sound that is out of place, sound that must be continually policed" (Stoever 2016, 68). With critical attention to the politics of noise involved in the Oromo protest, multiple and competing claims to peace become audible in ways that elucidate the contours and contradictory aspects of humanitarian government.

For years, representatives from the Kakuma camp's Oromo communities had performed their traditions during WRD events. Their coffee ceremony, in fact, had become a staple of UNHCR-sponsored public functions. Governing officials considered performances of Oromo identity peaceful when performers subsumed their cultural expressions under the national category of Ethiopia or when they conducted them as part of a wider multicultural Kakuma. It became a problem in 2014 when singers and dancers framed their traditional practices in opposition to the Ethiopian state. As music scholar George Kent suggests, "Music is peaceful or unpeaceful not because of the inherent character of the music itself, but because of the way it is used" (2008, 104).

The noise of the Oromo protest makes audible fundamental governing principles in the Kakuma camp. The UNHCR's decision to prevent Oromo protests at the 2015 WRD is once again indicative of the moral code of peaceful coexistence. Refugees did not have to like living among their enemies, but they had to refrain from violence. "Don't ruin it for everybody" was a common phrase I heard refugees and governing officials use to encourage refugees to eschew conflict in exchange for safety and relief aid. The propriety of peaceful coexistence was also linked to the humanitarian value of maintaining an apolitical stance. As political scientist Michael Barnett has suggested, "Many of the postwar international humanitarian agencies created by states, including the United Nations High Commissioner for Refugees (UNHCR), are defined as apolitical and are commanded to stay out of politics" (2011, 38). Proponents of this view believe that being political may generate negative outcomes—a politically minded doctor, for example, might refuse healthcare to a war criminal, or a refugee might attack an aid agency that disproportionately supports an opposing side. Similarly, the ideal refugee should be a peaceable subject who maintains an apolitical stance and avoids conflict and violence.

Contrastingly, the noise of the Oromo protest amplifies the inherently political nature of the seemingly apolitical humanitarian order. For many camp officials and refugees, the recognition of UN member states was so taken for granted that it was deemed apolitical. The fallout from the Oromo protest ruptured this view. More than just a celebratory event for acknowledging and respecting cultural diversity, the WRD event normalized the existing nation-state system. The Oromo protest exposed the humanitarian system's role in reproducing established political orders. It elucidated the fiction of a primordial political system of nation-states, amplifying the idea that identities, both individual and collective, are fluid, dynamic, and relationally constituted. As Malkki has suggested, "one of the most illuminating ways of getting at the categorical quality of the national order of things is to examine what happens when this order is challenged or subverted" (1995b, 6).

The recognition of the contours and fractures of the existing political system through analytical attention to the noise of the Oromo protest also elucidates competing claims to peace. For supporters of peaceful coexistence, the Oromo protesters infringed on other refugees' rights to live in safety. For

Oromo nationalists, on the other hand, the failure of the UN and the Ethiopian state to recognize a separate Oromo state was an infringement on their right to self-determination. For them, peace could come once the government stopped torturing and persecuting political dissidents, once they had established a new state. Their protest allowed them to make their claims in front of high-level political officials working for the UN and various diplomatic embassies.

Such attention to subjective interpretations of peace highlights another peculiar contradiction of the refugee camp: the simultaneous support and suppression of democratic principles. Journalists and politicians have widely recognized Kenya as a state where democratic systems have strengthened over the years, especially following 2008 postelection violence. Many UNHCR officials and aid workers in Kakuma subscribed to democratic ideals. In fact, UNHCR-Kakuma established a governing system whereby refugees had to elect one woman and one man to fill representative positions. From a gendered perspective, the Kakuma camp could be viewed as more democratic than its Western donor states. And yet, despite this appreciation for democratic principles, the UNHCR, Kenyan state, and aid officials compelled refugees to silence their political voices. Such a contradiction is indicative of how the Kakuma camp functioned as a "zone of indistinction" wherein notions of democratic rights no longer made sense (Agamben 1998, 171).

Critical attention to the depoliticized ideology of peaceful coexistence makes clear another vital issue concerning refugees' socioeconomic conditions. A main rationale behind this moral code suggests refugees should eschew conflict in exchange for humanitarian assistance. As stated throughout this book, however, a main facet of the Kakuma camp was its function as a spatializing technology of migratory control. Refugees in this context were expected to remain peaceful under a system that constrained movements, infringed on civil liberties, and generated precarity.

Fundraising for Negative Peace

"Resources are required to build a new camp," read a small poster tacked to the side of the UNHCR tent in the cultural exhibition area at the IOM Peace Centre Fairgrounds during the final ceremony for the 2015 WRD. This statement signified a main UNHCR/NGO objective for the day's event—fundraising. Next to the ethno-national cultural displays stood tents advertising the Kakuma camp's aid agencies. Between cultural dances and hip hop sets, UNHCR and NGO representatives gave speeches about the camp's dire socioeconomic situation. They highlighted the overcrowded classrooms and food shortages.

They reminded donors that refugees are "people like you and me." They pleaded for funding in front of a quilt of diverse institutional actors.[10]

Strategically positioned near the stage, preassigned seating for invited dignitaries indicated the types of institutional involvement required for maintaining a UN refugee camp. Seating cards affixed to red upholstered and gold-trimmed chairs reserved places for representatives from the UN Office for the Coordination of Humanitarian Affairs (OCHA), the World Health Organization (WHO), the UN Children's Fund (UNICEF-Lodwar), the Food and Agriculture Organization of the United Nations (FAO), the International Organization for Migration (IOM), the UN Population Fund (UNFPA), the Joint UN Programme on HIV/AIDS (UNAIDS), UN Women, the World Bank, the Kenya Red Cross, the Kenyan DRA Camp Manager, the local area member of parliament (MP) for Turkana West, the commissioner for refugee affairs, the UNHCR country representative, the UN goodwill ambassador, the governor of Turkana West, the European Commission Humanitarian Aid (ECHO), and the European Union (EU). Diplomats and other embassy staff arrived from Belgium, Ethiopia, Finland, France, Japan, the Netherlands, Senegal, Spain, Sweden, Switzerland, Uganda, the United Kingdom, and the United States.

WRD organizers positioned the invited guests as benefactors responsible for refugees' well-being. Embassy staff in particular assessed the UNHCR's financial needs for running daily operations. The racialized separation between the mostly white embassy employees from Europe and the United States and the black refugees from East Africa was apparent. Historically, the UNHCR's top donors have included state representatives from Western Europe, the United States, and Japan. Some may argue that wealthy countries meet their ethical responsibility by assisting more disadvantaged countries. More skeptical critics hold a different view.

In July 2012, journalists from *Kanere*, the first ever online newspaper established and run by refugees living in a refugee camp, asked refugees in the Kakuma camp to provide their thoughts on the performances and activities organized each year for WRD. The respondents' comments elucidate the ways structural violence was built into Kakuma's camp operations.[11]

> "Being a refugee is bad," stated Rukunda Jean. "You are deprived of most of your rights and freedom. I don't see the purpose of music and dances to make UNHCR and NGOs pleased yet there's no recognition in it."
> "World Refugee Day should not be celebrated," stated Mutichaw Mote,
> "because it encourages others to become refugees. Exile life is dangerous,

you don't have any rights, protection, justice or future. We are treated as
object for other people's business."

"It's hell in the camp, like in a prison," stated Bishar H. "I don't have rights like
other Kenyans."

"This day makes me feel very sad," stated Elros. "I am a voluntary prisoner in
Kakuma. I can't move freely. I don't see any reason for cheering the day."

This critical commentary about the WRD proceedings elucidates the
Kakuma camp's oppressive and exploitative dimensions. Rukunda Jean's comment exposes the UNHCR/NGO's use of music and dance as self-congratula-
tory expressions masking violations of refugees' rights. Mote's view of refugees
as people treated as "object for other people's business" is a damning critique
of how the camp's governing agents benefited economically from the regulated
care and control of forced migrants. Bishar and Elros's use of the concepts of
prison and prisoner highlights the punitive and carceral dimensions of the
refugee camp.

It is often the case that upholding negative peace serves the interests of the
powerful while maintaining the societal status quo (Galtung 1981 in Grewal
2003). Indeed, the idea that refugees should refrain from conflict in exchange
for humanitarian services in a site of precarity and constrained mobility up-
holds the interests of the more privileged and mobile class. Crucially, recognizing how this event functioned as a fundraising mechanism for segregated care
elucidates how celebratory musical signs enacted through tropes of unity and
multiculturalism not only masked but also reproduced structural violence.
And as the WRD critics demonstrated with their statements in *Kanere*, public
displays of unity through speeches and songs provided little solace to people
struggling against difficult and discriminatory conditions.

Music for Peacekeeping

Some might contend that my critique of peace songs and peace shows is mis-
placed. They may argue that refugee camps are unique spaces for peacebuilding and that creative expressions such as music, dance, and drama are potent
mediums for healing trauma and resolving conflict. These points are valid and
can be well supported with documentary evidence. They ignore, however, a
crucial dimension of the refugee camp—structural violence and inequality.

In the Kakuma camp, the UNHCR and police often responded to conflict
through prohibitive security measures such as compounds, curfews, and jail
cells. In addition to restrictions, however, more productive approaches were

deployed by those interested in curbing conflict. From public festivals to media production projects, the UNHCR's support of diverse cultural art forms was meant to foster cultural understanding. In contrast to infrastructures intended to quash and deter violence and instability, songs, dramas, and poems operated on principles of facilitation over suppression, encouragement over distrust, and creation over removal. In the wider context of segregated care, however, it is vital to recognize how seemingly different approaches to peace and security complemented each other.

A widely circulated narrative in Kakuma was that peace must be constantly built among refugees and between refugees and Kenyan-Turkana. My findings indicate that institutional support of peace songs and peace shows may be more aptly understood as a process of peacekeeping. The peacekeeping approach, Galtung explains, "is basically dissociative: the antagonists are kept away from each other under mutual threats of considerable punishment if they transgress, particularly if they transgress into each other's territory" (1976, 282). Whereas the term "peacekeeping" is often thought of as external intervention, usually military, intended to separate opposing members of warring factions, I suggest that we may usefully apply the peacekeeping concept to the wider practice of long-term encampment. When administrators and refugees in the Kakuma camp made speeches about peace, they typically did so in two thematic ways. The first called for establishing peace in refugees' countries of origin. The second called for maintaining peaceful coexistence within and around the camp area. Both interlocking discourses of peace located refugees as subjects requiring care and social control within a demarcated territory.

From this perspective, it was not a positive form of peace that was built through music and other artistic means in the Kakuma camp, but rather a listening ear attuned to ideologies that legitimized keeping forced migrants from crossing into wealthier areas of the globe. With an expanded scope of how peace songs/shows fit within the larger migratory order, it becomes evident that seemingly productive forms of peacebuilding through music were forever caught within a wider prohibitive practice of dissociative peacekeeping. Whether these projects were designed to make music for peace or make peace through music, they were interwoven within a larger mandate of ensuring the peaceful coexistence of a segregated population subjected to precarious living conditions. Musical performances may have appeared more productive and positive than fences and gates, curfews and compounds, but their objectives were the same.

My findings are indicative of the struggles of well-intentioned individuals and institutions involved in arts-based projects in a site where structural violence has been built into the design. This chapter provides a cautionary tale to those interested in applying music and other arts for the purposes of advancing sociopolitical change in situations of encampment. It is not enough to bring people together through the power of music. The limitations of these projects did not lie in their failure to generate peaceful feelings or positive social interactions. The problem was that these evaluative criteria ignore how music for peace projects relate to the broader aid/refugee industry, which is often required to conform to prevailing political orders that subjugate forced migrants. These same criteria ignore the ways refugees are denied basic civil liberties such as freedom of movement, access to formal employment, and the right to protest. They ignore the conditions of institutionalized precarity in the form of overcrowded schools and irregular food rations. They ignore the ways the peace discourse works to normalize social segregation. Over the years, institutional support of arts-oriented projects aimed at advancing peace has continued to grow in UNHCR-administered refugee camps. This growth in popularity necessitates developing critical tools that extend beyond the dominant evaluative criteria of project organizers.

Music for Positive Peace

Refugee camps are often perceived as safe havens for people fleeing violence, conflict, and persecution. And yet, when refugees inhabit these spaces, they can never say they have found absolute peace. Within the Kakuma camp, peace songs and peace shows aurally marked refugees as victims of war as well as advocates for and violators of peace. Contrastingly, these songs and shows never celebrated the idea that Kakuma's refugees were fully at peace. To perform such songs would negate the very idea of the refugee figure and the wider project of encampment. Thus, Kakuma's camp inhabitants faced a perplexing issue. On the one hand, they had to maintain the status of war-torn victims to justify their habitation of the humanitarian camp. On the other hand, this social distinction marked them as exceptional and unusual subjects in a discriminatory form of social segregation. Such lived realities lie in stark contrast to what Galtung calls "structural positive peace," a type of a peace that "would substitute freedom for repression and equity for exploitation, and then reinforce this with *dialogue* instead of penetration, *integration* instead of segmentation, *solidarity* instead of fragmentation, and *participation* instead of marginalization" (1996, 32).

Ndaliko and Anderson have noted that in postconflict situations, NGOs typically consult artists about "*how* to communicate; not *what* to communicate" (2020, 21). In the Kakuma camp, music for peace projects were often conducted in this manner. NGO staff typically asked local artists how they wanted to carry out music for peace projects through participatory approaches. The kinds of messages artists delivered, however, had to largely conform to the dominant ideologies that constituted the wider peace discourse—the propriety of peaceful coexistence and a depoliticized celebratory multiculturalism. This patterned practice aligns with what Ndaliko and Anderson describe as the tendency for "aid agencies [to] treat the arts as a kind of 'black box' (in the engineering sense), a device that accepts dry policy messages or painful memories as input and magically spits out entertainment, local legitimacy, or social healing" (2020, 22). Instead of a controlled messaging of arts-based activities, they suggest that "aid agencies, artists, and activists must be much more attentive to the work done by the unintended inputs, the unremarked internal processes, and the unexpected outputs of artists interventions" (Ndaliko and Anderson 2020, 22). This more open-ended approach to music for peace projects would provide opportunities for Kakuma's musicians to more freely and critically dialogue about the structural inequalities that constitute humanitarian encampment. If dialogue is indeed an essential aspect of building positive peace, then perhaps institutionally organized music for peace projects that enable more unintended and unexpected forms of artistic expressions can produce new knowledge for rethinking and restructuring the violence of aid interventions.

If music for peace projects predicated on advancing peaceful coexistence and musical multiculturalism do indeed reproduce structural violence, then what do music projects that advance positive peace actually look and sound like? The stories in the preceding chapters are instructive in this regard. Chapter 5 demonstrates how and why Dinka Christians fought for religious freedom and the right to practice their sacred ceremonies in a discriminatory and heavily securitized environment. Chapter 4 shows how and why Dinka youth leaders from pastoralist communities fought for their cultural rights to engage in weekly dance practices in a site where freedom of movement was severely constrained. Chapter 3 documents how and why popular musicians fought for greater labor equality in a country where refugees could not obtain formal employment. Chapter 2 elucidates how and why members of Afrostars Entertainment established spaces of social pleasure within a site where refugees were expected to suffer to prove their legitimacy. Or consider the LWF youth group's performative critique, recounted in the introductory chapter, and how it used artful theatrics to remind the dignitaries attending the 2011 WRD of the racialized inequities of the Kakuma camp's aid economy. These musical activities serve as examples of actions that opposed the structural violence of encampment by challenging repression and advancing dignity and equality.

As conflicts and wars continue unabated across the globe, it is important to create solutions for peace that go beyond reproducing structural violence through the humanitarian-governed encampment model. Listening to and supporting the ways Kakuma's camp inhabitants carried out initiatives that advanced a respect for difference and an acknowledgment of shared humanity serves as a crucial step toward building positive peace within the existing migratory order. "Peace has a structure," says Galtung. "To be of any value in the fight against violence it must be built within nations as well as between nations" (1976, 303).

Notes

1. Jonathan Clayton, "Grandi Says South Sudan's Leaders Must Restore Peace and Hope to 'Broken' People," UNHCR, February 2, 2018, http://www.unhcr.org /news/latest/2018/2/5a7446164/grandi-says-south-sudans-leaders-must-restore -peace-hope-broken-people.html.

2. Anonymous, interview with author, July 17, 2013, Kakuma Refugee Camp, Kenya.

3. "'Life Is a War' Refugee Hip Hop," Izzy Brown, January 26, 2011, music video, 7:43, https://www.youtube.com/watch?v=oJaPfkWKjTM.

4. UNHCR, "'United Drama for Peace' Project Launched in Kakuma," October 14, 2015, https://data2.unhcr.org/fr/news/9676.

5. The term "new arrivals" is commonly used in Kakuma for describing recently arrived refugees.

6. Wade Davis, "The Unraveling of America," *Rolling Stone*, August 6, 2020, https://www.rollingstone.com/politics/political-commentary/covid-19-end-of -american-era-wade-davis-1038206/.

7. "The Speech by H. E. Josphat Koli Nanok: The Governor of Turkana County on World Refugee Day Celebrations on 20th June 2015 in Kakuma," Turkana County Government, June 20, 2015, https://www.turkana.go.ke/index.php/2016 /10/24/world-refugees-day-speech-2015-final/ (page discontinued).

8. "Kakuma Rocks: A Music Video from Kakuma Refugee Camp," FilmAid Kenya, August 3, 2015, music video, 6:03, https://www.youtube.com/watch?v=6p LT4ejv4zo.

9. Kanere journalist and NGO workers, separate conversations with the author, May 2015, Kakuma Refugee Camp, Kenya.

10. Personal observation, June 2015, Kakuma Refugee Camp, Kenya.

11. Kanere, "Community Talking Point: World Refugee Day." *Kakuma News Reflector*, July 23, 2012, https://kanere.org/community-talking-point-world-refugee -day/.

RECOMPOSING AID

When I first came to the Kakuma Refugee Camp in 2011, I wanted to better understand how music could address the difficulties associated with forced migration. Initially, I attempted to fulfill this goal as a volunteer intern for the International Rescue Committee. My work entailed using research about music, dance, and drama to improve refugee health outcomes. Over the course of six months, I learned how cultural expressions can indeed be instrumentalized for this purpose. During this same period, however, I also learned that a larger problem existed beyond addressing refugees' immediate biomedical concerns. The refugee camp as a system was itself extremely flawed. This recognition compelled me to alter my research approach. During two subsequent visits to the Kakuma camp in 2013 and 2014–2015, I became more aware of how the camp's residents used music, dance, and performance to negotiate and oppose the negative effects of humanitarian rule. I became more attuned to moments of dissonance, silence, and noise. I came to recognize how certain forms of music reinforced normative ways of belonging while others constituted subversive and disqualified ways of belonging.

Sensing sound helped me understand how and why expressive culture served as a potent means through which forced migrants living in northwestern Kenya altered, opposed, and negotiated the disciplinary schemes of a UN-administered humanitarian encampment. Camp inhabitants transformed the standardizing effects of aid delivery through diverse forms of musicking in neighborhood compounds, bars, restaurants, churches, and fairgrounds. Songs and dances contributed to senses of normalcy, self-worth, and belonging—so much so that institutional attempts at curtailing them mobilized collective action. At the same time, these expressive practices became enmeshed with dominant norms, values, and ideologies that undergirded the encampment system. Attuning to the sonic politics of belonging thus illuminated the agentive capacities of Kakuma's camp inhabitants while exposing the limits and consequences of a system designed to segregate and control forced migrants.

What are the implications of these findings? At present, a privileged few are able to migrate relatively unencumbered as citizens and affiliates of wealthy and powerful states. Paradoxically, people who most need to move due to poverty and conflict face the greatest barriers to mobility. As studies have shown, the containment approach impinges on the lives of millions of people living in long-term refugee camps (Brankamp 2019 and 2021; Agier 2011; Verdirame and Harrell-Bond 2005). In addition, critical attention to the inequality of the aid industry and the refugee regime has demonstrated that this system does more for state officials and aid organizations than it does for forced migrants (Besteman 2016; Chimni 2004; Harrell-Bond 1986). With these pressing issues in mind, I discuss what can be learned from a politically engaged ethnographic account of music, dance, and performance in the UNHCR-administered Kakuma Refugee Camp.

Music, Migration, and Border Studies

Music and dance studies may seem irrelevant for addressing the concerns of forced migration. Indeed, I met scholars, aid workers, and refugees who viewed music-making and dancing as superficial aspects of life in refugee camp settings. If these individuals did acknowledge any social benefits associated with these activities, they often spoke of the healing aspects of music and dance for easing refugees' troubled minds. A deeper understanding of expressive culture, however, offers a different perspective. If music and dance are so irrelevant, then why are they so ubiquitous? It is precisely their enduring presence and reverberation in the homes, communities, and public spaces of the Kakuma camp that makes them so instructive for understanding and interrogating humanitarian government and the international refugee regime.

Scholars have long grappled with how best to confront the dangers of naturalizing the refugee experience. Employing a social constructivist approach, Liisa Malkki (1995b) has critiqued scholars for unwittingly reifying the refugee subject through academia. Roger Zetter (1991; 2007) has offered the conceptual term "labelling" for examining how state and humanitarian institutions have deployed the terms *refugee* and *asylum seeker* to identify, separate, and control human population. Many scholars have opted to use the broad categories of forced migrants and displaced persons to resist normalizing the refugee category. A host of scholars have addressed issues of state power and subjectivity to understand the effects of borders and refugee camps using critical theory, most notably Agamben's concept of *bare life* (Long 2006; Edkins 2000). It is crucial to note that while each of these theories offers different analytical benefits, they are not without limitations. Zetter's labeling framework elucidates the discursive effects of bureaucracy well, yet it does not attend to the complex facets of social life. The concept of bare life may describe the ways some institutional actors view people labeled as refugees, but it also obscures the latter group's social and political realities and conveys a limited understanding of human agency (Dunn and Cons 2014; Owens 2009). The terms *forced migrants* and *displaced persons* may resist reifying the refugee category, but they still define the lives of certain social groups through involuntary movement. The term *displaced persons* also articulates a social category of people as forever living in a situation of both physical and existential dislocation. In reality, it is crucial to recognize that involuntary movement is always only one aspect of larger social, political, and cultural processes (Malkki 1995b, 496).

Focusing on the political dynamics of expressive culture and belonging in the Kakuma camp challenges reductive ideas of what constitutes the refugee experience. Musicians and dancers countered stereotypes of refugees as helpless victims and objects of threat while emphasizing creativity and social strength. The intimate ways music and dance unfolded in Kakuma demonstrates the fallacy of presuming a person becomes bare life once they enter the camp area. The creation of social spaces through the enactment of hip hop and R&B shows, Dinka weekly dances, and Episcopalian religious ceremonies indicates that living in a refugee camp is a process not only of displacement but also of emplacement. Furthermore, the campaigns that musicians and local leaders conducted for advancing labor and cultural rights convey oppositional perspectives and discontent with the humanitarian status quo. Thus, focusing on songs, dances, and performances shows why living in a refugee camp is neither a form of totalizing abjection nor appreciative acceptance, but rather a complex and dynamic social and creative process that requires constant negotiation. Listening to and reflecting on camp inhabitants' voices and musical experiences foregrounds desired ways of belonging and offers crucial insights on ways of knowing and being that challenge common assumptions about how the refugee subject should belong.

Attuning to the sonic politics of belonging also offers keen insights on the role of aesthetics in humanitarian government. Unlike most city governments, the UNHCR's primary goal was not to use music and the arts to beautify the Kakuma camp to attract tourists and urban migrants. Rather, it funded arts programming to uphold camp operations. Aesthetics of care proliferated in songs with social messages and for entertainment. The former reproduced the subordinated status of the incomplete refugee, while the latter reaffirmed the imagination of the well-treated refugee and beneficiary. Aesthetics of minimalism had the complementary effects of signifying the aid agencies' "self-referential accountability" to instrumentalize the arts in an economical manner while reproducing the camp system's socioeconomic threshold (see Ndaliko and Anderson 2020, 16). Aesthetics of ethno-nationalism symbolically reproduced the dividing lines of the nation-state order, which in turn legitimized the very purpose of the camp. Collectively, these interlocking aesthetics had the effect of obscuring and reproducing the Kakuma camp as a site of social segregation. Studying humanitarian aesthetics is important because it calls attention to the obfuscating effects of the arts in masking the more hard-lined policies and practices of border externalization. As such, it is crucial to consider how artists and institutions can recompose humanitarian aesthetics to create a more just and equitable migratory experience.

Arts-Based Humanitarian Initiatives

Over the years, I have met NGO workers and volunteers in the Kakuma camp who came to improve refugees' lives through the power of expressive culture. They came with project plans on their laptops, musical equipment in their luggage, and good intentions in their hearts. They believed supporting musicians, dancers, and actors could make a difference in the lives of the disenfranchised. Artistic projects could offer refugees a creative outlet, raise their self-worth, address social problems, and help maintain cultural continuity in the face of social rupture. Each of these outcomes is indeed beneficial. Additionally, Kakuma's musicians and dancers often negotiated their roles in NGO-organized arts projects in ways that suited their own needs rather than the mandates of the sponsoring agencies. At the same time, however, my research findings demonstrate that these projects were interwoven with subordinating power dynamics. In chapter 3, I show how and why the aid agencies' recurring requirement for performing artists to sing songs and perform shows without payment exacerbated stress and reproduced socioeconomic inequality. In chapter 6, I examine how peace songs and shows positioned refugees as violators of social stability in ways that normalized encampment. It was not enough for the UNHCR to support peace through songs and dances that emphasized multicultural diversity, especially if we consider my findings in chapter 4, where I document how these same cultural expressions in their ritualistic contexts were subjected to prohibition and exploitation from police officials. These case studies offer keen insights for rethinking and recomposing arts-oriented program initiatives within refugee camp settings.

Part of addressing this issue requires moving beyond the needs-based approach widespread in arts-based humanitarianism. It is not enough to soothe an individual's troubled mind through music therapy programs if doing so merely enables and reproduces social segregation. A more critical approach would entail the UNHCR and its contracted agencies mobilizing resources and relationships with performing artists to redress structural inequalities plaguing the encampment model. In so doing, they would help advance the rights and causes not only of performers and audiences but also of other refugees facing similar injustices. As the number of camps have increased and endured over the years, there is an urgent need for ethnomusicologists and like-minded scholars and practitioners to adopt approaches that recognize and rectify the larger systemic forces that locate millions of people within the margins of the nation-state order. As Ndaliko has argued in her critique of NGO interventions in East Congo, "if music is ultimately going to prove viable as a means of sustainable sociopolitical change in any conflict the world over, it seems to me that it must be music produced from—or exposing—positions of power" (Ndaliko 2016, 161).

Indeed, it is crucial to consider that individuals and institutions dedicated to mobilizing the power of music and the arts have a unique tool at their disposal for rectifying social injustice—performance. Soyini Madison has argued that performances may be understood as "tactics" for "creating a means and a space from whatever elements or resources are available in order to resist or subvert the strategies of more powerful institutions, ideologies, or processes" (2011, 2). Relatedly, Christopher Odhiambo Joseph has argued that "theatre/drama as a tool of intervention should be framed in such a way that it provides possibilities for the oppressor to change instead of acting as an imaginary that only privileges the vanquishing of the oppressor" (2011, 53). As I have discussed throughout this book, Kakuma's aid agencies supported the work of theater for development (TfD) groups because of their focus on addressing refugees' social deficiencies. This needs-based approach to drama, however, had the effect of normalizing the hierarchy of the aid system and the use of the camp for regulating forced migrants. A more radical and critical approach to TfD programming would entail reconfiguring music, dance, and theatrical performances to interrogate, amplify, and transform the marginalizing forces of humanitarian encampment. Such performances would expose the hidden forces of altruistic subordination and planned precarity. They would educate the UNHCR, state officials, donors, and aid workers on the policies and procedures that hinder migrants' well-being. These kinds of TfDs would fall within the lineage of renowned Kenyan activist, scholar, and dramatist Ngũgĩ wa Thiong'o (2005 [1986]), whose ideas and work popularized dramas that exposed institutional oppression.

Individuals and agencies can join forces to amplify and rectify the injustices of segregated care. *Kanere*, for example, is an online newspaper established and run by residents of the Kakuma camp. It offers news stories and critical commentary on the difficulties that forced migrants face in Kenya. Its arts section includes letters, drawings, and poetry that highlight the agentive and creative capacities of Kakuma's camp inhabitants and the more problematic features of the long-term refugee camp. Contributors include refugees, researchers, journalists, and NGO staff. Aid agencies and researchers can join the voices of *Kanere*'s contributors and the chorus of other like-minded groups to amplify the widespread inequality of the refugee regime.

Skeptics might question the ability of researchers and agency staff to support critical arts-based initiatives in a refugee camp setting. They might point out that state officials and NGO workers would never allow such projects to occur. And they might be right. Such skepticism should not be ignored. Rather, it should provoke hesitancy to only engage in needs-based art projects. In other words, organizations should aim skepticism not toward their ability to support critical arts initiatives but toward a humanitarian system that disallows such actions.

Migration Policies and Possibilities

Political instability, violent conflict, economic insecurity, and climate change are just some of the factors that will likely cause forced migration to continue in eastern and central Africa for the foreseeable future. When it comes to addressing this phenomenon, talks concerning the viability of the long-term refugee camp have grown louder among state and UN officials in Kenya. In March 2021, Kenyan officials issued a two-week ultimatum to the UNHCR demanding a full-scale closure plan for the Kakuma and Dadaab camps on the grounds of protecting national security. The state's order generated swift backlash from individuals and institutions concerned with the fallout from dismantling a system affecting almost half a million people. Nevertheless, the UNHCR recognized the Kenyan state's sovereign right to dictate the terms of forced migration within its borders by submitting a closure plan that included the durable solutions of repatriation, resettlement, and local integration. The state-mandated June 30, 2022, deadline for the camp closures has since passed, and despite this plan, as of February 2023, both the Kakuma and Dadaab camps have remained in operation. As of 2022, the refugee populations of Dadaab and Kakuma were 226,000 and 189,000 respectively.[1] Meanwhile, people living in these sites face the uncertainty and possible ordeal of yet another situation of forced displacement. In what follows, I turn to policy plans surrounding the issue of encampment in Kenya, offering a few considerations for what this book's study on music, dance, and the politics of belonging in the Kakuma camp can contribute to these discussions.

Policy planners charged with rectifying the inadequacies of the care and maintenance approach to governing the Kakuma and Dadaab camps have developed an alternative model designed to take into account the more permanent realities of displacement. In 2016, the UNHCR and the World Bank Group (WBG), in collaboration with the Kenyan government, established the Kalobeyei Integrated Social and Economic Development Program (KSEDP) just 3.5 kilometers from the Kakuma camp. By 2020, the refugee population in Kalobeyei had grown to about 46,000.[2] Proponents of this fourteen-year project (2016–2030) have envisioned the creation of an urban center that fosters self-reliance and social integration in a manner that caters to the socioeconomic needs of both refugees and the host community. A main project objective is to better enable members of the often-marginalized local Kenyan population to access and benefit from foreign aid inflows in the region. According to the UNHCR, "Both refugees and host communities will benefit from: (a) investments in basic infrastructure and access to social services; and (b) increased opportunities for supporting income generating activities."[3] Recent findings on this project's efficacy have indicated that while integration between refugees and local citizens has not materialized at a significant level, the self-reliance model has led to improved nutritional outcomes and higher perceptions of autonomy as compared to findings from the Kakuma camp (Betts, Bloom, and Weaver, 2020).

And yet, behind these promising findings and the rhetoric of urbanism, social integration, and mutual benefits lies the reality that the KSEDP still functions as an instrument for migrant containment. According to Hanno Brankamp, refugee camps operate through a process he terms "carceral humanitarianism—the temporally unspecified storage of racialised human surplus through the subterfuge of aid, compassion and protective capture" (2021, 112). He notes that KSEDP's carceral qualities have included a lack of provisions for freedom of movement, political inclusion, and welfare, while simultaneously operating through militarized forms of policing (Brankamp 2021). Participants at an early KSEDP planning meeting raised a related critique when they pointed out how confining refugees to this site could turn it into a forced labor camp. Several NGO workers involved in the planning stages informed me that with the increased financial expenditures of European states toward preventing Syrian refugees from entering Europe, donors have even less capital available for addressing refugee situations in East Africa. From this perspective, the World Bank and UNHCR have championed the establishment of integrated settlements not merely because of a moral imperative to redress the wrongs of the care and maintenance model, but rather as a cost-cutting measure for upholding the containment model.

In my conversations with NGO workers in Kakuma, I often asked whether they would trade places with the refugees. Not a single NGO worker ever said yes. They knew that the conditions of encampment were difficult. They knew that refugees regularly complained about the camp's subpar services and discriminatory practices. And yet, many of them continued to support and administer the encampment system. Many believed that while the camp model was flawed, it was the most pragmatic approach for addressing forced migration. What they perhaps did not recognize was their own vulnerability to the consequences of war, persecution, disaster, and poverty. They failed to see what could happen if their positions became reversed. "If the Kenyans ever become refugees, we will abuse them," one of my interlocutors once said after I asked him and his friends what they would do if Kenyans were refugees in South Sudan.[4] Driven by feelings of anger and resentment over nightly curfews, police brutality, and limited job opportunities, he and his friends expressed their desire to exact revenge not only on the authorities that governed them but also the Kenyan population as a whole. This troubling statement points to how the debilitating aspects of encampment have the potential to turn the oppressed into the oppressor.

One way to address this issue is to better attune to disqualified but preferred ways of belonging. The desires and experiences of the Kakuma camp's musicians, dancers, and community members are instructive in this regard because of the ways these artists simultaneously negotiated, defied, and resignified normative understandings of how refugees are expected to belong while voicing and showing how they desired to belong. King Moses, Smart Djaba, and other members of Afrostars Entertainment strove to inhabit places of social pleasure, so much so that they organized club shows for like-minded audiences in the face of curfews, police bribes, and limited economic opportunities.

Leaders of the Dinka weekly dances and the Episcopal Church of the Sudan voiced opposition to their assigned belonging in a system where their community members were subjected to cultural bans as well as police exploitation and abuse. Professional musicians campaigned against a labor system in which their refugee status and musical labor were exploited by an unequal and subordinating aid economy. In addition to protesting, refugee-musicians voiced desirable forms of habitation through their artistry. With their music video "Mapenzi Gani," Queen Lisa and A Solution generated an aspirational sensory reality that resembles Nairobi's middle and upper-middle class areas. Meanwhile, the Street Boyz' music video "Let's Party" conveys a desired yet nonexistent reality in the Kakuma camp where young people can freely engage in nighttime revelry. Collectively, these findings are indicative of the kinds of preferred ways of belonging that should be considered when crafting policies addressing forced migration.

The defiance and artistry of the Kakuma camp's social actors point to the necessity of rethinking the encampment model. Their ideas and experiences elucidate the urgent need to generate policies and practices grounded not in monetary extraction, labor exploitation, social segregation, fear of difference, and imposed precarity but rather in advancing a life of mutual aid, labor equality, physical mobility, recognition of difference, and enhancement of social pleasure. Enabling the latter outcomes will require policies that generate greater belonging and social integration at local, state, regional, and global levels. It will entail building on the Kenyan state's recent revisions to the Refugee Act that enable greater opportunities to live and work in the East African Community by adding even more provisions for regional affiliation and inclusion. It will entail wealthy states increasing resettlement quotas from the current paltry figure of 1 percent, especially among countries, such as the United States, that have exacerbated conflict and forced migration in eastern and central Africa as well as other areas of the globe through politico-military interventions. It will entail supporting systems through which forced migrants can constitute meaningful social worlds free from abuse and exploitation. It will entail working in collaboration with governments, organizations, and communities to craft conditions that support dignified and diverse ways of belonging. It will entail working to establish places built on policies, institutions, and programs that better enable people facing the difficulties that come with forced migration to not just survive but thrive. Part of creating this reality will require listening to, reflecting on, and acting in solidarity with Kakuma's musicians, dancers, and artists to recompose the marginalizing effects of aid.

Notes

1. *Kenya Statistics Package: Statistical Summary as of July 31, 2022*, United Nations High Commissioner for Refugees, July 31, 2022, https://www.unhcr.org/ke/wp-content/uploads/sites/2/2022/08/Kenya-Statistics-Package-31-July-2022.pdf.

2. *Kenya Statistics Package: Statistical Summary as of July 31, 2022*, United Nations High Commissioner for Refugees, July 31, 2022, https://www.unhcr.org/ke/wp-content/uploads/sites/2/2022/08/Kenya-Statistics-Package-31-July-2022.pdf.

3. "Kalobeyei Settlement," UNHCR, accessed September 8, 2022, http://www.unhcr.org/ke/kalobeyei-settlement.

4. Anonymous, personal communication, June 2015, Kakuma Refugee Camp, Kenya.

BIBLIOGRAPHY

Agamben, Giorgio. 1998. *Homo Sacer: Sovereign Power and Bare Life*. Stanford: Stanford University Press.

———. 2005. *State of Exception*. Chicago: University of Chicago Press.

Agier, Michel. 2002. "Between War and City: Towards an Urban Anthropology of Refugee Camps." *Ethnography* 3 (3): 317–341.

———. 2011. *Managing the Undesirables: Refugee Camps and Humanitarian Government*. Malden, MA: Polity.

Ahmed, Sara. 2014 [2004]. *The Cultural Politics of Emotion*. Edinburgh: Edinburgh University Press.

Allen, Lara. 2004. "Music and Politics in Africa." *Social Dynamics: A Journal of African Studies* 30 (2): 1–19.

Appadurai, Arjun. 1996. *Modernity at Large: Cultural Dimensions of Globalization*. Minneapolis: University of Minnesota Press.

Aukot, Ekuru. 2003. "It Is Better to Be a Refugee Than a Turkana in Kakuma: Revisiting the Relationship between Hosts and Refugees in Kenya." *Refuge: Canada's Journal on Refugees* 21 (3): 73–83.

Avorgbedor, Daniel K., ed. 2003. *The Interrelatedness of Music, Religion, and Ritual in African Performance Practice*. Lewiston, NY: Edwin Mellen.

Bakewell, Oliver. 2014. "Encampment and Self-Settlement." In *The Oxford Handbook of Refugee and Forced Migration Studies*, edited by Elena Fiddian-Qasimiyeh, Gil Loescher, Katy Long, and Nando Signona, 127–138. Oxford: Oxford University Press.

Barnett, Michael. 2011. *Empire of Humanity: A History of Humanitarianism*. Ithaca, NY: Cornell University Press.

Barnouw, Erik, and Catherine E. Kirkland. 1992. "Entertainment." In *Folklore, Cultural Performances, and Popular Entertainments: A Communications-Centered*

Handbook, edited by Richard Bauman, 50–52. New York: Oxford University Press.

Barz, Gregory. 2006. *Singing for Life: HIV/AIDS and Music in Uganda*. New York: Routledge.

Barz, Gregory, and Judah Cohen, eds. 2011. *The Culture of AIDS in Africa: Hope and Healing through Music and the Arts*. Oxford: Oxford University Press.

Bergh, Arild, and John Sloboda. 2010. "Music and Art in Conflict Transformation: A Review." *Music and Arts in Action* 2 (2): 2–18.

Besteman, Catherine. 2016. *Making Refuge: Somali Bantu Refugees and Lewiston, Maine*. Durham, NC: Duke University Press.

Betts, Alexander, Louise Bloom, and Nina Weaver. 2015. *Refugee Innovation: Humanitarian Innovation That Starts with Communities*. Oxford: University of Oxford Refugee Studies Centre.

Betts, Alexander, Naohiko Omata, and Olivier Sterck. 2020. "The Kalobeyei Settlement: A Self-Reliance Model for Refugees?" *Journal of Refugee Studies* 33 (1): 189–223.

Bleiker, Roland, David Campbell, Emma Hutchison, and Xzarina Nicholson. 2013. "The Visual Dehumanisation of Refugees." *Australian Journal of Political Science* 48 (4): 398–416.

Bohlman, Philip V. 2011. "When Migration Ends, When Music Ceases." *Music and Arts in Action* 3 (3): 148–166.

Brankamp, Hanno. 2019. "'Occupied Enclave': Policing and the Underbelly of Humanitarian Governance in Kakuma Refugee Camp, Kenya." *Political Geography* 71:67–77.

———. 2021. "Camp Abolition: Ending Carceral Humanitarianism in Kenya (and Beyond)." *Antipode* 54 (1): 106–129.

Brankamp, Hanno, and Patricia Daley. 2020. "Laborers, Migrants, Refugees: Managing Belonging, Bodies, and Mobility in (Post) Colonial Kenya and Tanzania." *Migration and Society* 3 (1): 113–129.

Brinner, Benjamin. 2009. *Playing Across a Divide*. Oxford: Oxford University Press.

Brower, Lowell. 2020. "Mice, Cows, and Real Rwandans: The Folklore of Emergency in a Rwandan Refugee Camp." In *The Art of Emergency: Aesthetics and Aid in African Crises*, edited by Chérie Rivers Ndaliko and Samuel Mark Anderson, 280–308. Oxford: Oxford University Press.

Buzan, Barry, Ole Wæver, and Jaap de Wilde. 1998. *Security: A New Framework for Analysis*. London: Lynne Rienner.

Cardoso, Leonardo. 2019. *Sound-Politics in São Paulo*. New York: Oxford University Press.

Chávez, Alex. 2017. *Sounds of Crossing: Music, Migration, and the Aural Poetics of Huapango Arribeño*. Durham, NC: Duke University Press.

Chimni, B. S. 2004. "From Resettlement to Involuntary Repatriation: Towards a Critical History of Durable Solutions to Refugee Problems." *Refugee Survey Quarterly* 23 (3): 55–73.

Cohen, Cynthia. 2008. "Music: A Universal Language?" In *Music and Conflict Transformation: Harmonies and Dissonances in Geopolitics*, edited by Olivier Urbain, 26–39. London: I. B. Tauris.

Collins, Patricia H. 1998. *Fighting Words: Black Women and the Search for Justice.* Minneapolis: University of Minnesota Press.

Cormack, Zoe T. 2014. "The Making and Remaking of Gogrial: Landscape, History and Memory in South Sudan." PhD diss., Durham University.

Crenshaw, Kimberlé. 1990. "Mapping the Margins: Intersectionality, Identity Politics, and Violence against Women of Color." *Stanford Law Review* 43 (6): 1241–1299.

Crisp, Jeff. 2000. "A State of Insecurity: The Political Economy of Violence in Kenya's Refugee Camps." *African Affairs* 99 (397): 601–632.

Cusick, Suzanne G. 2008. "'You Are in a Place That Is Out of the World . . .': Music in the Detention Camps of the 'Global War on Terror.'" *Journal of the Society for American Music* 2 (1): 1–26.

Dave, Nomi. 2015. "Music and the Myth of Universality: Sounding Human Rights and Capabilities." *Journal of Human Rights Practice* 7 (1): 1–17.

———. 2019. *The Revolution's Echoes: Music, Politics, and Pleasure in Guinea.* Chicago: University of Chicago Press.

Deng, Francis Mading. 1973. *The Dinka and Their Songs.* Oxford: Oxford University Press.

———. 1976. "Music of the Sudan: Songs of the Dinka Sociological Context." Liner notes for *Music of the Sudan: The Role of Song and Dance in Dinka Society*, Folkways Records, LP.

Deng, Luka Biong. 2010. "Social Capital and Civil War: The Dinka Communities in Sudan's Civil War." *African Affairs* 109 (435): 231–250.

Diehl, Keila. 2002. *Echoes from Dharamsala: Music in the Life of a Tibetan Refugee Community.* Berkeley: University of California Press.

Dunn, Elizabeth. 2017. *No Path Home: Humanitarian Camps and the Grief of Displacement.* Ithaca, NY: Cornell University Press.

Dunn, Elizabeth, and Jason Cons. 2014. "Aleatory Sovereignty and the Rule of Sensitive Spaces." *Antipode* 46 (1): 92–109.

Edkins, Jenny. 2000. "Sovereign Power, Zones of Indistinction, and the Camp." *Alternatives* 25 (1): 3–25.

Eisenberg, Andrew J. 2012. "Hip-Hop and Cultural Citizenship on Kenya's 'Swahili Coast.'" *Africa: The Journal of the International African Institute* 82 (4): 556–578.

Erlmann, Veit. 2004. "But What of the Ethnographic Ear? Anthropology, Sound, and the Senses." In *Hearing Cultures*, edited by Veit Elrmann, 1–20. New York: Berg.

Evans-Pritchard, E. E. 1934. "Imagery in Ngok-Dinka Cattle Names." *Bulletin of the School of Oriental Studies, University of London* 7 (3): 623–628.

Fanon, Frantz. 2008 [1952]. *Black Skin, White Masks*. New York: Grove Press.

FAO. 2015. *South Sudan Livestock Strategy Paper*. Food and Agriculture Organization of the United Nations.

Fassin, Didier. 2007. "Humanitarianism: A Nongovernmental Government." In *Nongovernmental Politics*, edited by Michel Feher, 149–160. New York: Zone Books.

———. 2011. *Humanitarian Reason: A Moral History of the Present*. Berkeley: University of California Press.

Fast, Susan, and Kip Pegley, eds. 2012. *Music, Politics, and Violence*. Middleton, CT: Wesleyan University Press.

Feld, Steven. 1996. "Waterfalls of Song: An Acoustemology of Place Resounding in Bosavi, Papua New Guinea." In *Senses of Place*, edited by Steven Feld and Keith Basso, 91–136. Santa Fe: School of American Research Press.

Fiddian-Qasmiyeh, Elena, Gil Loescher, Katy Long, and Nando Sigona, eds. 2014. *The Oxford Handbook of Refugee and Forced Migration Studies*. Oxford: Oxford University Press.

Finch, Tim. 2015. "In Limbo in World's Oldest Refugee Camps: Where 10 Million People Can Spend Years, or Even Decades." *Index on Censorship* 44 (1): 53–56.

Flahaux, Marie-Laurence, and Bruno Schoumaker. 2016. *Democratic Republic of the Congo: A Migration History Marked by Crises and Restrictions*. Washington, DC: Migration Policy Institute.

Foucault, Michel. 1976. *History of Sexuality*. Vol. 1. Translated by Robert Hurley. London: Penguin Books.

Gabiam, Nell. 2016. *The Politics of Suffering: Syria's Palestinian Refugee Camps*. Bloomington: Indiana University Press.

Galtung, Johan. 1969. "Violence, Peace, and Peace Research." *Journal of Peace Research* 6 (3): 167–191.

———. 1976. "Three Realistic Approaches to Peace: Peacekeeping, Peacemaking, Peacebuilding." *Impact of Science on Society* 26 (1/2): 103–115.

———. 1990. "Cultural Violence." *Journal of Peace Research* 27 (3): 291–305.

———. 1996. *Peace by Peaceful Means: Peace and Conflict, Development and Civilization*. London: Sage.

Geertz, Clifford. 1973. *The Interpretation of Cultures: Selected Essays*. New York: Basic Books.

Gilman, Lisa. 2016. *My Music, My War: The Listening Habits of US Troops in Iraq and Afghanistan*. Middletown, CT: Wesleyan University Press.

Goldstein, Daniel M. 2010. "Toward a Critical Anthropology of Security." *Current Anthropology* 51 (4): 487–517.

Goldstein, Diane. 2015. "Vernacular Turns: Narrative, Local Knowledge, and the Changed Context of Folklore." *Journal of American Folklore* 128 (508): 125–145.

Grabska, Katarzyna. 2014. *Gender, Home and Identity: Nuer Repatriation to Southern Sudan.* Woodbridge, Suffolk: James Currey.

Greenwood, Davydd. 2008. "Theoretical Research, Applied Research, and Action Research: The Deinstitutionalization of Activist Research." In *Engaging Contradictions: Theory, Politics, and Methods of Activist Scholarship,* edited by Charles Hale, 341–366. Berkeley: University of California Press.

Grewal, Baljit Singh. 2003. "Johan Galtung: Positive and Negative Peace." *School of Social Science, Auckland University of Technology* 30:23–26.

Guarak, Mawut Achiecque Mach. 2011. *Integration and Fragmentation of the Sudan: An African Renaissance.* Bloomington: AuthorHouse.

Guilbault, Jocelyne. 2010. "Music, Politics, and Pleasure: Live Soca in Trinidad." *Small Axe: A Caribbean Journal of Criticism* 14 (1): 16–29.

Hale, Charles. 2006. "Activist Research V. Cultural Critique: Indigenous Land Rights and the Contradictions of Politically Engaged Anthropology." *Cultural Anthropology* 21 (1): 96–120.

Hammerstad, Anne. 2014. "The Securization of Forced Migration." In *The Oxford Handbook of Refugee and Forced Migration Studies,* edited by Elena Fiddian-Qasimiyeh, Gil Loescher, Katy Long, and Nando Signona, 265–277. Oxford: University of Oxford Press.

Harrell-Bond, Barbara E. 1986. *Imposing Aid: Emergency Assistance to Refugees.* Oxford: Oxford University Press.

Helbig, Adriana, Nino Tsitsishvili, and Erica Haskell. 2008. "Managing Musical Diversity within Frameworks of Western Development Aid: Views from Ukraine, Georgia, and Bosnia and Herzegovina." *Yearbook for Traditional Music* 40:46–59.

Hemetek, Ursula. 2010. "The Music of Minorities in Austria: Conflict and Intercultural Strategies." In *Applied Ethnomusicology: Historical and Contemporary Approaches,* edited by Klisala Harrison, Elizabeth Mackinlay, and Svanibor Pettan, 182–199. Newcastle upon Tyne, UK: Cambridge Scholars.

Holmes, Seth. 2013. *Fresh Fruit, Broken Bodies: Migrant Farmworkers in the United States.* Berkeley: University of California Press.

Hood, Mantle. 1960. "The Challenge of 'Bi-Musicality.'" *Ethnomusicology* 4 (2): 55–59.

Horst, Cindy. 2006. *Transnational Nomads: How Somalis Cope with Refugee Life in the Dadaab Camps of Kenya.* New York: Berghahn Books.

Hyndman, Jennifer. 2000. *Managing Displacement: Refugees and the Politics of Humanitarianism.* Minneapolis: University of Minnesota Press.

IASC. 2002. *Plan of Action: Codes of Conduct on Protection and Sexual Abuse and Exploitation in Humanitarian Crises.* Inter-Agency Standing Committee.

Impey, Angela. 2002. "Culture, Conservation and Community Reconstruction: Explorations in Advocacy Ethnomusicology and Participatory Action Research in Northern Kwazulu Natal." *Yearbook for Traditional Music* 34:9–24.

———. 2013a. "Keeping in Touch via Cassette: Tracing Dinka Songs from Cattle Camp to Transnational Audio-Letter." *Journal of African Cultural Studies* 25 (2): 197–210.

———. 2013b. "The Poetics of Transitional Justice in Dinka Songs in South Sudan." UNISCI Discussion Papers no. 33. 57–77.

———. 2018. *Song Walking: Women, Music, and Environmental Justice in an African Borderland.* Chicago: University of Chicago Press.

Jaji, Rose. 2012. "Social Technology and Refugee Encampment in Kenya." *Journal of Refugee Studies* 25 (2): 221–238.

Jansen, Bram J. 2008. "Between Vulnerability and Assertiveness: Negotiating Resettlement in Kakuma Refugee Camp, Kenya." *African Affairs* 107 (429): 569–587.

———. 2018. *Kakuma Refugee Camp: Humanitarian Urbanism in Kenya's Accidental City.* London: Zed Books.

Johnson, Bruce, and Martin Cloonan. 2013. *Dark Side of the Tune: Popular Music and Violence.* Burlington, VT: Ashgate.

Joseph, Christopher Odhiambo. 2011. "Theatre of the Oppressor: A Reading of Butake's Play, 'Family Saga.'" *Journal of English and Literature* 2 (3): 53–59.

Juma, Monica Kathina, and Peter Mwangi Kagwanja. 2013. "Securing Refuge from Terror: Refugee Protection in East Africa after September 11." In *Problems of Protection: The UNHCR, Refugees, and Human Rights*, edited by Niklaus Steiner, Mark Gibney, and Gil Loescher, 225–236. New York: Routledge.

Kaiser, Tania. 2006. "Songs, Discos and Dancing in Kiryandongo, Uganda." *Journal of Ethnic and Migration Studies* 32 (2): 183–202.

———. 2008. "Social and Ritual Activity in and out of Place: The 'Negotiation of Locality' in a Sudanese Refugee Settlement." *Mobilities* 3 (3): 375–395.

Kartomi, Margaret. 2010. "The Musical Arts in Aceh after the Tsunami and the Conflict." In *Applied Ethnomusicology: Historical and Contemporary Approaches*, edited by Klisala Harrison, Elizabeth Mackinlay, and Svanibor Pettan, 200–213. Newcastle upon Tyne, UK: Cambridge Scholars.

Kent, George. 2008. "Unpeaceful Music." In *Music and Conflict Transformation: Harmonies and Dissonances in Geopolitics*, edited by Olivier Urbain, 104–111. London: I. B. Tauris.

Kidula, Jean N. 2012. "The Local and Global in Kenyan Rap and Hip Hop Culture." In *Hip Hop Africa: New African Music in a Globalizing World*, edited by Eric Charry, 171–186. Bloomington: Indiana University Press.

———. 2013. *Music in Kenyan Christianity: Logooli Religious Song.* Bloomington: Indiana University Press.

Kun, Josh D. 2000. "The Aural Border." *Theatre Journal* 52 (1): 1–21.

LaBelle, Brandon. 2018. *Sonic Agency: Sound and Emergent Forms of Resistance.* London: Goldsmiths Press.

Lienhardt, Godfrey. 1961. *Divinity and Experience: The Religion of the Dinka.* Oxford: Clarendon Press.

Le Lay, Maëline. 2020. "Humanitarian Theater in the Great Lakes Region: In Pursuit of Performativity." In *The Art of Emergency: Aesthetics and Aid in African Crises,* edited by Chérie Rivers Ndaliko and Samuel Mark Anderson, 229–248. Oxford: Oxford University Press.

Lipsitz, George. 2008. "Breaking the Chains and Steering the Ship: How Activism Can Help Change Teaching and Scholarship." In *Engaging Contradictions: Theory, Politics, and Methods of Activist Scholarship,* edited by Charles Hale, 88–114. Berkeley: University of California Press.

Long, Joanna C. 2006. "Border Anxiety in Palestine–Israel." *Antipode* 38 (1): 107–127.

Long, Katy. 2014. "Rethinking 'Durable' Solutions." In *The Oxford Handbook of Refugee and Forced Migration Studies,* edited by Elena Fiddian-Qasimiyeh, Gil Loescher, Katy Long, and Nando Signona, 475–487. Oxford: University of Oxford Press.

Lorde, Audrey. 2007 [1984]. "Uses of the Erotic: The Erotic as Power." In *Sexualities and Communication in Everyday Life: A Reader,* edited by Karen E. Lovaas and Mercilee M Jenkins, 87–91. Thousand Oaks, CA: Sage.

Lutz, Catherine, and Geoffrey M. White. 1986. "The Anthropology of Emotions." *Annual Review of Anthropology* 15 (1): 405–436.

Madison, Soyini D. 2010. *Acts of Activism: Human Rights as Radical Performance.* Cambridge: Cambridge University Press.

———. 2011. *Critical Ethnography: Method, Ethics, and Performance.* Thousand Oaks, CA: Sage.

Malkki, Liisa. 1995a. *Purity and Exile: Violence, Memory, and National Cosmology among Hutu Refugees in Tanzania.* Chicago: University of Chicago Press.

———. 1995b. "Refugees and Exile: From 'Refugee Studies' to the National Order of Things." *Annual Review of Anthropology* 24 (1): 495–523.

———. 1996. "Speechless Emissaries: Refugees, Humanitarianism, and Dehistoricization." *Cultural Anthropology* 11 (3): 377–404.

Marriage, Zoë. 2020. *Cultural Resistance and Security from Below: Power and Escape through Capoeira.* New York: Routledge.

Martin, Alison. 2021. "Plainly Audible: Listening Intersectionally to the Amplified Noise Act in Washington, DC." *Journal of Popular Music Studies* 33 (4): 104–125.

Mbembe, Achille. 2001. *On the Postcolony.* Berkeley: University of California Press.

———. 2005. "Variations on the Beautiful in the Congolese World of Sounds."
    Politique Africaine (4): 69–91.

McCabe, Terrence J. 2011. *Cattle Bring Us to Our Enemies: Turkana Ecology,*
    Politics, and Raiding in a Disequilibrium System. Ann Arbor: University of
    Michigan Press.

McDonald, David. 2009. "Poetics and the Performance of Violence in Israel/
    Palestine." *Ethnomusicology* 53 (1): 58–85.

———. 2013. *My Voice Is My Weapon: Music, Nationalism and the Poetics of*
    Palestinian Resistance. Durham, NC: Duke University Press.

Merriam, Alan. 1964. *The Anthropology of Music.* Evanston, IL: Northwestern
    University Press.

Montclos, Marc-Antoine Perouse de, and Peter Mwangi Kagwanja. 2000.
    "Refugee Camps or Cities? The Socio-economic Dynamics of the Dadaab
    and Kakuma Camps in Northern Kenya." *Journal of Refugee Studies* 13 (2):
    205–222.

Ndaliko, Chérie Rivers. 2016. *Necessary Noise: Music, Film, and Charitable*
    Imperialism in the East of Congo. New York: Oxford University Press.

Ndaliko, Chérie Rivers, and Samuel Mark Anderson. 2020. *The Art of Emergency.*
    New York: Oxford University Press.

Ndĩgĩrĩgĩ, Gĩchingiri. 2017. "Popular Songs and Resistance: Ngũgĩ wa Thiong'o's
    Maitũ Njugĩra." *Popular Music and Society* 40 (1): 22–36.

Novak, Paolo. 2007. "Place and Afghan Refugees: A Contribution to Turton."
    Journal of Refugee Studies 20 (4): 551–578.

Ntarangwi, Mwenda. 2009. *East African Hip Hop: Youth Culture and Globalization.*
    Champaign: University of Illinois Press.

Ochoa-Gautier, Ana Maria. 2015. *Aurality: Listening and Knowledge in Nineteenth-*
    Century Colombia. Durham, NC: Duke University Press.

O'Connell, John Morgan. 2011. "Music in War, Music for Peace: A Review
    Article." *Ethnomusicology* 55 (1): 112–127.

Oka, Rahul. 2014. "Coping with the Refugee Wait: The Role of Consumption,
    Normalcy, and Dignity in Refugee Lives at Kakuma Refugee Camp, Kenya."
    American Anthropologist 116 (1): 23–37.

Oring, Elliott. 2004. "Folklore and Advocacy." *Journal of Folklore Research*
    41 (2/3): 259–267.

Owens, Patricia. 2009. "Reclaiming 'Bare Life'?: Against Agamben on Refugees."
    International Relations 23 (4): 567–582.

Perman, Tony. 2010. "Dancing in Opposition: Muchongoyo, Emotion, and the
    Politics of Performance in Southeastern Zimbabwe." *Ethnomusicology* 54 (3):
    425–451.

Perullo, Alex. 2011. *Live from Dar es Salaam: Popular Music and Tanzania's Music*
    Economy. Bloomington: Indiana University Press.

Pilzer, Joshua D. 2014. "Music and Dance in the Japanese Military 'Comfort Women' System: A Case Study in the Performing Arts, War, and Sexual Violence." *Women and Music: A Journal of Gender and Culture* 18 (1): 1–23.

Pinto García, María E. 2014. "Music and Reconciliation in Colombia: Opportunities and Limitations of Songs Composed by Victims." *Music and Arts in Action* 4 (2): 24–51.

———. 2016. "Cesar Lopez and the Escopetarra." In *Music, Power and Liberty: Sound, Song and Melody as Instruments of Change,* edited by Olivier Urbain and Craig Robertson, 185–203. London: I. B. Tauris.

Ramadan, Adam. 2012. "Spatializing the Refugee Camp." *Transactions of the Institute of British Geographers* 38 (1): 65–77.

Rasmussen, Anne, Angela Impey, Rachel Beckles Wilson, Ozan Aksoy, Denise Gill, and Michael Frishkopf. 2019. "Call and Response: SEM President's Roundtable 2016, 'Ethnomusicological Responses to the Contemporary Dynamics of Migrants and Refugees.'" *Ethnomusicology* 63 (2): 279–314.

Rawlence, Ben. 2016. *City of Thorns: Nine Lives in the World's Largest Refugee Camp.* New York: Picador.

Reed, Daniel. 2016. *Abidjan USA: Music, Dance, and Mobility in the Lives of Four Ivorian Immigrants.* Bloomington: Indiana University Press.

Reyes, Adelaida. 1999. *Songs of the Caged, Songs of the Free: Music and the Vietnamese Refugee Experience.* Philadelphia: Temple University Press.

Ritter, Jonathan. 2012. "Contemporary Discourses of Truth and Memory: The Peruvian Truth Commission and the Canción Social Ayacuchana." In *Music, Politics, and Violence,* edited by Susan Fast and Kip Pegley, 197–222. Middletown, CT: Wesleyan University Press.

Robbins, Joel. 2013. "Beyond the Suffering Subject: Toward an Anthropology of the Good." *Journal of the Royal Anthropological Institute* 19 (3): 447–462.

Rose, Tricia. 1994. *Black Noise: Rap Music and Black Culture in Contemporary America.* Middletown, CT: Wesleyan University Press.

Sandoval, Elaine. 2016. "Music in Peacebuilding: A Critical Literature Review." *Journal of Peace Education* 13 (3): 200–217.

Scalettaris, Giulia. 2007. "Refugee Studies and the International Refugee Regime: A Reflection on a Desirable Separation." *Refugee Survey Quarterly* 26 (3): 36–50.

Schmidt, Anna. 2003. "FMO Thematic Guide: Camps versus Settlements." *Forced Migration Online,* ALNAP, https://www.alnap.org/system/files/content/resource/files/main/fmo021.pdf.

Scott-Smith, Tom. 2016. "Humanitarian Neophilia: The 'Innovation Turn' and Its Implications." *Third World Quarterly* 37 (12): 2229–2251.

Shank, Michael, and Lisa Schirch. 2008. "Strategic Arts-Based Peacebuilding." *Peace & Change* 33 (2): 217–242.

Small, Christopher. 1998. *Musicking: The Meanings of Performing and Listening.*
Middletown, CT: Wesleyan University Press.

Steingo, Gavin. 2015. "Sound and Circulation: Immobility and Obduracy in
South African Electronic Music." *Ethnomusicology Forum* 24 (1): 102–123.

———. 2016. *Kwaito's Promise: Music and the Aesthetics of Freedom in South
Africa.* Chicago: University of Chicago Press.

Stoever, Jennifer L. 2016. *The Sonic Color Line: Race and the Cultural Politics of
Listening.* New York: New York University Press.

Stokes, Martin, ed. 1994. *Ethnicity, Identity and Music: The Musical Construction
of Place.* Providence, RI: Berg.

Stone, Ruth. 2010 [1982]. *Let the Inside Be Sweet: The Interpretation of Music Event
among the Kpelle of Liberia.* Bloomington: Indiana University Press.

Sugarman, Jane C. 2010. "Kosova Calls for Peace: Song, Myth and War in an Age
of Global Media." In *Music and Conflict,* edited by John Morgan O'Connell and
Salwa El-Shawan Castelo-Branco, 17–45. Champaign: University of Illinois
Press.

Sylvan, Robin. 2002. *Traces of the Spirit: The Religious Dimensions of Popular
Music.* New York: New York University Press.

Teferra, Gerawork. 2022. "Kakuma Refugee Camp: Pseudopermanence in
Permanent Transcience." *Africa Today* 69 (1–2): 162–189.

Thiong'o, Ngũgĩ wa. 2005 [1986]. *Decolonizing the Mind: The Politics of Language
in African Literature.* Nairobi: James Currey.

Turino, Thomas. 2000. *Nationalists, Cosmopolitans, and Popular Music in
Zimbabwe.* Chicago: University of Chicago Press.

———. 2008. *Music as Social Life: The Politics of Participation.* Chicago:
University of Chicago Press.

Turner, Thomas. 2007. *The Congo Wars: Conflict, Myth and Reality.* New York:
Zed Books.

Turton, David. 2005. "The Meaning of Place in a World of Movement: Lessons
from Long-Term Field Research in Southern Ethiopia." *Journal of Refugee
Studies* 18 (3): 258–280.

Tyler, Imogen. 2013. *Revolting Subjects: Social Abjection and Resistance in
Neoliberal Britain.* New York: Zed Books.

UNHCR. 2015. *UNHCR Global Appeal 2015 Update: Ensuring Protection for
People of Concern.* United Nations High Commissioner for Refugees.

———. 2021. *UNHCR Global Trends: Forced Displacement in 2021.* United
Nations High Commissioner for Refugees.

UNHCR and Save the Children UK. 2002. *Sexual Violence and Exploitation:
The Experience of Refugee Children in Liberia, Guinea, and Sierra Leone.* United
Nations High Commissioner for Refugees, Save the Children UK.

Urbain, Olivier, ed. 2008. *Music and Conflict Transformation.* London: I. B. Tauris.

Van Buren, Kathleen J. 2010. "Applied Ethnomusicology and HIV and AIDS: Responsibility, Ability, and Action." *Ethnomusicology* 54 (2): 202–223.

Verdirame, Guglielmo, and Barbara Harrell-Bond. 2005. *Rights in Exile: Janus-Faced Humanitarianism.* New York: Berghahn Books.

Wadiru, Stella. 2012. "Sounding the War: Acholi Popular Music in the Peace Process in Northern Uganda." In *Ethnomusicology in East Africa: Perspectives from Uganda and Beyond,* edited by Sylvia Nannyonga-Tamusuza and Thomas Solomon, 177–187. Kampala, Uganda: Fountain.

Walters, William. 2011. "Foucault and Frontiers: Notes on the Birth of the Humanitarian Border." In *Governmentality: Current Issues and Future Challenges,* edited by Ulrich Bröckling, Suzanne Krausman, and Thomas Lemke, 138–164. New York: Routledge.

Waseda, Minako. 2005. "Extraordinary Circumstances, Exceptional Practices: Music in Japanese American Concentration Camps." *Journal of Asian American Studies* 8 (2): 171–209.

Webster-Kogen, Ilana. 2018. *Citizen Azmari: Making Ethiopian Music in Tel Aviv.* Middletown, CT: Wesleyan University Press.

Western, Tom. 2020. "Listening with Displacement: Sound, Citizenship, and Disruptive Representations of Migration." *Migration and Society* 3 (1): 294–309.

Willson, Rachel Beckles. 2011. "Music Teachers as Missionaries: Understanding Europe's Recent Dispatches to Ramallah." *Ethnomusicology Forum* 20 (3): 301–325.

———. 2013. *Orientalism and Musical Mission.* Cambridge: Cambridge University Press.

Wirtz, Elizabeth. 2017. "The Inhumanity of Humanitarian Aid: Gender and Violence in a Kenyan Refugee Camp." PhD diss., Purdue University.

Wright, Terence. 2002. "Moving Images: The Media Representation of Refugees." *Visual Studies* 17 (1): 53–66.

Yuval-Davis, Nira. 2011. *The Politics of Belonging: Intersectional Contestations.* London: Sage.

Zetter, Roger. 1991. "Labelling Refugees: Forming and Transforming a Bureaucratic Identity." *Journal of Refugee Studies* 4 (1): 39–62.

———. 2007. "More Labels, Fewer Refugees: Remaking the Refugee Label in an Era of Globalization." *Journal of Refugee Studies* 20 (2): 172–192.

INDEX

abjection, social, 128–131, 133
activist research, 10–16
aesthetics: and belonging, 23, 49, 99, 154, 166; of ethno-nationalism, 167; of humanitarianism, 2, 8, 23, 32–33, 56, 153–154, 166–167; of intervention, 8
affective economy, 43; of pleasure, 50, 59; of suffering, 51, 61
Africa's Great War, 44
Afrostars Entertainment, 18, 43, 162, 171; and labor issues, 71–72, 85–86; mantra of 47–48; performances by, 51–53, 57
Agamben, Giorgio, 78, 132, 157, 166
Agier, Michel, 22
Ahmed, Sara, 43
aid: apolitical aspects of, 156; economy of, 29, 82; inequality of, 7, 32, 45; performative critiques of, 3; technologies of, 95–96. See also arts-based humanitarianism / musical aid; humanitarian labor
Allen, Lara, 53
altruistic subordination, 76–78, 168
Anderson, Samuel Mark, 145, 161–162

Appadurai, Arjun, 31
Arts-based humanitarianism / musical aid, 11, 32; impacts of, 8, 57, 72–73, 145, 162; intangible benefits of, 67, 72, 142; rethinking of, 68–73, 167–170; in systems of inequality, 32, 58–59, 75, 78, 110–112, 142. See also edutainment activities; music production projects; peace; theater for development (TfD) groups
A Solution, 56, 172
asylum seeker, as label, 9, 48, 165
aurality 23–24, 145; and the peace discourse, 146–147. See also listening; listening ear
Avorgbedor, Daniel Kodzo, 117

Bakewell, Oliver, 5–6
bans: on cattle herding, 95, 111–113; on Christian activities, 14, 115–116, 120, 127–133; on Dinka weekly dances, 24, 91–92, 104–106, 129, 130
bare life, 166
Barnett, Michael, 156
Barnouw, Erik, 47

Barre, Siad, 26
belonging: disqualified ways of, 38, 164, 171–172; multiscalar forms of, 124; music and types of, 22; to music scenes, 43, 60; nation-state logic of, 21–22, 28; politics of, 22–23; through religion, 117, 124, 137–138; social spaces of, 31, 106, 108–109, 124, 166; sonic forms of, 30–32; sonic politics of, 21–24, 37–38, 165–167. *See also* identity
Besteman, Catherine, 28–29
bi-musicality approach, 13
Black, Chris, 48, 49
Black Snake Swagger, 49
Boal, Augusto, 83
borders: and European colonialism, 26; externalization of, 8, 28–29. *See also* containment; international refugee regime (IRR)
Born Town Creations, 81
Brankamp, Hanno, 7–8, 36, 74, 120, 170–171
Brower, Lowell, 4, 98–99
Buduburam Refugee Camp (Accra, Ghana), 5
bul (double-headed drum), 100, 101
Burundi, 26, 44

carceral humanitarianism, 170–171
Cardoso, Leonardo, 23
Carter, Jimmy, 150
cattle: and conflict, 93–95; and herding bans, 95, 111–113; and personality oxen, 94; and portability of culture, 98–99; and significance to Dinka, 93–94. *See also* Dinka refugees; Dinka weekly dances; pastoralism
Chávez, Alex, 23–24

Christian activities: bans on, 14, 115–16, 120, 127–133; campaign for, 131–133; on Christmas Day, 134; coping through, 117, 124, 127, 133–137; and midnight services, 17, 115, 116, 128, 135, 138; on New Year's holiday, 135–37; and security, 116–117, 131, 137–139. *See also mathira* (religious ceremonial procession)
Christianity: and colonialism, 134; in Kakuma 115–116; and nonheteronormative identities, 138–139; transnational, 31
civil liberties, denial of, 78, 92, 145, 157, 161
colonialism, 25–26, 74, 84; and Christianity, 134; and pastoralism 96–97, 112
composing aid, as concept, 16
Comprehensive Peace Agreement (CPA, 2005), 29, 93
Congo, Democratic Republic of the, 17, 20–21, 26, 29, 32, 44, 72
Congolese Kinyarwanda-speaking people, 98–99
containment, 27, 143, 165, 170–171; beyond culture of, 111–113; culture of, 91–93; subject-making effects of, 108–110; and xenophobic attitudes, 129. *See also* borders; encampment(s)
Cooper's Camp (West Bengal, India), 6
Copenhagen School, 116
COVID-19 pandemic, 20
cultural flows, 31
cultural violence, 144–145
curfews, 144, 171; and Dinka dances, 93, 104; and entertainment, 57–58; and NGO events, 66; and the police, 14, 36, 112, 120, 129, 137; and sexual misconduct, 34–35

Dadaab Refugee Complex (Kenya), 5–7: establishment of 27; insecurities of, 118–119; relocation from, 29; precarity of 33; and threats of closure, 137, 169–170

Daley, Patricia, 74

dance, 1–4, 69, 91; and curfews, 57–58; and immobility, 93, 108–112; social cohesion through, 103. *See also* curfews; Dinka weekly dances; music

Danish Refugee Council (DRC), 69

Dassanetch of southern Ethiopia, 97

Dave, Nomi, 72–73

decolonial performance, 83–85

Democratic Republic of the Congo, 17, 20–21, 29, 41; and the First Congo War (1996–1997), 44; independence of, 26; NGO art projects in, 32; and the Second Congo War (1998–2003), 44

Deng, Francis Mading, 94, 98, 103, 135

Deng, Luka Biong, 94

Department of Refugee Affairs (DRA), 12, 106

deregel dance style, 100–101, 103, 114n8

Dharamsala, India, Tibetan refugees in, 5, 29

Dinka music, 13; audio-letters, 99; ox songs, 98, 103, 109, 110; wrestling songs, 100, 109. *See also* Dinka weekly dances

Dinka refugees, 17, 91; cattle's significance to, 93–94; and civil unrest (2014), 126; and ethno-national politics, 109; and Pan-Dinka alliance, 109, 113; regional affiliations of, 106–107, 109; violent stereotypes of, 105–106. *See also* Christian activities; pastoralism

Dinka weekly dances, 99–101, 112, 162; ban on, 24, 91–92, 104–106, 129, 130; campaign to reinstate, 106–108; conflicts at, 104–105; and courtship, 102–104; and curfew restrictions, 93, 104; and *deregel* dance style, 100–101, 103, 114n8; and encampment, 109–110; and herding traditions, 92; and institutional constraints, 92–93; instruments in, 100–101, 107, 108; locations of, 101; LWF support of, 107–108, 109–110; as place-making activities, 108–109; and political tensions, 106–107. *See also* cattle; Dinka music; pastoralism

displaced persons, as category, 166

dissent, 24, 35–38. *See also* protests; resistance

dissonance, 24, 35–38, 84–85

"Do 1 Thing" UNHCR campaign video, 3

Don Bosco Kakuma, 35, 116, 132

durable solutions, 28, 92, 169

East Africa: colonialism and migration in, 26, 74. *See also individual countries*

East African Community (EAC), 86

East African music industry, the 31, 49, 55, 58; belonging to, 49, 83–86; commodification of music in, 68

East African Protectorate, 26

Ebei (Turkana war leader), 96–97

edutainment activities, 11; as bottom-up approaches, 69–70, 84; radical approaches to, 83–85; and social problems, 50–51, 56, 60, 67–69, 84–85. *See also* arts-based humanitarianism / musical aid; music production projects; theater for development (TfD) groups

Eisenberg, Andrew, 80

El-Shabaab, 12, 137

emotion, 42, 61; and camp governance, 110; cultural politics of, 43; and social abjection, 129

encampment(s), 5–8; and border externalization, 28; humanitarian, 8; and music for peace projects, 71, 143, 145–46, 150–155; precarity of, 7, 14, 33–35; problems with, 7; as protracted refugee situations, 6; protraction of in Kenya, 24–30; rethinking of, 170–172; structural inequalities of, 15–16, 22–23, 32, 35, 59, 78, 162, 168; variety of, 5–6. *See also* containment; international refugee regime (IRR)

entertainment: commodified, 46–47, 65, 68, 172; limits of, 57–60; nighttime, 9, 35, 57–58, 80–81, 112; politics of, 46–48; social role of, 47, 56; and youth talent competitions, 49–50. *See also* pleasure

Episcopal Church of the Sudan (ECS), 18, 115. *See also* Christian activities; *mathira* (religious ceremonial procession)

erotic, the, 59

E-Squad, 17, 79–80, 86

Ethiopia, 24, 29, 96, 150. *See also* Oromo

ethnomusicology: critical activist, 12–16; of migration, 9;

Europe: and durable solutions, 28; and the Refugee Convention (1951), 27; and Syrian refugees, 137, 171. *See also* colonialism

exile, politics of, 4–5

Fanon, Frantz, 11

Fassin, Didier, 6

Feld, Steven, 109

FilmAid International (FAI), 12, 55, 69, 148; and music competitions, 20; and studio recording, 79, 83; and youth talent competitions, 50

Food and Agriculture Organization of the United Nations (FAO), 93

forced migrants / forced migration, 3–9; as category, 166; causes of, 150, 169; debates about, 21–22; and economic migrants, 85–87; protection of, 64; representations of, 9. *See also* borders; encampment(s); international refugee regime; refugee(s)

Foucault, Michel, 108

fundraising activities, 3, 157–159

G4S (British multinational security company), 66, 129

Gabiam, Nell, 45

Galtung, Johan, 144, 160, 161, 163

garden, refugee camp as, 15–16

Garissa University attack, 137

Geertz, Clifford, 15

Gifted Music Group, 81

Global Appeal Update (UNHCR, 2015), 70, 76

Global Trends (UNHCR report), 6, 61

Goldstein, Diane, 70

Grabska, Katarzyna, 97

Grandi, Filippo, 141

Great Lakes refugees, 48, 70, 83, 126, 153–154

GTZ (German agency) solar cooker project, 95–96

Guilbault, Jocelyne, 43, 49

Hale, Charles, 12

hardship post, 45–46

Harrell-Bond, Barbara, 3, 16, 78

hip hop: and belonging, 21; in East Africa, 64–65; as multicultural performance, 153–154; and pleasure, 51–57; and refashioning identities, 48–49
Holmes, Seth, 14
Hood, Mantle, 13
Horst, Cindy, 118
humanitarian border, 8
humanitarianism: carceral qualities of, 170–171; innovation in (neophilia), 75; politics of, 4–10, 20. See also arts-based humanitarianism / musical aid; humanitarian labor
humanitarian government, 6, 33, 161
humanitarian labor: and British colonialism, 74; and cost of music-making, 17, 54, 76, 79–81; inequality of, 73–76; and refugee incentive workers, 34, 74, 96, 110. See also altruistic subordination
humanitarian violence, 36
Hyndman, Jennifer, 32–33, 92

identity: bureaucratic labeling and, 48, 94; formation of, 7, 31, 48; herder, 98–99; intersectional, 24; music and national, 5; music and religious, 116; nonheteronormative, 138–139; through popular music, 64–68. See also belonging
immobility, 93; and music/dance, 93, 108–112; politics of, 93, 109, 112. See also mobility
Impey, Angela, 22, 98, 99
Imposing Aid (Harrell-Bond), 16
incentive workers, refugee, 34, 74, 96, 110
"innovation turn," 75
insecurities, 14, 35, 104, 111; and Christian activities, 116–117,

135–137; of protection, 117–20; types of, 118. See also precarity of refugee camps; security
Inter-Agency Standing Committee, 130
international days, 1–4, 30, 32, 53
International Organization for Migration (IOM); Peace Centre of, 30, 141, 151–152, 155, 157; radio station of, 50, 69
international refugee regime (IRR), 27–29
International Rescue Committee (IRC), 11, 12, 69, 164
intersectionality, 24, 153
intervention, aesthetics of, 8
IsraAid, 12

Jal, Emmanuel, 50, 153–154
Jansen, Bram J., 28, 97, 119–120, 127
Jesuit Refugee Service (JRS), 12, 116
Jolie, Angelina, 3
Joseph, Christopher Odhiambo, 168

Kaiser, Tania, 4, 108–109
Kakuma, 18n1
Kakuma, town of (Turkana County, Kenya), 25, 33; and curfew policy, 35; nightlife in, 57
Kakuma Refugee Camp (northwestern Kenya), 1–4; establishment of, 25; insecurities of, 118–119; protraction of, 24–30; and threats of closure, 29, 169–170; as urbanized site, 44, 57, 65, 96, 97. See also sonic politics of belonging
"Kakuma Rocks" (song and music video), 50, 153–154
Kakuma Sound, 69
Kakuma Youth Peace Ambassadors (KYPA), 148

Kalobeyei Integrated Social and Economic Development Program (KSEDP), 170–171
Kalobeyei refugee camp (Kenya), 5, 27, 152, 170–171
Kamĩrĩĩthũ Popular Theater Experiment, 83–84
Kanere, 17, 158–159, 169
Kent, George, 156
Kenya: and the East African Protectorate, 26; migration to, 26–29; protraction of encampment in, 24–30; refugee policies in, 86, 92, 169–170, 172
Kenyan-Turkana people: and arts-based peace programs, 148–149, 151–152, 160; and British colonialism, 96–97; and Dinka pastoralists, 94–95; and foreign aid, 170; marginalization of 34, 45, 82, 96–97, 113n5
Kenya Television Network (KTN), 45
Kenyatta, Uhuru, 137
Kerry, John, 137
Kidula, Jean Ngoya, 64, 65, 116
Kiir, Salva, 93
King Moses, 17, 20–21, 36–38, 46, 86, 171; as Afrostars Entertainment leader, 20, 31, 48–49; and cost of music-making, 79; "Ma Champagne" by (with Queen Lisa), 56; "Maesabu Yasiku" by 20; "Mkali" by, 20, 52; performance by, 52–53
King of the Dance, 48
Kirkland, Catherine, 47
kwaito music, 47, 56

labeling, refugee, 9, 19n8, 42–43, 48–49, 165–166
LaBelle, Brandon, 24, 82

labor rights of refugees, 15, 64, 73–76, 83–87; infringements on, 74–75, 77, 81–82, 85; and the Refugee Act (2022), 86–87; and work permits, 74, 86. See also humanitarian labor
läc (Dinka wooden staffs), 99
Lienhardt, Godfrey, 94
"Let's Party" (Street Boyz), 56, 172
"Life Is a War" (song and music video), 146–147
listening, 10; intersectional, 24; politics of, 37–38; and precarity, 33; situated forms of, 23–24. See also aurality
listening ear, 145–147, 154, 160
local integration, 28, 92, 169
Lodwar, Kenya, 80
Lorde, Audre, 59
Lost Boys of South Sudan, discourse of, 139
Lutheran World Federation (LWF), the 2, 12, 116: arts programming by, 20, 50, 69, 148; compound administered by, 63; Peace Building Unit of, 104; and the Youth Congress, 35

Machar, Riek, 93
Madison, Soyini, 168
Mae La Camp (Thailand), 6
Maitũ Njugĩra (Thiong'o), 83–84
Malkki, Liisa, 28, 58, 156
"Mapenzi Gani" (Queen Lisa and A Solution), 56, 172
Martin, Alison, 24
mathira (religious ceremonial procession), 115–16, 120–24; as communal activity, 122–124; marginalization of, 128–130, 138; reinstatement of, 133.

See also Christian activities; religion

Mbembe, Achille, 9, 47

media: humanitarian responses to, 6–7; representations of refugees in, 126–127, 147

Meheba refugee settlement (Zambia), 5

Menelik, King, 96

Migration Policy Institute, 44

minimalism, aesthetics of, 167

Ministry of State for Immigration and Registration, 2

mobility: of humanitarian aid, 32; of music, 30–31; restrictions on, 5–6, 32, 86, 92, 95–96, 158–60, 170. *See also* immobility

modernity, notions of, 97

Mombasa refugee camps (Kenya), 27

Mukarwego Refugee Camp (Rwanda), 98

multiculturalism, 150–156, 159, 162

music: as aid and for aid, 78; belonging through, 22; boundary-making effects of, 23, 109, 150, 153, 154, 167; and immobility, 93; and peace, 143; and state security, 117; studies of in refugee camps, 4–5; synergistic capacity of, 116–117; valuations of, 23–24. *See also* belonging; Christian activities; dance; Dinka weekly dances; *mathira* (religious ceremonial procession); theater for development (TfD) groups

musicking, 23, 38, 38n2, 84, 164

music production projects, 8–9, 55, 79, 152; limits of, 58–59; *Refugeenius* (Octopizzo) project, 56, 60; and studio recording, 55, 59, 79, 83. *See also* arts-based humanitarianism / musical aid; edutainment activities

Nanok, H. E. Josphat Koli, 152

Napata Fairgrounds (Kakuma Refugee Camp), 1, 30, 53, 54, 151

National Council of Churches of Kenya (NCCK), 12, 35, 69, 116

national security, 119, 137, 169

nation-state system, the: abject subjects of, 130–131; and belonging, 21, 28; and the humanitarian system, 156

Ndaliko, Chérie Rivers, 8, 9, 32, 72, 144–145, 161–62, 167, 168

neoliberalism, 68, 75, 129

nighttime entertainment, 80–81; restrictions on, 9, 35, 57–58, 80, 112

noise, 23–24, 38, 84, 138, 146, 155–157

nongovernmental organizations (NGOs): arts-based projects of, 2, 50–51, 63, 67, 68–69; and compensation, 71–73; and rights-based rhetoric, 64. *See also* arts-based humanitarianism / musical aid; *and specific aid organizations*

non-refoulement, 7, 64

Norwegian Refugee Council (NRC), 35

Ntarangwi, Mwenda, 64–65

Nuer refugees, 97, 125–126

occupied enclave, 36, 120

Octopizzo, 55–56

Octopizzo Foundation (OF), 12, 55, 69; and the Artists for Refugees project, 152; and studio recording, 79

Oromo, 29, 45, 155–157

orphans and vulnerable children (OVC), 45

Oxford Handbook of Refugee and Forced Migration Studies, 42

Palestinian refugee camps, 5, 6, 29, 45

Pan-Africanist ideology, 49, 154

participatory approaches: to aid, 69–70, 84, 148, 162; to research, 8 12

pastoralism, 91–93; and conflict, 93–95; and encampment, 93–97; recognition of, 111–113; silence of, 94–98. *See also* cattle; Dinka refugees; Dinka weekly dances

peace: aural imaginaries of, 146–48; discourse of, 142; loudness of, 141–144; and multiculturalism, 150–155; negative, 144, 157–59; positive, 161–163; segregating sounds of, 145–146; structure of, 163; and uneven power relations, 142–143; violence and, 143, 144

people living with HIV and AIDS (PLWHA), 45

permits, 57, 80, 86, 120, 129, 133

persons with disabilities (PwD), 45

Perullo, Alex, 68

Philippines, refugee camps in, 4–5

Place-making activities, 108–109, 166

pleasure, 171; affective economy of, 50, 59; bureaucratic limits on, 45; as collective force, 53; limits on, 59–60; in live performance, 51–53; in material goods, 46–47, 51, 52; as political, 37–38, 43, 47, 53, 60–62; and public intimacies, 49; and sound quality, 53–57; and suffering, 61–62. *See also* entertainment; hip hop

policing, militarized, 7–8, 36, 120, 129, 170–171

politics: of entertainment, 46–48; of music production, 58–59; of national self-determination, 29; of pleasure, 37–38, 43, 47, 53, 60–62; sonic, of belonging, 21–24, 37–38,

165–167; of suffering, 45. *See also* power; sound-politics

power: and biopolitics, 9, 75, 139–140n2; of the erotic, 59–60; as productive force, 108. *See also* dissent; protests; resistance

precarity of refugee camps, 7, 14, 33–35; and food rations, 7, 118, 161; and sound quality, 53–54. *See also* insecurities

protection: insecurities of, 117–119; through religious worship, 135–136; types of, 117

protests, 2–3, 37, 63–64, 74, 84–85, 139, 155–157

protracted refugee situation (PRS), 6

pseudopermanence, 7

Queen Lisa, 48–49, 56, 172

recording studios, 55, 59, 79–80, 83

refugee(s): definition of (Refugee Convention 1951), 27; as infantile, 105–106, 129, 133; 130; as out of place, 28; status determination of, 45; as suffering subjects, 42, 48, 58; as violent, 105–106, 128–31, 144, 149. *See also* forced migrants / forced migration; labeling, refugee; voices

Refugee Act (Kenya, 2022), 86, 172

refugee camps: conditions in, 13–14; as designated areas, 5–6; as garden, concept of 15–16; political role of, 29; proliferation of, 168; as protracted refugee situation, 6; socioeconomic thresholds of, 33–34; as sites of control, 7, 22, 33, 109, 157; uses and functions of, 5–8; varieties of, 5–6. *See also* encampment(s)

Refugee Consortium of Kenya (RCK), 12

refugeeness, social, 58

Refugeenius (Octopizzo), 56, 60

Refugee Studies Center (Oxford), 75

religion: belonging through, 117, 124, 137–138; and music, 116–117. *See also* Christian activities; Christianity; Episcopal Church of the Sudan (ECS)

repatriation, 28, 61, 92, 118–119, 169

resettlement, 28; 45, 92, 169; quotas for, 14, 28, 113n3, 172

resistance: micro forms of, 148; through music, 2–3, 8–9, 85–86, 117; and the politics of belonging, 23; and social abjection, 131. *See also* dissent; power; protests

Robbins, Joel, 62n1, 62n2

Rose, Tricia, 48

Rwanda, 26

Rwanda, Mukarwego Refugee Camp, 98–99

Sahrawis, 29

Sandoval, Elaine Chang, 150

-scapes, 31

Schirch, Lisa, 141–142

Scott-Smith, Tom, 75

securitization, 116–117, 120, 139–140n2; and social abjection, 128–131, 133

security: concepts of, 116; discursive approach to, 116; humanitarianized forms of, 9; national, 119, 137, 169; and nighttime entertainment, 35, 58; and power inequalities, 116; and restrictions on Christian worship, 115–117; rethinking of, 137–139. *See also* insecurities

segregated care: and musical aid, 78; sounds of, 32–35, 167. *See also* curfews; nighttime entertainment

sexual and gender-based violence (SGBV), 45, 63, 95, 118, 120, 149; and culture of disbelief, 120; as sexual misconduct, 34–35, 130; and social abjection, 130

Shank, Michael, 141–142

silence, 38, 64, 76; of pastoralism, 94–98; and the peace discourse, 149–150

Smart Djaba, 31, 41, 43, 46, 47–48, 61, 171; "Born to Shine" by, 65–67; "From Refugee to Superstar" by, 67–68; "I Am the Director" by, 67; on NGO arts-based projects, 77–78; "Nimedata" by, 50; performance by, 52–53, 65–66; "Piga Photo" by, 53; popularity of, 66–67; "She Want" by, 81; "Show Dem Love" by, 81

Somalia, 6, 150

Somali refugees, 26–27, 45, 86

sonic color line, 145

sonic politics of belonging, 21–24, 30–38, 165–167

sound-politics, 23

South Sudan, 17, 24, 106; civil war in (2014), 25, 93; conflict in (2013), 126, 112; independence of, 93; and migration to Kenya, 25, 27, 29. *See also* Sudan

speaker systems, sound of, 53–54

state of exception, 132

Steingo, Gavin, 47, 56, 93

Stoever, Jennifer Lynn, 145, 146, 155

Stone, Ruth, 14–15

Street Boyz, 56, 172

structural positive peace, 161

structural violence, 120, 144–45, 158–163

subjectivity: and Christianity, 138; 153; and Dinka dancing 109–110; and emotion, 43; and music 22–24, 65, 68, 84, 145; and pastoralism, 97, 153; and research, 17–18

Sudan, 29, 93, 97. *See also* South Sudan

Sudan People's Liberation Movement (SPLM), 29

suffering: affective economy of, 51, 61; in forced migration studies, 42; and humanitarianism, 6; and pleasure, 61–62; politics of, 45, 51, 60

Sylvan, Robin, 116–117

symbolic violence, 59, 78, 127, 144–145

Syrian refugees, 137, 171

Tanzania, 26, 68

Teferra, Gerawork, 7

theater for development (TfD) groups, 11, 68–69, 168–169; radical approaches by, 83–85. *See also* arts-based humanitarianism / musical aid; edutainment activities; United Drama Group (UDG)

Theater of the Oppressed (Boal), 83

Thiong'o, Ngũgĩ wa, 83–84, 169

Tibetan refugees, 5, 29

Turkana County, Kenya, 24, 44; and British colonialism, 96; governor of, 152

Turkana pastoralists, 25, 30, 96

Turktribe and Turkland entertainment companies, 80

Tyler, Imogen, 129

Uganda, 24, 26, 96

United Drama Group (UDG), 70, 75, 148–149

United Nations (UN) international days, 1–4, 30, 32, 53

United Nations High Commissioner for Refugees (UNHCR) 2, 69; apolitical aspect of, 156; compromised position of, 118–119; development agenda of, 33; funding of, 28; and the Youth Initiative Fund, 70, 75, 148

United Nations High Commissioner for Refugees (UNHCR)-Geneva, 70, 75

United Nations High Commissioner for Refugees (UNHCR) in Kenya, 2–3; arts programming by, 1–4, 50, 150–155; and the international refugee regime, 27

United Nations Relief and Works Agency (UNRWA), 29

United States, 28, 150

Universal Declaration of Human Rights, 64, 87n1

Verdirame, Guglielmo, 3, 78

vernacular culture, 70

violence: cultural, 144–45; direct, 144; discourse of, 105–106, 128–131, 149; of encampment, 78, 125–127, 162; humanitarian, 36; liberal, 8; and peace, 143, 144; slow, 8; structural, 120, 144–145, 158–163; symbolic, 59, 78, 127, 144–145. *See also* sexual and gender-based violence (SGBV)

voices: of refugees; 17–18, 35–37, 84, 172; silencing of 157

vulnerable populations, 45

warscape, 127

Western, Tom, 9

Wirtz, Elizabeth, 120

work permits, 74, 86
World Bank Group (WBG), 170
World Food Program (WFP), 7, 35
World Refugee Day (WRD), 1–4, 151–159; Dinka dances at, 104, 110–111; and fundraising activities, 3, 157–159; invited guests at, 158; multicultural activities in, 151–155; refugees' views on, 158–159

Youth Congress, 35–38
Youth Education Programme Development (YEPD), 1, 148
Youth Initiative Fund (UNHCR), 70, 75, 148
youth talent competitions, 49–50
Yuval-Davis, Nira, 22–23, 24

Zetter, Roger, 48, 165, 166

Oliver Shao is Assistant Professor of Liberal Arts at the School of the Art Institute of Chicago.

For Indiana University Press

Tony Brewer, Artist and Book Designer
Brian Carroll, Rights Manager
Allison Chaplin, Acquisitions Editor
Sophia Hebert, Assistant Acquisitions Editor
Samantha Heffner, Marketing and Publicity Manager
Brenna Hosman, Production Coordinator
Katie Huggins, Production Manager
Nancy Lightfoot, Project Editor and Manager
Dan Pyle, Online Publishing Manager
Pamela Rude, Senior Artist and Book Designer

www.ingramcontent.com/pod-product-compliance
Lightning Source LLC
Chambersburg PA
CBHW030330270326
41926CB00010B/1568